MERCY
NEVER
SLEEPS

MERCY NEVER SLEEPS

SLEEPLESS THOUGHTS ON FAITH, HEAVEN, AND THE FEAR OF HEIGHTS

JAMIE BLAINE

W Publishing Group

An Imprint of Thomas Nelson

Published in Nashville, Tennessee, by W Publishing Group, an imprint of Thomas Nelson.

Author is represented by the literary agency of Alive Communications, Inc., 7680 Goddard Street, Suite 200, Colorado Springs, CO 80920.

Thomas Nelson titles may be purchased in bulk for educational, business, fund-raising, or sales promotional use. For information, please e-mail SpecialMarkets@ThomasNelson.com.

ISBN 978-0-7180-3297-5 (eBook)

Library of Congress Control Number 2017944424

ISBN 978-0-7180-3272-2 (TP)

Printed in the United States of America

17 18 19 20 21   LSC   10 9 8 7 6 5 4 3 2 1

CONTENTS

CONTENTS

PART III: GENESIS AGAIN

PART IV: CODA

I MISSION

I hope you will put up with a little more of my foolishness.
—2 CORINTHIANS 11:1 (NLT)

When you are young and foolish and have no healthy fear of death, when you feel like, quite honestly, you have nothing to lose and can never ever truly die, you might pray some truly reckless prayer. Something scandalous and rash like, "God, give me adventure."

Later, you may regret this request. But by that time it's probably too late.

—JAMIE BLAINE

SOME KINDA HELP, RIGHT NOW

I have become a brother to dragons and a companion to owls.
—JOB 30:29 (JUB)

SOME NIGHTS IT SEEMS LIKE THE WHOLE WORLD IS coming apart at the seams.

I'm driving down Sixth Street with the rain coming down in sheets, on my way from one psychiatric crisis call to the next, from hallucinations at the city jail to a suicidal math professor in Skylark ICU to a distraught divorcee at the Malibu II apartment complex out past the mill. I'm on my way to see a lapsed prescription-pill addict at the Westwood ER when my cell buzzes with another call.

A hysterical voice rushes in before I can say hello. "Oh my gosh, thank you, thank you. I need help! I need help right now!"

"Whoa. Calm down," I answer. "Tell me what's going on."

"I can't do this anymore," the woman cries. "I've got the pills laid out. They're right here. I'm looking at them now."

The phone hisses and with a click it dies. I pull over to the side of the road, dial back, and she answers on the first ring. "Sorry," I explain. "I'm driving, and the reception's real bad. Tell me what's too much to take."

"I got fired at work, my husband's been running around with some girl I thought was my friend, and I had knee surgery and now it's even worse than it was before." She spits everything out rapid fire. "How many reasons do y'all need? 'Cause I've got plenty more."

"There is no y'all," I tell her. "It's just me. But I'll try and help you best I can."

She's fading in and out, so I start the truck again and drive in circles, searching for a steady signal on higher ground, trying to find a place where we can hear each other clearly enough to talk more than one broken sentence at a time. I catch garbled snippets about a pistol and lots and lots of pills. It's a tough decision, and I've got to make it on the fly. Can I try and direct this person over the phone, or is it best to simply go to where she is?

It takes four tries, but I confirm her address and let her know I'm headed that way, keeping her on the phone as it crackles until the line finally goes dead. The highway splits at a boat landing and disappears into thick black forest. I dial Westwood ER.

"I'm hung up in some drama," I tell Dr. Black. "But I'll be there. Probably bringing another one with me."

"Roger that on the drama." Black sighs. "We'll save a room."

I'm deep into the trees when the crisis line rings again. "Will God forgive me for this?" the woman asks, crying harder now.

"God forgives us," I tell her.

"How do you know?"

Working psych crisis requires someone equal parts missionary, daredevil, detective, magician, tracker, and theologian. You wear a lot of hats once the sun goes down. You wing it and do your best.

"If humans can forgive each other for so much terrible stuff, then don't you think God's gotta be bigger and better than us?"

"That's what I'm hoping," she says, her voice cracking but clear.

"Me too," I reply. "Listen, I just turned off the highway. Hold tight, okay?"

There is a long pause and the sound of one deep breath. "I'm holding best I can," she says, and the line goes silent again.

I turn left at the wagon-wheel mailbox and drive three-quarters of a mile to a long driveway in the middle of a serpentine curve. One low light shines in the distance from a small brick rancher in the middle of a barren field. I pull in close and take a minute to ready myself for whatever comes next.

The front door flies opens. A woman rushes onto the porch, wrestling a bag behind her. The rain is heavy in the headlights. I reach for the door to make a run for her, but before I can get out she is hobbling toward me fast as she can. She yanks the passenger-side handle, but it's locked. I reach over and pop the latch as she beats against the glass.

"Take these," she says, hustling her stuff inside and shoving a Ziploc bag full of pill bottles into my hand. "And wherever we're going, go quick. My husband's coming."

"Whoa, lady," I protest. "I'm just, like, the crisis counselor guy. You shoulda called the police."

"My husband *is* the police."

My head drops against the window, and a sound comes out of my chest like air from a punctured balloon. *"Ohhff . . ."*

"Look, I didn't know what else to do!" she says. "I was too chicken to use a pistol, but I had the pills all poured out and said, 'Hey, God? If you're really up there and if you care and if there's some reason you need me sticking around, then you're gonna have to send me some kinda help, right now.' And not thirty seconds later your TV commercial came on and said, 'Need help? A crisis professional is standing by. Call now.' Well, if sitting three hours on your bathroom floor crying and trying to get up the courage to take enough pills to end your life isn't a crisis, I don't know what is. Now hurry, or we'll both be in it deep."

"Both?"

"He's just a small-town cop who thinks he's big and bad," she says, curling her lip with disgust. "But if you can get me to my sister's in Spring Hill, her stepdaddy is the judge. He might be able to help me there."

I hold up the baggie of pills. "Were you really gonna take all these?"

"Seriously," she says, measuring a millimeter between her finger and thumb. "I was this close."

"I don't know about Spring Hill," I tell her. "But I think I can get you somewhere safe."

I hit the gas and throw gravel all down the side of her Taurus as we fishtail back up the drive and turn right onto the break in the serpentine curve. She whips around to look behind us.

"Car coming," she warns.

I check the rearview mirror. Twin beams approach from the other side of the bend. I pull over and kill the lights.

"Why are you stopping? Go! Go!"

I lock the hubs into four-wheel drive and barrel through the field, driving blind. She braces herself with one arm on the console and the other against the door. We hit a series of ruts, the wheels of the Trooper bouncing hard but plowing on. She cusses with every rut until I slide around a patch of thicket at the far end of the curve and park. Distant headlights gleam toward us through the pines. They turn and motor slowly away.

"Ma'am?" I say, my heart still pounding in the side of my neck.

"Yeah?"

"This is a little beyond my level of crisis expertise."

"Sorry."

The engine ticks as we sit in silence, waiting until the tail-lights vanish from sight. I reverse to unlock the hubs and ease back onto the road.

"Where'd you learn to drive?" she asks.

"*Dukes of Hazzard* reruns."

"Yeah." She pries her fingers from the door. "That makes sense."

We wind back up the same highway with rain pelting the windshield and an old green suitcase between us on the seat. "I'm Jamie," I say, reaching over to offer my hand. "Nice to meet you. Sorry it's under circumstances like this."

"April," she replies, pushing wet hair from her face and ducking her eyes. "I sat next to you in Dr. Engle's class, freshman year. Just my small-town luck. It's okay if you don't remember me."

I glance at her. "I remember. Been a few years."

"Seems like twenty, with all that's happened to me since then. You meet this person and they seem so perfect at first. Then you get married, and everything starts falling apart. Money problems and in-law problems and fightin' all the time. The one thing I never thought he'd do was cheat. You think you know somebody, but you don't ever know." April starts to say more but stops herself and looks away. "We don't have to talk about all this right now, do we?"

"We can talk about whatever you want."

"I wish I'd just stayed in college like you." She leans in and looks across the suitcase. "So you're the crisis professional standing by?"

"Six at night 'til six in the morning. Six days a week."

"How in the world did you end up with that job?"

I keep a pair of knock-off Wayfarers in the side-door pocket. I reach down and slip them on. "I'm on a mission," I tell her. "From God."

She doesn't catch the reference, so I take off the shades and tell her straight. "I was splitting the shifts with my boss and dee-jaying at the roller rink to make ends meet. But then the rink got hit in that freak storm about the same time my boss relapsed and had to go back to rehab. So now I'm the crisis professional standing by all the time."

April stares like maybe I'm making a joke. "For real?" she says.

"Seriously," I reply.

The windshield wipers mark time as white lines and telephone poles blur by. "I remember you used to show up for class looking like you just woke up, wearing that same black cowboy hat you got on now," she says. "You were real quiet back then. I thought you were majoring in astronomy."

"I did too."

"What happened?"

"What ever happens?" I ask, shaking my head and flipping up my hands before grabbing the wheel again. "Life gets strange."

She settles back in the seat, and we ride awhile without speaking.

"Math," I confess.

"Math?"

"Astronomy math was kicking my behind, so I switched to psych. Psychology is like science without all the calculus." The words hang before I clarify. "Or maybe it's emotional calculus instead."

"Never was much good at calculus," April says.

"Me neither."

The hum of tires is hypnotic in the rain. Secrets seem safer in the dark. Sometimes it's easier to trust a half stranger than a friend.

"I made a deal with God," I tell her.

She adjusts the air vent down and away. "What kinda deal?"

"You ever wonder how you ended up where you are? Like if it's God's plan or the choices you made or just the way things go down here?"

"Yeah," April says, leaning against the door. "I think about that all the time."

"Two weeks ago I applied for a job putting together bicycles at Toys"R"Us. Before that I was gonna give guitar lessons at the music store. I'm no counselor. I made it through grad school on grace and magic tricks. But every time I try to do something else, it falls through. So whether it's a total fluke or mission, I told God I'm in—whenever, wherever, whatever comes my way. And if they fire me, who cares? It's not like I've got a lot to lose. I'll go back to sacking groceries at the Pig. One way or another, I'll figure something out."

She's giving me that Is-this-guy-serious? look again. Sometimes I do get carried away, but this is one of the parts of crisis I really like. When you meet people in dire straits, you can skip the small talk and get to the deeper stuff of life. Or at least you can try.

The highway comes to a stop at the boat dock. A tangle of balloons hang tied to a cardboard sign: *FOUR-FAMILY RUMMAGE SALE: furniture, guns, lots of baby clothes.*

Tacked to the marina post, there's a black-and-white flyer for a lost dog. In the photo a mangy little shepherd sits in the back of a pickup next to a grinning kid with dirt on her flowered dress. *$20 reward*, the flyer says. *Answers to Jake.*

"So I guess this is why you were willing to come help some strange woman in the middle of the night, no questions asked?" April says.

"Pretty much," I maintain, turning right at the sign. "Plus, I need the cash."

The rain lets up as we approach the lights of town. I pull into Westwood's ambulance entrance and grab a nearby wheelchair.

"Jump in and look pitiful," I tell her, throwing the sack of pills in her lap. "Lot quicker this way."

I roll April through the back door and a nurse swoops in to take her away. "I don't know about the whole mission thing," April calls back over the chair, "but I'm pretty sure you're on one tonight. You saved my life."

"Nah," I tell her, laughing it off. "I was just crazy enough to show up and give you a ride."

"Well, I ain't no great Christian," she says, right before they round the corner to her room. "But maybe that's what your mission is."

Dr. Black steps into the hall beside me. He reminds me of Robin Williams—if Robin was a bass-fishing ER doc from Birmingham. "God must be hard up for angels," he says, flashing his toothpaste-commercial, TV-doctor smile. "You look rough."

"If you're looking for a briefcase and a tie, call somebody at three in the afternoon. This is the best you get at three a.m."

"When's the last time you slept?"

"What's today?"

"Thursday," he says, checking the Baker Brother's Funeral Home calendar nearby. Somebody drew a caricature of Dr. Black rising like Dracula from their Champagne Velvet model casket. Marked in big red letters below they advise, "DON'T GET SICK ON A FRIDAY NIGHT."

"I think I slept some Tuesday? For a little while?" I calculate, doing the eyes-up, chin-scratching thing. "You don't look so hot either, y'know."

"Night shift makes you gray," he says, pinching the skin under his eyes. "Our prescription forger's in bed sixteen, pretty cut and dry. Clear him quick and go home. Get yourself some rest."

"Ugh, addicts," I mumble. "My compassion meter's about tapped out."

I knock at sixteen's door before walking in. There's a guy, late twenties, asleep in the bed. His left arm is mangled, and burn scars stretch up to the side of his face. A silver-haired woman in brown slacks and a sweater sits bedside, clutching a rosary, nervously working the beads.

"Sorry I'm running late," I say, sitting in the chair beside her. "Been one of those nights."

The rosary is wrapped between her fingers. She reaches over to take my hand. The stones are cool and smooth, the metal edges sharp against my skin. "It's okay," she says, clutching tight. "God has a plan. If you can help us, it's worth the wait."

The city is a shadow at four in the morning—abandoned streets and dark store windows. I close the ER side door behind me and step out into the lot. In the moment of crisis you simply react, but once things settle, the pieces play back through your mind.

Just my small-town luck, she said. My former classmate was right. Most everybody I see on crisis is some distant relative or friend of a friend, someone I went to church or school with, an old babysitter or the girl who used to cut my hair. Pretty strange finding out your high school crush is hooked on meth or your best friend's dad wears T.J.Maxx dresses in neighboring towns. We are all so many secrets inside.

When I started working in psych wards, I was still naïve and judgmental enough to believe that addicts and mentally struggling people were somehow different. Soon enough the truth hit home: the people I was seeing weren't any less spiritual or smart or privileged than me. Nothing but grace and circumstance lay in the thin spaces between us.

The hospital power plant pumps giant clouds of steam into the sky. Climbing the scaffold to the second-floor rail, I can see the mall where I bought my back-to-school clothes, the library where I checked out stacks of books on magic and space, the apartments where I spent the summers after my parents went separate ways.

I cut through a short stretch of trees at the pavement's end and stand eye level with the back balcony of my dad's old townhouse, 3E. Everything looks different. Everything looks so much the same. A semicircle row of brown-cedar units with yellow bug lights by front and back doors. The slim silver mailboxes sitting between the laundromat and sky-blue kidney-shaped pool.

It's not hard to imagine my scruffy nine-year-old self riding a battered BMX bike down the red-dirt hill that spills just around from where I stand. I walk over and look down to where I crashed into the handrail and knocked a dent in my head, over to apartment 7C where I tried to steal my first real kiss from Ashley Braddock and she blushed and stuttered that she was pretty sure she didn't like boys. The steady trickle of Chance Creek still runs off to the left. Back in the day, the older boys had built a ramp out of plywood and cinder blocks, calling me chicken (and worse) when I was too scared to try and jump to the other side.

Strange what stays with you, the things you remember so clearly. I can still feel the heat of the southern sun, the sting of their taunts as I sat with one foot on the pedal and the other in the dirt. Still see the People's Bank Time and Temperature sign flashing *2:15 p.m./102°*, the look on Ash's face as the big kids cackled when I turned and rode back into the trees.

How did I end up here, in the place I am today? Was it choices? Or fate?

I used to sneak out after my dad was sleeping to sit on the hilltop and talk to God. Not official prayers or anything fancy— just talking as if to a schoolmate about music and hopes and girls and dreams. Sometimes, when it was quiet and the wind whipped through the trees, it felt like God was right there, close by, listening and talking too.

You think back to your kid-sized concept of God before so much religion and living and grown-up changes and wonder if you're closer now or were closer then, or if you ended up missing it somehow.

I wonder what my nine-year-old self would think if I could meet him here and tell him how things turned out. Wonder if he would have ever dreamed he'd become some still scruffy late-night crisis guy working at the ER behind the apartments. If he knew he'd still be coming back to the top of this red dirt hill on so many nights.

I close my eyes and wait—for the wind, for God, for my kid self to show. For something. But there's nothing here but old memories. I'm tired, wired from drama and overthinking things again. But as I turn to go, the slightest breeze drifts through the trees. I wait, listening to the nothing-sounds of the night. And when I open my eyes, 3E's porch light flickers back to life.

Never underestimate the power of magical thinking. My grad school psych professor taught us that. "But before you turn cynical, remember," he would suggest, "every now and then miracles really happen. The things we cannot explain—those are the most beautiful in the end."

I walk back to my truck and head for home. There's an oldies station at the far end of the dial that plays classic R&B in the midnight hours. It sounds crackly and surreal, like they're broadcasting from some faraway and desolate place like Zero Meridian, Mars, or Memphis, Tennessee.

Sometimes you need some all-night DJ to guide you home

with just the right song, one you wouldn't have thought of on your own, one that makes you not feel so alone in this world. Something like Sam and Dave's "Goodnight Baby," while you drive slow with the lights reflecting off wet pavement and the air smelling all rich and mystical after the rain.

How did I end up driving these downtown streets while all my old friends are asleep in their beds with kids and spouses and happy normal lives? Is it God's fault, mine, or simply life among billions in a fallen world? Do we invent meaning because otherwise it's simply too bleak? Does God have some quantum equation or sanctified pi to calculate the balance between choices and fate, or is the sum total of our existence fuzzy math that we can never fully comprehend until we step from this world into whatever lies on the other side?

"You wait and wait for life to begin, and all the while it's passing you by." A fifty-eight-year-old investment banker in for a failed overdose attempt once told me that as I dropped him off at the Trailways station with a one-way ticket to rehab. Eleven million dollars had passed through his hands, and not one penny of it brought him peace. "Don't waste it, Jamie," he said. "Don't let it pass you by."

They should have church in the middle of the night when the mind most ponders life and the state of all things. I bet sermons would be a lot different then.

"Four forty in the morning," DJ Cleavon Swan says. "Sixty-four degrees and starry skies as the nighttime ends and day begins again." His voice is as deep as a river and Cadillac smooth. Sam and Dave fade away as Al Green slides in testifying how Jesus is close and waiting for all the lonely and broken down.

"Love is right there waiting," Swan promises as the Reverend Al spirals high on the refrain. "Peace is right there waiting. No matter where you go . . . no matter where you've been . . . he's right there waiting all the time, guiding with his love and light. This is DJ Cleavon Swan saying, 'God bless, my people. Wherever you go, you are always going home.'"

I pull through iron gates guarded by twin granite sphinxes and park beneath the giant live oak. A Southern mansion grand as Graceland looms before me. I slip past an ivy-clad obelisk through hidden gardens, back beyond statues of Venus and David to a secret set of spiral stairs. I live in what might be the South's ritziest poolhouse. Still a poolhouse, though. Which is at least a small bump up from finishing college and moving back in with your folks.

Inside, I drape a blanket over the stairwell to keep out the morning sun and climb into bed. Purple Christmas lights are strung across the ceiling like twinkling stars, and a sound machine lulls me with "Endless Surf." Before sleep I read the Bible to try and get my mind right. Psalm 4 about gladness and wine, how you'll lie down in safety and peace. Proverbs 3 promising sleep that's sweet to all those God loves. Just for fun, that verse that says it's useless to get up early and work too hard.

I like those scriptures they rarely mention in church—the prophet who lost his cool and called down bears to maul a couple of mouthy kids, that sneaky naked disciple in Mark 14, a tricky woman in Judges who lulled the cruel commander to sleep and drove a tent stake through his skull, Noah finally climbing off the ark and getting sloshed, foreskin piles and massive concubines and talking mules. One broken character after another, in seemingly hopeless situations, struggling to make it through.

Scripture doesn't try to sugarcoat the strange nature of life or the desperation of man. The Bible is brutally honest. That helps me believe it truly was written by some all-knowing, all-seeing Someone Bigger up above. Humans would have made the Bible so much tamer. Human nature is to camouflage and hide. The nature of God is no fakery, to see things for what they really are. Who knows? Maybe that's the balance between choices and fate.

Gideon put out a fleece. The disciples threw dice. You can't just be complacent. Sometimes you've got to get in the ring and wrestle God, refusing to let go until he shows you the way.

The sea rolls endlessly as stars twinkle above. I lay the Bible to the side and drift into the dreaming.

DRIVE HOME BACKWARDS

For God speaks in one way,
and in two, though man does not perceive it.
In a dream, in a vision of the night,
when deep sleep falls on men,
while they slumber on their beds.

—JOB 33:14–15 (ESV)

FIRE CREEPS UP THE SIDES OF AN IMPOSSIBLY HIGH skyscraper, crackling sparks and walls of wavering heat. The floor buckles beneath me as smoke and cinders choke the air. I race down a long, dark hall where all the doors are locked and the walls start crumbling in.

There is a stairway that leads to heaven, but it has no rails. The lights of the city dwindle as I climb, and the stairs disappear behind me. I scramble faster, but suddenly the stairway turns.

You got close, a voice rings out as I start to fall. *But not quite.*

I can't sleep. Crazy, broken dreams again—volcanic mazes and endless falling from terrible heights, lost in an army of locked doors.

These are not the worst dreams. The worst are looping

scenarios from crisis, the recurring dreams where I can never get there in time. A woman on the phone whose car is running in the closed garage. Her voice is fading, but I cannot find her house. A desperate man perching on the rooftop, but I'm too scared and dizzy to climb. A college student stranded with a pistol, but my truck won't start and I can't find my clothes.

I get stuck in the most anxious moment, and it plays out over and over again like a needle skipping on a record, like a scene on repeat, until I finally wake up, too shaken to sleep again.

"Some say dreams are wish fulfillment," Dr. Stephens taught us in Abnormal Psych. "Others theorize they are jumbled snippets from a sleeping brain or a product of unresolved hopes and fears. There are those who contend that dreams are symbolic. But that's largely confirmation bias—inventing significance that supports what we desperately want and need to believe."

I raised my hand. "What do you believe?"

"It's only my opinion," Stephens offered. "But I don't believe dreams mean anything."

Pastor Reddy promised that young men would dream dreams and the older would see visions. He said that dreams were messages from the other world: When you lie down, your sleep will be sweet. For God gives sleep to those he loves.

What do you do when you can't sleep and all your dreams are disturbing? You pray it's not evidence that God never liked you much to begin with, that you were marked to be a goat before the world even started to turn. You shove towels under the door to block out the sun and face the clock away so you can't see that it's 8:41 a.m., and you've only had two hours' sleep. You pray for help and mercy, to silence an anxious mind, that the preacher was wrong and your psych professor was right. You take two Benadryl, pour a mixer bowl full of Cocoa Pebbles, and turn on *Ferris Bueller's Day Off* again.

I found a junky old VCR at the Goodwill off St. John for six bucks, and it still works. It's like going back to vinyl, only hipper. Or maybe not.

For the longest time I didn't have a TV to go with it, but then somebody gave me their ancient set, and I plugged it up so I could watch stupid movies and Christian broadcasting. The best part is whoever gave Goodwill the VCR left an old Sony videocassette inside. Marked in Sharpie, the label reads: *FAST TIMES, CLUELESS, BLUES BROTHERS, FERRIS BUELLER.* And, crammed at the bottom in tiny letters, *laura's b-day.*

Jackpot. Double jackpot that the movies were all taped off some station in Savannah with the local commercials intact. Do we really need more blood and curse words added to our lives? The edited-for-TV versions suit me fine.

I had curious hopes for *laura's b-day,* but it turned out to be some old woman of questionable sobriety with bad blonde highlights, squinting into the sun and singing about twenty seconds of "Wind Beneath My Wings" before smoke from a barbecue pit blew into her face and the video switched to a commercial for Oglethorpe Mall followed by the last half of *Zapped!*

When I can't sleep, it helps to zone out and watch some mindless video I've seen a hundred times—so often that every scene feels like a familiar old friend. That grainy bottle-blonde woman warbling about heroes and eagles and hacking as some comb-over guy squirts half a bottle of lighter fluid on the pit always makes me feel a little better. Kind of like, *Relax, we're all crazy. Nobody knows this better than God. So trust him to make things right. Life is far too bizarre to live uptight.*

I watch the smoky old woman's moment of inspiration almost every day. Then I settle in and let the movie play until I can sleep again.

"It's simple," Ferris explains after they hijack Cameron's dad's

Ferrari for adventure downtown. "Whatever mileage we put on, we'll take back off again."

"How?" Cameron asks.

"We'll drive home backwards."

The weight finally lifts, and anxiety subsides, just enough to close my eyes. *Drive home backwards,* I think. *That's a pretty good idea.*

The alarm starts pinging at 5:17 p.m., the sound of satellites in deep space segueing into the blood-rousing rhythm of "It's a Long Way to the Top (If You Wanna Rock 'n' Roll)" fixed to hit maximum volume if I don't mash the button in time. Bon's bagpipe kicks in before I can reach over, but instead of hitting Snooze I turn it down a notch and let it play.

Why is the sweetest sleep always at the end? It's like God says, "Okay, yes, I love you. Have some delicious slumber"—just as it's time for the alarm to ring. Unfair. Totally backward from the way things should be. Sleep should start out delicious and end up light and revitalized, leaving us eager and ready to go. Did God create sleep that way and then humans messed it up? Didn't he realize we are capable of ruining everything?

I hope God has a bicycle, a sweet blue cruiser with a fat seat and big fenders. I hope he lives in a really big house way back in the suburbs of heaven, out there on the lake—that house with the long, winding driveway and all the tall magnolia trees with lights strung in the top branches to look dramatic in the evening. And I hope when I get to heaven, God will ride bikes with me on that long stretch of road that rambles around the lake. And after we've pedaled in silence for a good spell while I adjust to the strange gravity of heaven and time beyond time, God will nod at me and say, "All right, go ahead. Ask me anything you like."

And even though my head will be swirling with a million questions about the fallen and frustrating nature of man in an immeasurable universe, I hope that riding bikes with God in heaven is so completely perfect that all those questions won't matter anymore. And if hoping something like that makes me naïve or spiritually immature, then so what? I hope I stay naïve and hopeful all through this one tiny life into the next.

I am the king of magical thinking.

Grabbing my parallel Bible, I read through Psalm 91. I start each day the same, with promises of rescue and safety, guardian angels to guide me in all my ways. The crisis psych business sends you to the war zone but doesn't offer insurance benefits. I need all the coverage I can get.

I roll to the floor and try to get my bearings. The room is pitch black, with windows layered in heavy drapes and towels stuffed under doors. One Benadryl used to help, but now it takes two. Two leaves me groggy, so I trudge downstairs, grab the two-liter of Diet Coke, and turn it up. If I keep it in the top back shelf of the fridge, it stays icy, just the way I like. Never have been one for coffee.

Recently, a youth pastor sporting ochre skinny jeans, the facial hair of a Civil War reenactor, and one of those Smokey the Bear hats suggested I might be more relatable to Jesus culture if I'd start drinking lattes or craft beers at the coffeehouse where all the cool Christians hang. I allocate myself thirteen curse words a year, just to stay grounded and meek, and I used one that day. It was the only truly appropriate response.

On second thought, last night I hung out in the alley behind the 7-Eleven with a drunk named Lenny wearing a Meat Loaf tour shirt. So Ochre Smokey youth pastor might have a point.

I'm not really awake yet.

One way I get moving is to fill the mixer bowl full of cold water, dump two ice trays inside, and stick my head under for as long as it takes me to say the Lord's Prayer. You think I'm kidding. I had maybe four hours' sleep today, and another long night of mental-health calamity likely lies ahead, so I say the Lord's Prayer twice, one Hail Mary, a somewhat fumbled Apostles' Creed, the Carny's Creed, and a rushed pass through the Pledge of Allegiance. When I was a kid, I practiced holding my breath underwater a lot.

I dry my face and refill the ice trays, feeling a bit more coherent. There's a picture on my freezer door of Jesus laughing. My buddy Jules gave it to me. *JESUS IS LAUGHING*, she wrote at the top. Then, in small letters at the bottom, *at you*. Over on the back: *So quit worrying. Everything's gonna be all right.*

I'd never seen a picture of Jesus laughing before. I hope he laughs a lot. I hope Jesus and Jules are laughing at me from someplace happy and grand right now. That would give me hope. That would help me believe things really could be all right.

One more long pull of caffeine. I slide back the side door, turn a kitchen chair backward, and watch the sun sitting fat and sleepy in the west. Plenty of people wake up in time to watch the sun rise. How many wake up to watch it set?

I don't get to enjoy it long before the crisis line rings.

I'LL JUMP IN

Crafty fellow that I am, I caught you by trickery!
—2 CORINTHIANS 12:16 (NIV)

T'S NEARLY DARK BY THE TIME I PULL UP TO CHARTER House, the group home for the terminally mentally ill located right behind the zoo. If any of Charter's thirty-five clients make a comment insinuating self-harm, protocol dictates they have to call crisis to evaluate. Charter calls me at least four or five times a month. The place is dank, dark, depressing, and in the most dangerous part of town.

There are worse places to go.

If you look through the crack in the courtyard bushes, you can see the zebras, Jacko and Janet. (I didn't name them.) Tonight Jacko stands placidly munching grass. It's always weird to see zoo animals after dark. You think they'd be kicked back relaxing, watching Animal Planet or whatever it is zebras do when they're off the clock. But they're standing there on show just like when people pay good money to look.

When God showed Adam that first zebra, I bet it blew Adam's mind. I wonder if Adam uttered the first swear word then—or later, when Eve told him the story of what went down with the fruit and the snake. Probably the snake.

When you grow up in the Bible Belt, your thoughts are a constant tug-of-war between the sacred and profane.

I walk to the staff entrance around back. From the top of the picnic table there's a good view of the monkey house where I did all my research in grad school. Just one low fence separates the group home from the animals.

I saw a zoo worker fall into the alligator pit one day. The drain got clogged, and he had to clear it out with a long-handled scoop. "Want to help me on a little adventure?" he said, not telling me beforehand exactly what "adventure" might entail.

"Sure," I said, hustling my bored monkeys back to their cage.

"It might involve a wee bit of danger," Mires said, his Irish eyes smiling with the sort of deranged glee you might expect from the zoo's reptile guy—a man who had been bitten so many times he was immune to most venom and would often be called on to fly around the country and donate blood.

"Danger is my game!" I replied, misquoting *Fast Times*'s Spicoli, as foolishly eager as Mires had hoped. He smirked like Nicholson in *The Shining*, handing me a pair of rubber boots and a pole with a big metal hook at the end.

"Are we chasing skunks?" I asked.

"Don't you wish?" Mires replied. "C'mon. Let's go."

We hiked back through a swath of palms and entered the alligator pit from the rear. The water was thigh deep, and gators were piled near the drain, dark green masses and curvy spined tails.

"You're seriously going in there?" I asked.

"No, we are. You can hang back a bit, but if I call, I need you to jump in."

Mires was such a joker. "Okay, yeah," I said. "Sure."

Much to my surprise, he charged forward, pushing gators aside with his boot, attacking the drain's spindles with his spade. "Come snag Big Alice," he grunted. "I can't get this witch to move."

Wanting to be helpful (and not seem like too much of a wuss), I crept in and extended the hook as far as it would reach. Mires grabbed the clasp and latched it around her neck.

"Pull!" he commanded.

I gave it a yank. Alice hissed, thrashed lightning quick, and knocked Mires flat with her tail. With a yelp he vanished beneath the waters.

And for one epic second, it was far too still.

"Ah! Jesus!" I cried, not at all taking the Lord's name in vain but voicing a sincere and desperate plea for help. I rushed forward. The lurking mass swirled. I rushed back. Then onward again with a surge of courage that I could only credit to adrenaline and divine assistance. A spiked tail cut me down with one swift hammer to the knee.

"JesusKnievelcomehelp!" I wailed, swamp moss clinging to my face, clutching the rail and pedaling back again. My brain was bewildered and sleep deprived—hoping, I suppose, that somehow, in being all things to all people, our Savior was also part daredevil who could rescue idiots from a concrete death bog teaming with razor-sharp tails and teeth. Or maybe it had something to do with watching Evel's last interview on the gospel channel the night before, where he said he was ready for "the final jump" and trusting in God and mercy to cushion his fall.

"Je-sussss!" I said a third time, just in case the Knievel part was offensive or he hadn't caught my call on the first two rings. Plato and Lieutenant Colonel Warren Clear were right: there are no atheists in murky gator ponds.

Mires burst up from the waters, a blue stream of curses cutting the semiconsecrated air. He plunged his hands into the water, seizing tails and dragging alligators to opposite sides. Then he took his scoop and calmly cleared the drain. The alligators dozed in the sun as the water receded to knee-deep again.

"Whoa," I said, quoting Spicoli once more. "Righteous!"

Mires grabbed a midsized gator around the belly and lifted him up. "By nature, alligators are generally docile," he told me, kissing the beast above its sleepy yellow eye. "It's the crocs you gotta watch for."

"We don't have crocs here, right?" I brandished my hook.

Mires flashed that Nicholson grin again. "Two guesses where we're headed next."

"What are you doing up there?" Barbie, the group home administrator, asks, shaking me from my memory. Barbie's mid-forties, divorced, and devotes her life to the group home now. She tried lipo and a facelift after her husband split, but ended up with a botched discount job and kind of gave up after that. Now she wears track pants and cake-face makeup to cover the scars.

There are so many stories in this spinning world.

"Thinking about the zoo," I reply. "Back when I worked there."

"If they really want to see some exotic wildlife, they oughta take that fence down and let visitors gawk and throw peanuts through here. Maybe that way I wouldn't have to stretch the food budget from beans and rice to biscuits every month."

"What y'all having tonight?" I ask, still on top of the picnic table.

"Tacos. With cheese and real meat and everything. First week of the month is big money. You're welcome to stay."

"Pass."

"You better reconsider," she says. "Next week's tacos is soy crumbles." She nods toward the fence. "Third week's tacos, you don't want to know."

"Maybe just one," I tell her. "You still got those little cartons of chocolate milk?"

"Like in grammar school? Yeah, I can find you one, if chocolate milk and tacos is your thing."

"We've all got our thing," I reply, climbing down.

"Ain't that the truth. Hey, you picked a good night. After supper the residents are having a talent show."

"I didn't pick anything. You called me."

"Aww." She pats my back in a pitiful sort of way. "Is somebody feeling grumpy? Do you need a hug?" She points to the posterboard stuck to the back of the door that offers *FREE HUGS* in puffy letters, signed by all thirty-five of the Charter House guests.

"Right over that fence one day," I tell her, "I fought back an army of alligators. Almost all by myself."

"Well, then," she says, faking awe. "Your task here today should be cake."

"Let me guess: Milton's suicidal again."

"I think he just likes talking to you."

"Great," I reply. "Story of my life."

"Free hugs?" Barbie offers again.

Truth is you have to kid around or else the mentally ill group home is way too sad. These people aren't ever going home. They are home. And home is a dilapidated old middle school where the classrooms have been converted into four-bunk patient quarters. Many rooms still have decorations on the wall—bulletin boards celebrating the first day of fall and flannelboard cutouts of George Washington Carver chopping down his parents' peanut tree for Ms. Peaches's sixth grade History Re-Re-Remix.

Amazingly, most residents are upbeat. Except for the frequent paranoid delusions and episodes of psychosis, they don't seem that bothered at all. In fact, a lot of them have a better attitude than me.

I find Milton in his room, sitting on the edge of his bed, looking like a cross between a skid row Mr. Rogers and Rodney Dangerfield in *Natural Born Killers*, an electric-orange alphabet playfully arranged on the wall behind his head.

"Hey, Jamie," he says, except all his vowels are drawn out, so the way it sounds is "Heeyyyyyy, Jaaaamieeeee."

"Milton!" I greet him like a long-lost rich uncle with no remaining heirs. "What's up, buddy? I hear you're feeling bad."

"Yup. I shore am. Mi-ghty looow."

"What's going on?"

"Aww, I was just thinking about my dog, Lucy. Jamie, I don't know if you heard this, but, well, Lucy passed away."

"Dang, man," I say, flopping onto the opposite bed, offering a moment of silence. "Nothing in the world worse than losing your dog."

"Yup."

"Was Lucy that black-spotted dog that slept in the shed out back? I used to pet her."

"Nope. That's Muffins. She's still livin'. Lucy was my dog when I was twelve."

I let my breath out slow and lay back across the bed, staring at a constellation of glow-in-the-dark stars stickered across the ceiling.

"You know what I miss most about her, Jamie?" Milton asks.

The room smells like crayons, paste, and Bengay. Edgar, in the far corner bunk, is sawing logs. "What's that, Mr. Milton?"

"Well. Let me tell yooooou . . ."

I roll my head back, like one might do if they were watching the Goodyear blimp glide overhead, half listening while Milton tells the story of Lucy, the tan-and-white collie he found by the dumpsters at Winn-Dixie. The one who somehow learned to blow the horn of his dad's Datsun Honey Bee and steal sausage from the grill. Then it hits me. Once upon a time Milton had parents and a dog and at least a seminormal life before something went terribly wrong. If it could happen to him, who's to say it couldn't happen to me?

I prop up on my elbows and pay closer attention. Still, my eyes wander. Fastened behind the door is a laminated poster. *Classroom Rules: Listen carefully. Be kind. Help others.* It strikes me there are worse ways to make a little money. Maybe I'm on a mission after all.

Edgar stirs and shuffles past, poking his cane toward Milton's chest. "He pees in the sink," he mutters in a croaky mechanical tone.

"Do not," Milton denies.

For a moment I wonder if I'll have to step between them like some sort of World's Lamest Bouncer, but Edgar waves it off and shuffles on. Once he's gone, Milton leans in.

"Edgar lies," he whispers. "You oughta see what he does at night."

"Huh," I reply, which is my go-to phrase when I want to steer the conversation from its current track. Funny how I can go from feeling inspired to tragic in seconds flat. Maybe my mission is to make Jesus laugh.

"Jamie," Milton asks. "You think there might be dogs in heaven?"

"I don't know. What do you think?"

"God forgive my soul, but if it says our loved ones is waiting in heaven, well, there's a lot of dogs I'd rather see there before kin. Ain't right to say, but it's the truth."

"I reckon so, Mr. Milton."

We both sit for a while not saying anything. The silence is not uncomfortable.

"Hey, Jamie?"

"Yeah?"

"I'm hungry."

"Yup. Me too."

A clattering racket ricochets from the lunchroom as we cross down the back hall and head closer. It's Ronnie from housekeeping on drums, his cousin Leon on bass, and C-hall resident Fast Eddie Leray on guitar/vocals, singing something that sounds sort of like Creedance Clearwater's "Bad Moon Rising," if you scratched up the CD and threw the boom box into a concrete mixer on the moon. The patients are all clapping off beat, and it's a little sensory-overload and devastating, like you're not sure whether to burst into tears or laughter at how sad/happy/crazy life on planet Earth can be.

"Will ya dance with me, Jamie?" Neta barges in, about fourteen WWJD bracelets piled around her wrist. I can't quite imagine Jesus dancing with a heavy-set schizoaffective lady wearing candy-cane shortalls while a delusional man with Down syndrome warbles about a bathroom to the right. But the apostle Peter might. And I'm pretty sure that with as much wild hair as King David had, he'd get right on down too. So I compromise and hold Neta's hands while she shimmies around. If only I were cool enough not to worry about being cool.

The song wraps up, and all the residents cheer. Next up is karaoke from Mrs. Nicey. Ronnie steps over to where we stand, wiping the sweat from his face with a rag. "My man, Blaine!" he says, shoving the guitar into my hand. "Glad you could make it. You, sir, are up next."

There's a sixty-year-old woman up front lip-syncing "Rainbow Connection" with a Cookie Monster puppet, and nearly everyone sings along. This might be a moment when a person is tempted to wonder whether God is with or against him. But if you think about it, I guess the answer oughta be clear.

Barbie trots over and sets a carton of chocolate milk on the table beside me. "See?" she says. "Told you. You picked a good night."

"I never pick," I reply. "I just show up where they call me to go."

Leon walks over with his bass still around his neck. "If you know 'Jesus Will Fix It,' Brother Turner over there used to be a preacher. His mind left him long time ago, but ol' dude can still sing."

"Y'all just start," I tell him. "I'll jump in."

THE HOUSE OF GOD
AND GATE OF HEAVEN

Nighttime was preferred by fishermen in ancient times.
—ARCHAEOLOGICAL STUDY BIBLE

THE OLD DOWNTOWN IS DESERTED, LONG-DEAD pharmacies and vacant department stores, neon bail-bond signs and barred-up pool halls, the sad, swaggerless tags of two-bit street gangs scrawled across walls and the corpses of old junk cars.

Ninth Avenue's alley is tight and low, shadowed by the heights of small-town skyscrapers. Steam rises from underground vents and the blacktop is marred with potholes and scattered bits of trash. Thomas Towers stands king at thirteen stories high, with art-deco arches and crumbling stone, a beacon at the peak that cuts across the sky. The building sits empty now except for the homeless outreach that occupies the first two floors.

I park between the dumpster and the wall. There's a gap in the locked gate behind People's Bank with just enough space to squeeze through if you turn sideways and hold your breath.

DANGER. DO NOT ENTER. AUTHORIZED PERSONS ONLY.

Being the late-night crisis guy gives you a bit of creative license. You're sort of full-on authorized. That part I really like.

There's another warning sign tacked to the grate of the fire escape. They tore out the first story, but it's an easy climb up the frame to where the second floor begins. Once you're there, it's five flights to the top, metal stairs and a gridwork of rails to hide from passing eyes.

If I go home and try to lie down, the crisis line never fails to ring just as I'm drifting away. So I stay awake most every night 'til dawn, loitering in airports and all-night grocery stores, driving aimlessly, revisiting the old ghosts of town. Lately I've been climbing things. Radio towers, water towers, fire towers, fire escapes, football stadiums, the second tallest building in town.

There are worse troubles than insomnia. I can catch a few hours after the sun rises. Until then, I can watch while the city sleeps.

Halfway up the fire escape hangs a VIOLATERS WILL BE PROSECUTED sign, but some clown turned it upside down and drew a smiley face underneath with an addendum noting prosecutors might be violated too. I sing the chorus of "Breaking the Law" with fist up, taking steps two at a time.

I am not actually breaking laws. An undercover ATF agent first showed me how to get up here. "Just in case, Jamie," he said.

Beer bottles and graffiti clutter the fifth-floor mooring, a none-too-flattering take on the university mascot spray-painted on the wall. School spirit is a bit more jaded at a small state college. Students sneak up here to goof around, just as we did and those before us. Dorm rooms get tight, and college kids have a restless nature and need to discover new things. Some of us keep that nature even after college is done. For all the trouble it causes, I hope I never lose that. Once desire is gone, you might as well be dead.

Still, God should have put a volume knob on restlessness. Too little and you're complacent. Too much and you can't sleep, even when there're no calls and nothing to do but climb the side of People's Bank. God should have put tiny sliders on our stomachs so we could adjust emotional balance. And thermostats on trees for nights when it's still 86 degrees at 11:57 p.m.

Dogs should live at least thirty years. Kids should be invincible and death spectacular, like a Roman candle shooting stardust back to paradise, the happiest day of one's life.

I've got this whole mental list of ideas for God. This either makes him angry or proud. I am not sure which.

At the very top of the building, a slim ladder leads to the roof. I was born afraid of heights, fever dreams of falling without end. Sometimes I am flying high in an overcrowded airplane, and someone has to go. I step through a random office door to find myself miles high and plunging toward the sea. I am shot into the sky by a giant sling. They say you always wake up before you hit. Not me.

"Some say that falling in a dream is a subconscious red flag," Dr. Stephens taught us. "It means something in your life is going rapidly off course. But I have a hard time believing those theories. A dream is just a dream. Nothing more than that."

In Genesis, Jacob dreamed of a ladder to heaven, angels going up and coming down, and when he woke, he said, "Surely the Lord is in this place, and I did not know it. This is the house of God and the gate of heaven."

Verily, the Bible says, Jacob was afraid.

The roof-access ladder is positioned near the landing's rail, a seven-story drop just off to the right. I grab the bottom rung and pull myself up, clinging to the left side. *Face your fears*, the sages suggest. *Kill the old ghosts before the old ghosts kill you.*

With one leg thrown over, I am on the roof. It helps when I'm restless to sit up high and look out over the town. Elevation brings perspective. If I climb high enough and sit still long enough, then I don't think so many scrambled thoughts. When it's late and still and the lights of the city are dim, that's often when God slips out from the shadows and draws near.

From the rooftop I can see from the yellow smolder of the box plant, rising in the west, to the fires at the refinery by Bellano Lake, from the psych ward to the roller rink, both ERs, and the bend of the river where I got baptized. A few steps to the other side of the building finds me eye level with the steeple of the church where I was on staff not long ago.

I can trace the maze of streets to find the nightclub off St. Paul where I deejayed underage and people waved their hands in the air, the neighborhoods where I learned to ride a bike and drive a car, first grade to grad school, yesterday to now, triumphs, regrets and absolute catastrophes, the best and worst of times, the zigzag story of my life so far.

Those people I've met in their darkest hours—they're all down there, too, from trailer parks to gated mansions, from barstools to prison cells to megachurch pews. Trouble makes the ground level. Everybody's struggling to do the best they can.

If I were God, I would have made life a little easier, the wages of sin less nebulous, the benefits of prayer and right living quick to pay off. Humans have a hard time learning cause and effect. The faults of others seem obvious while our own are so difficult to see. If I were God, I would have made it the other way around so we wouldn't keep making the same mistakes age after age.

Every day reminds me I am not God.

There are really only three choices: God is responsible for everything, we are responsible, or it's some mysterious balance between. If God is in total control, then we cannot be held accountable. If we are in total control, then why would God trust such incompetent and careless drivers to take the wheel of something so important as an eternal soul? And if it's a balance, why do we all feel so wobbly down here?

I used to think I was the only one who felt this way. But I am not the only one.

Giggles and high-pitched voices echo through the heights. I cross to the other side. Shoes and T-shirts lie in a pile by the statue of Geronimo Perez. Four skinny bodies romp through his namesake fountains, smack in the middle of the town square.

I took a filmmaking class once. The professor said you could take a scene like that and film it one way where those kids looked like living-in-the-moment heroes, fully alive. Or you could capture the same scenario from another take and make them look like law-breaking punks. The difference between hero and villain depends on the director's point of view.

"But the best stories show both sides," he told us. "Because all true characters are deeply flawed. Contrast brings depth. It's struggle that gives a story flesh and blood."

There was a girl student who chewed pencils and wore boy's clothes and purple berets. "Like what?" she asked.

"Well," the professor replied, "the Bible comes to mind."

I grab a piece of loose slate and sail it toward the fountain. It skids across the street, throwing sparks up through the air. The illicit swimmers stop, spooked and searching. I lift my hands high.

"Wooooo!" I call down.

They shade their eyes, find me, and eight hands salute back toward mine. "Wooooo! they call back. "Aw-right!"

A sliver of moon cycles across the sky. The kids gather their clothing and wander away. Ambulances exit from the highway to the hospital, some fast with lights flashing, others morbidly slow. The crisis line does not ring. A flurry of stars falls just south of Perseus before the sky steadies again. Finally, my mind goes still, and it occurs to me that just maybe everything will work out okay in the end. Falling stars aren't even really stars. The Creator who shakes the heavens has a plan.

I think about all these things, Genesis to Revelation, beginnings and ends, all the strange stuff that happens in between. Then, for the longest, I don't think about anything at all.

Dawn breaks over the river, a thin crimson slash piercing the edge of night. I climb down and drive home, praying before bed for the people whose paths I crossed, for those I'll see tonight, for sleep that is restful and sweet.

In the dream a staircase spirals into the stars. Sometimes you have to face your fears. I begin to climb, higher, faster, as the rails end and the steps behind me disappear. Suddenly there is a blinding light, and I can feel warm rays against my face. The stairway shifts without warning, and I stumble off the side. It is a fearful and endless fall.

UNKNOWN JOURNEYS

And whether you turn to the right or to the left, your ears
will hear a message behind you: "This is the way, walk in it."
—ISAIAH 30:21 (ISV)

MS. NETA WAS FOUND WALKING THE HALLS WITH A
rope knotted around her neck, so I'm back at Charter House
again. She said it was to remind her of something she could not
quite recall but later changed her story and claimed it was a neck-
lace. Barbie thought I'd better check to be sure.

It's cooler out, so we sit at the back picnic table sampling the
pistachio Snack Pack that some nice local church donated along
with some leftover VBS shirts and Noah's Ark coloring books.

"Can we color?" Neta asks, wearing an XXXL tee that says,
JOURNEY OFF THE MAP. Unknown to Us, Known to Him.

"Sure." I grab a Blizzard Blue from the cigar box of broken
Crayolas and flip through pages. "Hey, they left out that scene
after Noah got off the boat."

"Which scene you talking about?" says Neta.

"Never mind."

She picks an early page—animals standing in queue while
storm clouds brew torrential rains. Two rhinoceroses wait toward
the back of the line. Neta takes a Periwinkle nub and starts shading

a flank. "Right over that fence at the zoo," I tell her, "I tried to ride a baby rhino one day and nearly got gored."

"What you did that for, Jamie?"

"Thought it'd make a funny picture."

"You coulda got yourself real bad hurt."

"Coulda," I say, draping her rope around my neck. "If you saw me like this in the hall, would you worry I might get hurt?"

"Yes," she says, eyes lowered, taking a bite of pudding. "But I would ask you why."

"I'm listening."

She pulls several shades of brown and yellow from the box and starts detailing the giraffes. Sharpening the crayons with the side of her spoon, the tones become lifelike.

"Sometimes I can't quit thinking about things I don't wanna think about no more." She sets her palm against her head. "It's like my mind's got a mind of its own sometimes."

"Mine, too, Ms. Neta." I'm struggling to stay in the lines, coloring up the final page in bright primary colors, doves and rainbows, happy Noah with his hands to the sky. Sometimes it's less intimidating to talk while you're working on something else.

"I wasn't gonna do nothing crazy, I promise," she says. "It just helped to have it close by. You understand, doncha?"

"Yes, ma'am," I tell her. "I do."

We color quietly for a minute or so. Neta reaches over to sharpen my Sunset Orange, then scrapes out the last of her pudding. "Jamie," she says, tipping the container to its side. "My snack pack's expired."

"I thought I was your snack pack."

She laughs into her hand. "What you said?"

"I said, 'Why are you wearing a shirt three sizes too big?'"

"This and smalls were all they got," she says. "Figured too big's better'n too small."

"Good point." I thump my pudding cup over and point to the date. "Hey, mine's expired too."

"It's just bad by a little. That won't hurt nothin', will it?"

"We can hope."

Sometimes that accidental, unrelated thing you say ends up being the most helpful and relevant of all. Pretty cool when it happens like that.

She holds up her finished picture, which for a box of broken crayons and a hand-me-down church coloring book looks like a total Van Gogh. I hold mine up in response. Which looks like it was done by a color-blind kindergartner with a sippy cup full of hobo wine. "This is my interpretation of Noah after the vineyard," I explain.

"What's that mean?"

"Never mind."

"Don't take this wrong, Mister Jamie," she says, easing her words with a sympathetic grimace. "You're real good to talk to, but you ain't much good at coloring at all."

"You're not ever gonna color with me again, are you?"

"No, no," Neta swears. "We'll keep working. It'll get better. You can't just give up."

Barbie steps out on the back patio, wearing the same colossal VBS shirt and a yellow Playtex glove on her left hand. "When you were at the zoo, how'd y'all wash the elephants?" she asks, arm up to block the setting sun.

"I am not having this conversation with you."

"No, seriously," she says. "What'd y'all do?"

"Long brush, bucket of soapy water, and a garden hose."

"Hmm," she says, heading back.

"Hey, can I have one of them 'Unknown to Us' shirts?"

"You want ginormous or teeny?"

"Ginormous."

"All right, then. Drag that hose around and meet me in the back hall. Wilda's refusing to bathe again."

"You go ahead. I'll be right there."

Ronnie flags me down while I'm sneaking out the lunchroom door and tells me Edgar and Milton finally got in a fistfight. "Well, not really fists," he admits. "More like a couple of slaps and some light pushing before we had to heavily medicate them both. Miss Barbie got 'em in different rooms now."

"Wonder why didn't I have to come talk Milton down?"

"Oh, Milton's good now," Ronnie says, spreading red sawdust in the corner. "Happier than I've seen him in a long time."

Split between feeling relieved and unneeded, I bump fists with Ronnie and head out. "We had that good groove goin' at the talent show," he calls. "Let's do it again sometime."

"Absolutely," I agree. "Anytime y'all want."

Tina, the super-Christian case manager with *Too Blessed to Be Stressed* and Jeremiah 29:11 plaques all over her office, catches me at the truck. "Oh! Jamie!" she says, breathless. "Lately, God's had you so heavy on my heart."

I point to her nearly condemned rat trap of a facility full of highly unstable, deeply damaged, and constantly needy clients. "Cut it out, Lord," I mockingly implore, angling my chin to the clouds, reminding him silently that she also has a daughter with three kids by three different fathers and an unemployed son on drugs. "Tina's got enough."

"I just love you," she replies. "You are so funny. Anyway, I wanted to be sure and give you this."

She holds out a slim workbook, the front cover showing a woman with her arms wide and face lifted to the sunrise. It's got that flimsy self-published look, and the title is in swirly script: *The Divine Secret of Life: Forty Days to Finding God's Purpose Through the Everyday, Ordinary Pages of Your Life.*

"Huh," I tell her, not knowing what else to say.

Is she giving me this for my patients? I don't work with patients. I'm the night crisis guy.

Finally, I figure out from the tone of her voice that it's meant for me. "Oh," I reply, avoiding eye contact. "Okay, thanks."

"I think this will really be a blessing on your journey," Tina says, resting her hand on my elbow to show concerned support.

"Um, yeah," I tell her, bristling as usual at the term *journey* unless it refers to the anthems of Steve Perry and Neal Schon. "I gotta go."

I climb into my Trooper, pull out of the drive, and toss Tina's well-intentioned gift in the wayback, along with twenty-seven other books about Mötley Crüe, black holes, and the discovery of the Dead Sea Scrolls. Draped across the passenger-side mirror is a gigantic *Unknown Journey* shirt. I reach over and fetch it, waving to Barbie as I drive away.

"Divine secret of life," I mutter, rooting for Trident to erase the tang of bad pistachio from my tongue. "Sure could use some of that."

HOW HEAVEN BEGINS

Language is always inadequate in the face of pain.
—JOHN GREEN

I T'S ONE OF THOSE NIGHTS—CALL AFTER CALL, CRISIS
into crisis, a new dispatch before the previous one is even done. I
fall through a porch in Twinny Town, and the German shepherd
on watch for Apache's Wrecking Yard barks the whole time I'm
trying to listen to someone's sweet grandmother lay out plans to
fasten a plastic bag over her head and fall asleep.

"There's nothing anymore," she says. "And it only gets harder
every day."

A pile of cars is on fire, gusts of wind swirling sparks up over
the yard. The shepherd barks louder before trailing away. "How
long have you felt this way?" I ask.

Her eyes are milky with cataracts, but when she stares into
me, they turn clear. "Long time," she replies. "Probably before you
were even born."

Across town, the sister of an unabashed methamphetamine addict
begs me to intercede, neglecting to tell her brother she'd called me

until I walk through the door. I stutter and make apologies and resolve again to find some other job, anything. But I'm here now and the situation sounds grave, so I try to be as helpful as I can.

He refuses to talk, threatens to sue, and swears that his sister is the crazy one, far more in need of mental intervention than him. They squabble, barbing each other with dark family secrets while I stand by with a look on my face like a housecat forced to wear an Uncle Sam costume on the Fourth of July.

Jesus? Is that your laughter I hear? Could you possibly throw a rope ladder down instead?

The hospital buzzes my cell. Another call waits. I slip away quietly without saying good-bye.

A lady living in one of the beautiful A-frame cabins out on Sherman's Bay is suffering paranoid delusions and requires commitment to the psychiatric ward. Due to the volatile nature of extreme paranoia, it's suggested I call for police backup in situations like this. But I rarely do because it slows down the process.

I park, knock, and walk in with my hand out, greeting her like an old friend. She accuses me of being in league with Satan's army and pulls an ax from under the sink.

Shoulda called for backup.

I bolt through the back door and into the woods. She pursues with a banshee scream.

Psychosis makes you strong and fast, but so does fear, so we run a tight race through a snaky patch of briars and low-hanging vines. Until . . . in the clearing I catch enough light to see that she's wielding a plastic hatchet—a Halloween prop. I stop and shoot her a withering glare.

"Really?" I ask. "Seriously?"

She drops her ax and agrees to go peacefully. "On one condition," she adds.

"What's that?"

"Can we stop and get some of those white-chocolate cookies at Subway? I've had a craving like crazy lately. Those are the best."

There's a haze sitting over the water, a tricycle spilt sideways on the pier. A rope swing taunts from the bluff, and the moon is not even close to full.

"Sure," I say, ushering her toward the truck. "I don't see why not."

The sister calls again, asking if I could please come back, saying that her brother has changed his mind and is now willing to get help. When I pull up, he is pacing the driveway, both of them crying and sharing one cigarette, squeezing tightly to each other's hands.

"I am so sorry, sir," he says, gripping my sleeve. "I lie to everybody. I have made a complete mess of my life. But if you're still willing, I'll do whatever it takes."

"Wow. What brought this on?" I ask, brushing cookie crumbs from my shirt onto the grass.

"After you left, we fought, and then we prayed, and then we had another cuss fight until we finally settled down," the sister says. "It was real ugly, but we both said some things that's needed saying for a long time now. We had a real messed-up childhood, Darrell and me. He realizes he needs help, and so do I. So if you're not fed up with us, we're both ready for whatever you recommend."

I like to pause sometimes before I respond, letting the drama simmer and anticipation build, like the outlaw Josey Wales or some aloof detective in a Raymond Chandler film. A woman at the psych ward once suggested that in stressful situations I should pretend I'm someone else, like an actor playing a scene. A patient suggested this, not a therapist. It's turned out pretty well so far.

They pass the cigarette and wait.

"You're in luck," I reply, cold serious with a trace of Eastwood's gruff. "We just happen to be running a buy-one-get-one special this week." Then I blow it with a goofy grin.

"For real?" Darrell asks, flicking the spent cigarette into the street. "Y'all really do specials like that?"

I can be calm and even comical in moments of crisis, but later my chest gets tight and I struggle to catch my breath. When you hear traumatic stories all the time, eventually you start buckling under the weight. Vicarious empathy it's called. Burnout. Compassion fatigue. A lot of things that didn't use to bother me are starting to bother me now. Then again, I didn't use to work crisis every night.

Sometimes in working mental health, you think you're somehow exempt or above it. I came in as a researcher, not a therapist. That's what kept me from going over the edge. I approached it like a scientist, studying from a safe distance with microscopes and telescopes, putting on the lead apron so the radiation from all those broken stories didn't seep into my blood and bones. But you can't wear a lead apron 24/7. The fallout is in my blood. I'm not exempt or above. I am down in it. My story is broken too.

God, if you want me to keep doing this, I'm gonna need some help.

I pray that prayer at least twenty times a night. Maybe God's got his own crisis line for desperate helpers trying to keep from losing their mind.

I'm downing forty-eight ounces of fountain Diet Coke in a frantic attempt to stay awake when a relapsed alcoholic calls begging to be admitted, saying that he can't hang on another day. "If you can hurry over here," I reply. "I'm at the rehab getting someone else in now."

He shows up, beating on the back entrance all six sheets to the wind, totally plastered, shirt inside out, staggering with hands on his knees. "Johnny?" he gasps. "I'm lookin' for Johnny."

"Jamie?"

"Uh-uh, man. My name's Jim."

"No, I mean I'm Jamie. You're looking for me." I reach to catch his elbow. "Weren't you at least kind of sober when we talked?"

"I ain't been sober since my kid's sixteenth birthday." He leans headfirst against the lamp pole, closing his eyes, anticipating my next question. "She oughta be 'bout twenty now."

I step outside beside him. The moths are giant in the light. "That's a long time drinking."

"Sorry, man," he says. "I've been having a hard time ever since her mama died."

"It's okay. You made it. You're here now."

"I can still come in? You'll take me?"

"This is rehab, my man. You don't have to clean up first. Come on in. You're gonna be all right."

"Sir," Jim says. "I don't know what you believe, but the only thing that could make me right would be Jesus or a time machine."

"I believe it," I tell him. "More than you could know."

"Y'all got any time machines in there?"

"'Fraid not." I guide him inside. "But maybe we can find Jesus."

"Tried that already," Jim says, tearing up. "This time I need Jesus to come find me."

The door shuts behind us, and everything is dead silent, the glass half-silvered and walls soundproofed, an airlock between the ward and the world. Jim turns his head, wiping his face with his shirt. "Sorry for the crying," he says.

"It's cool, brother. One of them days. Everybody's crying tonight."

Our church just had a six-part series on evangelism and how to steer any conversation toward God, but really, it seems to me, all you have to do is listen. Give people a safe place to talk unedited and resist the urge to direct, lecture, or make judgments. It's more important to be honest than smooth and theologically astute. Nobody hurting wants a religious debate. Everybody's hurting. We're all desperate for something bigger and better than self. We are all trying to find our place and a way to be okay down here.

"The summer I was sixteen we followed a stray inlet and found a little island on the far side of the lake," the blue-eyed stranger says. "The trees were thick at the perimeter, but there was a clear spot in the middle, and we built a big treehouse there. If you climbed on the roof, you could look out past the lake and see the lights of town where the land dipped low."

Inside cell six of the county correctional center, a deadbeat bandit paints pictures from his youth. He's sitting back against the slab while I lean on the opposite side, both of us staring at the cinderblock wall. "Sounds pretty magic," I reply.

"I want that summer back again, to rewind it and relive it with no rush, just being able to appreciate it better this time. I want to climb that tree and watch lightning strike the water and bounce back into the sky. Lay on the sandbar staring at the stars with Jessie Newton, back before we'd ever kissed, just when we were still best friends."

"That's good stuff right there," I tell him.

"Been thinking a lot lately," he explains, running his hand over a spot on the wall where someone scratched *CONSIDER YOUR WAYS*. "'Cause there's nothing else to do in here but think."

"I've been thinking about things like that lately too."

"Like what?" he asks.

"Like summer nights and best-friend girls," I say. "How it's so hard to appreciate anything until it's gone. But there's no going back. Not in this life."

I can hear the river far away and the wind as it rushes through the branches by the slats. An airplane passes high, signals flashing across the stars.

"Maybe that's what heaven is," Bandit says. "The best moment of your life a million times, a million different ways. Maybe a memory in heaven is like your favorite song and you can play it again anytime you like."

"Maybe," I suggest, "that's just how heaven begins."

The cell is quiet for the longest. "Yeah, man," he says, his voice low. "I think about stuff like that all the time."

Last call of the night. Westwood ER. Dr. Black shakes his head when I stumble in. "Here," he says, scribbling out a prescription. "Try this."

"What is it?"

"Zombien. A sleep med, non-narcotic. Sometimes it's the only way I can get a little rest."

"This job kinda scares me off pills, y'know?"

Black's tone turns serious. "You need to sleep, my friend. We're not much help to anyone when we're too exhausted to think."

"You've got a point," I say, pushing the script away. "But let me try some natural stuff first."

"You haven't tried anything?"

"Just Benadryl. I hate taking stuff."

"Counselors," he says, already walking away. "Why are you all so strange?"

"I am not a counselor," I reply. "I'm not that crazy."

"Keep it up," Black calls back, "you will be."

I head out to sit in the parking lot, waiting for my current patient's insurance company to return my call. Insurance is the devil. God should just wipe out insurance companies and fix it where bad things don't happen much anymore.

Brother Benny preached a sermon last Sunday where he assured us that everything evil would one day be defeated. I said to God, *Why wait?* I wonder if that makes me more faithful or faithless? I wonder about everything.

God should send out report cards once a year so we could get an idea of how we're doing. I figure I'm about C-minus—average, give or take. But if a person believed themselves to be an A-plus Christian, wouldn't that border on arrogance? Jesus didn't come looking for gold-star students. He trusted the kingdom to a bunch of reprobates.

I'm bored, so I grab Tina's workbook and start flipping through. Seems pretty dippy in places, but it talks a lot about God's perfectly imperfect path, and there's a picture on page 28 of Jesus guiding a person across a tightrope over Niagara Falls. Not a photograph (although that would make it, like, the coolest book ever). An illustration. Life often feels like a long tightrope-walk over perilous falls. I need a seven-hundred-foot-tall Jesus to be my balance beam, to steady my walk and provide a focal point to carry me to the other side.

From page 66:

> Remember that moment you felt most alive? Likely, it wasn't anything expected. God loves to catch us by surprise. Write about one of those moments without worrying about what someone might think if they stumbled upon your words. Write like you are free.

Maybe I should give this book a try. It can never be bad to learn something about yourself. Can it? Plus it cost twenty-five bucks, and I'd hate for Tina's money to go to waste.

It looks simple enough. A brief devotional thought and then questions that lead you to write, "picking out the story of God through the stray pieces of your past, as little or as much as you can recall." *The Secret of Divine Life* promises to help "tap into deep wells of the divine creative within" and "open the windows of heaven to defeat age-old strongholds and self-destructive thoughts."

Lingo like that usually pegs the limit of my fertilizer scale, but I think about all the stray pieces of life scattered around me now, history and memories in the streets of my youth. Every night I listen to people's stories, encouraging them about the importance of the rough and messy parts, even the parts that don't seem to make sense.

I did some hospice work once. It wasn't as depressing as one might think. People facing the end can be surprisingly upbeat. I was too intimidated to do anything other than ask about their favorite memories.

When dying people review their best moments, they rarely talk about weddings or graduations or the days we mark as most important. They talk about that day in sixth grade when it snowed in April and school let out. The night they snuck past the barricades and went skinny-dipping in the river, hiding behind bridge pillars when the cops passed by. That time the car broke down, way out in the country, and fireflies lit the fields as far as the eye could see. The days and nights that life caught them by surprise, and they felt totally, completely alive.

I like listening to people's uncut stories but never give much thought to my own. My story seems too trivial, too silly, too meandering thus far. It's all loose pieces. Besides, there's another reason I never give my history much thought: I can't remember a lot of it. I've racked up a number of concussions, some from high jinks, others from too many nights of crisis psych. I hide the holes in my memory well, playing it off as being absentminded. Everybody's a little foggy, right?

I confided it a while back to my old psychology mentor, Dr. Stephens. He asked me a string of odd questions and nodded a lot while making a tent with his fingers. Finally, he offered advice. "Try writing things down," Stephens said. "There are many triggers—songs, sights, smells. But mostly, memory triggers memory. You should be able to reclaim some of what's lost, but it'll take persistence."

Then he reminded me of how I'd skipped out on the therapy sessions second-year grad students were required to take. The notion was that before we helped others make peace with their past, we needed to work through our own. "They let you talk your way out of that one," Stephens said. "But maybe you're ready for it now."

My phone buzzes. I put the workbook down to take the insurance company call and finally head home. In my driveway I pick it up again. Maybe it'll be something to work on when I can't sleep. Maybe it'll put me to sleep.

I grab it in a stack with *The Dirt*, Neil Strauss's modern-day retelling of Ecclesiastes, and a collection of essays concerning the radioactive curse of King Tut's tomb. Balance is the key to all things. I got a fortune cookie last week that said, "Don't be cynical, the path home is often unexpected."

Maybe this is a start.

DAY 1

While it's important not to get stuck in the past, the experiences of yesterday are what make us who we are today. The best place to begin is where you are right now—starting with recent events and working your way back through your life. What lessons has God revealed in this most recent season of life? What series of events brought you to this place? Remember, there are no hard and fast rules. It's your story to tell however you like.

THE SEASON OF
MAD EPIPHANIES

[THEN]

Nothing gets any easier; we just find better
ways to admit how vulnerable we are.
—SEAN BEAUDOIN

WAS A CLUELESS C-PLUS COLLEGE STUDENT, SEMI-
active in local ministry and deejaying at Skate City on the side.
Blacklights and birthday cakes, fog machines and thumping bass—a
great little gig, but it didn't quite pay the bills. A psych nurse stopped
by for her niece's party one night and offered me a job at the mental hospital out past the edge of town. "You seem pretty good with
people," she said. "Could you use a little extra cash?"

My church considered psychology a second cousin to Ouija boards
and witchcraft, so I caught Pastor Reddy in the foyer after service to
see what he thought. Reddy had this thing: he'd stare you straight in
the eye, then half smile while looking around you like he was checking
out your aura or something. Then he would speak.

"I feel a peace about it, little brother," he said, sliding his long arm around me. "You can help teach those people about Jesus. God could use you to change a person's heart."

Given Reddy's blessing, I accepted the job. The psych ward was severely understaffed, so they rushed me through orientation and threw me in over my head. I covered every unit, drove the van, and answered the helpline overnight. I delivered addicts to AA, talked suicidal jumpers off the ledge, chased naked patients through the woods behind the interstate, hacked through nooses, led support groups for obsessive-compulsive recluses, and broke out windows in run-down single-wides to rescue hallucinating prostitutes.

I felt justified, prosperous, and super spiritual to boot. I was reaching down to the "least of these," the worst of the worst, bringing hope to the hopeless, charging into the fire with reckless faith. Or at least that's the way it seemed those first few weeks. Then I prayed this crazy prayer: *All right, God, let's go. Show me everything you want me to see.*

Late one Sunday a drunk who looked like Blue from *Old School* told me that maybe grace was amazing because God came down, walked a mile in our shoes, and saw how difficult and confusing life can be. Then Ol' Blue climbed up the base of a U-turn sign and sang "Amazing Grace" to drive his point home. He might have been a little tipsy, but as Sunday night sermons go, it was a strong and stirring word, one that stuck with me for a very long time.

When my girlfriend dumped me for the youth pastor of a rival church, an anorexic stripper struggling to kick cocaine took my hands and said, "Jamie, we gotta learn to let go of the things we can't control, change, or ever understand."

Back at church, the couple that taught the marriage seminar split and the music minister vanished and the preacher's wife chewed me out for accidently parking in her space one Thursday afternoon.

Everything I thought I knew was being turned upside down. I

didn't know what to think anymore. So I pushed on and tried not to think.

I had a van full of schizophrenic patients and stopped at a gas station to fill the tank. A trio of street thugs started harassing me when I walked up to pay. I tried talking calmly as the lead goon grinned and twisted a short piece of chain. The van door slammed open. My patients stormed over. Even the toughest street thugs won't tangle with a pack of wild-eyed schizophrenics.

"Thanks, guys," I told them. "But y'all didn't need to be getting mixed up in this."

"No, no way," said Norman, whose forehead was laced with stiches and scars. "Ain't nobody messin' with our man. We gotta watch out for each other. Each other is all we got."

The church finance manager got caught siphoning cash. An associate pastor was fired without notice and forced to tell the congregation that God was calling him to other pastures. An evangelist packed the altars, then two weeks later I admitted him into rehab.

A tattooed genius with increasing episodes of self-harm shook his head and told me, "Brother, listen: most everybody feels like they're doing the best they can."

I didn't share this with many, but I thought I might be called to work at the church in full-time ministry. I'd been working on a little collection of messages and had some pretty clever bullet points and catchphrases. That's what I thought ministry was: speaking and teaching and telling people how to fix their lives. But my church was falling apart and the psychiatric hospital was starting to feel like home. Mental health was the most difficult, fascinating, frustrating, tragic, comedic job I'd ever had, and even though it drove me nuts sometimes, I loved it. So much that I changed my major to psych.

A bulldozer mechanic suffering with panic disorder and poor impulse control tutored me on statistical analysis the night before a big exam. A bipolar card shark slipped me two twenties so I could buy a textbook for class. I had midnight Bible study with a jumper on the rail of the Black River Bridge and prayed with a pair of repentant Jezebels in a beat-up Ciera rolling toward the psych ward.

Truth came from a lot of strange places in the Bible. Misfits and loners and loose women. Outcasts, outlaws, oddballs, and thieves. Jesus ran with a rough crowd. And he warned the religious about labels and easy assumptions. Those people you're calling *lost* might be closer to the kingdom than you.

One patient bit me and another kicked me, and I racked up my umpteenth concussion when a guy who thought he was Satan smashed me with a chair. Junkies taught me Greek and a schizoaffective kleptomaniac gave me a motel Bible in which he had drawn an elaborate ink-pen illustration of me standing on a mountain surrounded by an army of crows. "Jamie, ah," he explained, pointing to the lightning he'd drawn around my hair. "In Hebrew that means 'one who was born for revolution.'"

I graduated with a degree in psychology, and the dean (whose daughter I'd taught to skate backward) offered me a full paid assistantship for graduate school. My adviser counted all my hospital work as internship and practicum. "You'll learn more there than here," Dr. Cryer said. "So just keep on doing what you do."

A homeless woman called the crisis line when her husband ran out of meds and started hearing voices in the night. I met them at a diner off Ninth, figuring I could at least buy them something to eat while I heard their story. But when I pulled out my wallet, the waitress informed me they had already paid. "Aw, we don't mind," the husband said, nearly too quiet to hear. "We just happy to have some comp'ny for a change."

In the parking lot, they laid hands on my shoulders. "Bless him, Lord," they prayed. "Open his eyes to your mercy." So I did right then. I opened my eyes and we laughed at the big truck's air horn blaring as it passed us on the street. Then the woman smiled sweetly and added this: "God, lead Jamie. Show him what you want him to see."

The backslidden evangelist turned out to be a model patient and returned often to encourage his peers. "Call me anytime," he told me. "You got somebody I can help, I don't care how late it is."

The church couple that split emerged a lot humbler, and when the music minister showed back up, he told me that for once in his life, he finally felt honest and real. And that preacher's wife who lit into me for parking in her space? She snuck a stack of money into my hand and said, "Honey, I know you meet a lot of people in need."

It was truly a season of mad epiphanies. I stopped trying to figure things out. I stopped talking and tried to listen better and learned to appreciate silence. I gave up any notion of ministry beyond showing up and trying to live in that one small moment struggling people share. The things that divide us grow dim in desperate hours. We are all so much the same. We are all the least of these.

It was Sunday evening, several months after I started working at the psych ward. Pastor Reddy caught me in the foyer after service. "How's the mental-health mission field going?" he asked.

I tried to find a way to sum it up, to compose the right words to where my pastor could understand. "Remember when you said God could use me to change those people?" I said. "To teach them about the Lord?"

"Yuh," he said, half smiling and sliding his arm around me. "How goes it?"

"Pastor, they're teaching me about Jesus," I told him. "God's using those people to change me."

NO RUSH

[NOW]

If I take the wings of the dawn,
If I dwell in the remotest part of the sea,
Even there Your hand will lead me,
And Your right hand will lay hold of me.

—PSALM 139:9-10 (NASB)

AFTER A FITFUL EFFORT TO GET SOME DECENT REST, I am finally hovering at the entrance to dreams—that thin place between awake and asleep, in a hot-air balloon drifting over endless fields of wheat and stark white cotton, headed somewhere yet unknown but hopeful and right.

Bzzt-bzzt.

Storm clouds dot the distance, moving in as I climb higher.

Bzzt-bzzt.

A rising wall of fire rages at the horizon, devouring the harvest while the balloon pitches and battles against the wind.

Bzzt-bzzt.

I grip the sides of the basket to keep from falling.

Bzzt-bzzt.

Closer, looming, the clouds are mechanical, formed from

swarms of angry locusts with their low, greedy hum. The balloon catches fire, tipping and twisting in the backdraft. Flames surround me as I spiral up into the sky.

BZZT-BZZT.

Finally, the locusts descend.

I jerk myself awake and snatch the buzzing phone. "'Lo?"

"You weren't sleeping, were you?" It's my relapsed boss calling from treatment.

"What's up, Marlboro?" I mumble, sitting up, shaking off the dream. "How's rehab?" I call him Marlboro because he looks like the Marlboro Man, hard-eyed and mustache rugged.

"Ah, well," he says. "There's been a small hitch."

Marlboro doesn't have any sort of psychology or social work degree. He graduated from the treatment program ten years back and never left, volunteering at first, then getting hired on as a tech and working his way up to program director. Helping others keeps you straight to a certain point. Past that, it drags you down. In a way I was shocked when he started using again. In another sense I'm not surprised at all. He was working the same nonstop schedule that I am now.

"I flipped my bunk the other night and trashed my room," Marlboro explains. "You dig up all those old feelings in therapy and I guess it gets to you. Long story short, the team thinks I need to extend my stay."

"How long?"

"At least ninety days."

"*Oof*," I groan. "So they put you in lockdown? Like me and you did to a thousand other patients back when we were techs?"

"That's exactly what happened."

"What was that like?"

"I guess it can be helpful to see things from the other side. Your day's coming."

I pull the blanket off the rail, head downstairs, and grab the two-liter of Diet Coke. "Closer than you know," I tell him, tipping the bottle for a long, harsh pull.

"Can you hang on a little longer?" he asks. "If I start using again, it's not going to end well."

I fill the bowl with ice cubes and turn the water on. "Sure, man, I'll figure it out. Do what you need to do."

It feels like the place to hang up, but Marlboro's holding on. "You know, sometimes we feel like since we're helping sick people the rules don't apply to us," he says. "But Jamie, man, that's not the way it works. If anything, that just makes it more dangerous."

Jesus watches from the freezer door. It's one of those strange Jesus pictures where straight on he's laughing, but then his eyes follow you to the side, turning serious and concerned. "I know, brother," I tell Marlboro, pulling the shades back to let in some light. "Trust me, I know."

We say our good-byes and end the call. The sun is slowly sinking in the west. I duck my head beneath the icy waters and start to pray.

The inside of my head is like flipping through extended-tier cable. Old movies and how-to shows, bombastic news flashes, hype, comedies, tragedies, ghost chasers, slick preachers that sometimes sound good, commercial distractions offering programs and merchandise to fix your life.

What if crisis intervention is my calling and it doesn't matter if it drives me nuts? What if I'm stuck with it? I didn't pick this. But what else am I going to do? Besides, you gotta make money somehow. It'll do for now. I'll figure it out.

"Figure it out" means I'm wandering around Piggly Wiggly

searching for ways to stay asleep and awake for under twenty bucks. Everything marked PM is simply Benadryl, and I've already tried that. I started with one tablet, then two, then guzzling the liquid in Berry Burst until eventually it didn't work anymore.

I grab some melatonin, four tiny bottles of Snooze Water, and a box of Wiggly brand sleepytime tea. For maximum vigilance, a fistful of five-hour energy drinks, blister packs of Sudafed, and a vat of caffeine pills marked down to $1.99. I'm going to beat this thing or die trying.

Scratch that. Bad choice of words. With God's help and practical methods, I will beat insomnia.

While I'm in the self-check line, Squiggly, the dispatch operator, rings with a crisis call. I scribble the info on the back of my receipt and hit the road. A lady on the helpline describes the knot in her stomach while I speed down the interstate. I listen, waiting for her to get to the point, but she just rambles on.

"Ma'am?" I finally interrupt. "I'm psychiatric crisis. What is it I can help you with?"

"Okay," she says. "So I saw y'all's commercial on channel 12, and here's my question. Does it sound like a hernia? Or do you think it's maybe just gas?"

Not five minutes later a girl calls in, too hysterical to understand, and after that, a man with a Colombian accent gets indignant because I refuse to referee a fight between him and his fiancée on a three-way call. Then some backwater hospital, out past Wickyville, lets me know its patient should be medically cleared soon, so put it on my list; and Skylark CCU buzzes in to tell me the client I just finished with there changed her mind and wants to do outpatient now.

"We'll need you to come back," the nurse informs me. "Her father called a family meeting and wants you involved."

"I don't do families," I tell her, always a little guilty when I have to stand my ground. "Plus, I'm forty-five minutes away now. I'm crisis. Once I'm gone, I'm gone." She huffs and hangs up without saying good-bye.

Just off the highway there's a road hidden in the brush, marked with two orange ribbons tied to a pine. After a half mile or so the asphalt turns to gravel and then to dirt. The dirt road dead-ends into the trees. A couple hundred yards through the trees lies one of the last remaining fire towers. The Forestry Commission knocked the first fifteen steps out, but I can make my way past it by inching up the frame. A cabin sits at the top with just enough space for a desk and lookout. From there you can see nothing for miles but shadows and shades of black, no lights, only trees and night.

Once my eyes adjust, the distance to the ground makes my stomach spin. It's good to feel the panic, to sit with it and make yourself breathe through.

You have to take small breaks from crisis response, find a place to stop and switch gears. I've got a perfectly good excuse: my cell shows no service. I lay flat and stare through the trapdoor, straight to the ground. Vertigo churns me. I think about the legs of the tower collapsing while I'm on top.

Deep breath. Calm. I'm a hundred feet high in the middle of the woods. It's peaceful—until the phone rings. Great. One tiny bar of reception slipped through the trapdoor.

I hear you laughing, God.

Rose County Jail calls to request assistance on an inmate arrested for D&D. "Dungeons & Dragons?" I reply, wondering what might happen if I threw my phone off the fire tower, far into deep forest. "My preacher warned me about those weirdos."

"Blaine, you know good and well what D&D is. This old fool was drunk in the Dollar Tree parking lot, and that Yankee manager down there called the cops. Can you come tell us what to do with him?"

"On my way."

I head down the tower, the trees and sky around me brighter now. With every step the fear and dizziness lessen, but I really can't breathe right until I'm standing back on solid ground, staring back up at the cabin, a silver speck against the night.

Rose County is a good hour's drive up the highway. It's the last of the country jails—a white wood-frame house with cells in the basement and lots of good-ol'-boy officers with flattop haircuts and Copenhagen tucked between their gums and cheek.

"Inmate's right down there, last door," Sergeant Riley says when I arrive, wiping his mouth and handing me a big bronze key with round tumblers and *#4* stamped on the side. "I know you don't need me to go witcha, do ya?"

On the counter before him there's a baked potato with chili dumped over the top and a large Frosty. Riley catches my hungry stare. "Hey, you want something? I know you ain't had no time to stop. You can have Glaser's. He obviously don't need no more food."

Glaser leans out from the booking desk, jarhead blonde and baby-faced, already stuffing a double-stack cheeseburger into his mouth. "You ain't one to talk, Riley," he snorts.

"I'll catch something later if it slows down," I say. "Besides, I'm more of a Subway guy. Let me take care of my man here. What'd you say his name is?"

"Thomas Paul," Glaser calls.

"Nobody calls him that, though," Riley corrects. "Been Deuce long as I've knowed him."

"*Doooose,*" Glaser hoots.

"Deuce ain't crazy," Riley explains. "He's just an old drunk."

"I like old drunks," I reply. "Me and old drunks get along just fine."

A long hall with brown-paneled walls and green pile carpeting leads to the basement stairs, where I'm buzzed through a thick steel door. Beyond, in general population, guys are gathered around a TV watching *The Andy Griffith Show*. Parnell's on guard, leaning back in a straight chair, picking at his teeth with his pinky nail. I linger a moment, long enough to watch Barney speed away on a motorcycle, leaving Andy stranded in the sidecar. The old men of Mayberry laugh, and Parnell laughs with them, slapping the arm of the trustee next to him.

"You kin see it five hundred times," Parnell says, "and it's still funny as the first." He spots me and tips his head. "Blaine!"

I shout back and duck down the other hall. There's a set of four doors on the right, each with a slot in the middle wide enough to slide a food tray through. I walk to the last one and turn the key in the lock.

Inside is a six-by-nine cell with a concrete bench along the wall and steel commode in the corner. A tall, scrawny fellow is splayed over the bench, like he tripped over backward and stayed there, one leg up and his arm hanging over the edge. Wayward white hair falls over bony shoulders. His skin is pockmarked and scarred, red stars tattooed between his first finger and thumb. He looks like a welfare Johnny Winter from South Arkansas.

"What's shakin', boss?" he asks in a raspy cackle. "C'mon in here. Have you a seat."

The toilets in jail are cold steel, seatless, and low to the ground. I slide up on the other end of the bench.

"Boy, what you doin' out here this time a night?" Deuce grins like he's known me all my life.

"Come to see you," I tell him. "Hey, remind me why they call you Deuce."

He rolls his arm over to show me the two of diamonds inked on his right shoulder.

"I've seen jacks and kings and jokers, and one time I even saw

Jesus holding the ace of spades. But can't say I've ever seen a two-of-diamonds tattoo."

He taps the two. "Won fifty bucks bluffin' on a pair when I was twenty-two. Buddies started callin' me Deuce. Guess it stuck." He's wearing boot-cut jeans, no shoes, and a faded old shirt that says, *SKYNYRD '93 The Last Rebel Tour.*

"So," I say. "Drunk at the dollar store, huh?"

"Ah, you know how it is," he says. "Or maybe not. You mighta been smarter'n me and not ever took up with no foolishness."

I point to his shirt. "Me and my buddy Jules used to ride around on nights like this singing 'Simple Man' loud with the windows down."

"Naw, you didn't." Deuce grins, his eyes lighting up.

It's Sunday night, 10:45. I've got nothing to lose, not one thing. So I bounce it off the cell-block walls, that old song about love and trouble passing by, not living so fast you miss what really counts, never forgetting there's a God above ready and willing to catch your fall.

Deuce sits up, slaps my back, and leans in on the chorus. A voice from down the hall joins in, and we both bust out laughing. "How old was you then?" he asks.

"Seventeen," I reply.

"In high school? That's what we was doin' when I's in school. The Lord watches out for ol' drunks and babies, I guess."

"God watches," I agree.

A tiny porthole sits at the top of Deuce's cell, and the smell of burning leaves floats in on the wind. We sit there in the thought of things, old memories rattling around.

"I remember one night we were out riding," I begin. "It was storming and the windows were fogged, and this lady ran the light. Jules hit the brakes, and the car started spinning, skidding straight toward the gully. And then we stopped, like some big hand held us back, just inches from the ledge." I hold my hands apart to show how far.

"Every bit of fog cleared except for one place in the middle of the windshield," I continue. "Jules said, 'Dude! It's Jesus!' And I gotta admit, it did look just like him. We sat there staring until the lady came over and knocked on the glass. I cracked the window, turned the music down, and she said, 'Never seen nothing like that. Good Lord must be with you both.'"

Deuce sits forward now, hands on his knees, head leaned close to mine. "What happened then?" he asks.

"She was on her way home from bingo. Said she had thirty-five hundred dollars' cash in the car and didn't want to call the cops. We didn't either. Guess the Lord really was with us."

"Oh, he was," Deuce says, in a sure sort of tone. "Matter of fact, he's right here in this cell. I don't live right, but I know Jesus; he's always with me."

"I don't know," I confess. "Some places I go, I have to wonder if Jesus is anywhere around."

"Ain't no such thing, son," says Deuce. "You can go to the worst part of hell, and Jesus'll whip the devil's tail to come find you. Says so right in the Bible. I can show you." He pulls up his shirt. In hard black script against his ribs: *Though I make my bed in hell / thou art with me.* There's a soaring eagle over his heart and next to that a crude tattoo of a redhead with a huge rack, winking and holding a pool cue.

"That's Donna," Deuce explains. "She was a good girl." He traces her outline with his finger. "She's long time gone now, though."

"Sorry to hear that," I say.

"What happened to your friend?" he asks, his pale eyes piercing, knowing, somehow.

"What friend?"

"One that was with you when Jesus stopped the car."

"Long time gone," I reply.

"Everybody been through something, ain't they?" Deuce says, shaking his head. "Make you wish you could do it all over, knowing what you know now."

"Is it ever too late to start over?"

He smiles and points to the words beneath the soaring eagle: . . . *and this bird you cannot change.* "Maybe," he says. "Maybe not." He lets his shirt down and leans back against the wall. One foot on the bench. Arm hanging off the side.

"Anything I can do to help you, sir?" I ask.

"I'll be all right, friend," he says. "Appreciate you comin' to visit tonight. You be careful out there. Hope to see you again."

I walk back up to the front office. Just outside the screen door there's a porch swing at the bottom of the steps. Riley's rocking while Glaser pulls at the dirt with his boot. "What y'all wanna do with Deuce?" I ask, flopping down into the swing.

"Chief said it was up to you," says Riley.

"What you gonna do if I don't send him somewhere?"

"Turn him loose," Glaser says.

An unmarked squad car squeezes into the sally port while another exits, slowly motoring toward the town square. Magnolias bloom in the prison yard, sweet flowers on the wind.

"Turn him loose, then," I reply.

Riley recites a few codes into his radio and holsters it back. We swing for a minute or so. "Hey, Glaser," he says, snapping his fingers.

Glaser reaches into his cruiser and hands me a Wendy's bag, still hot. They both grin, watching. Inside the bag is a footlong chicken on flatbread from Subway. "Oh, man, I'm starving," I tell them. "How'd you know what I like?"

"Glaser looks all tough," Riley says, "but he's real sensitive inside. Y'all oughta give him a job. He listens to people and stuff."

"Shut up, man." Glaser laughs, kicking dirt Riley's way. Then to me, "Least Rose County can do for you, coming all this way."

"Take it with you if you're in a hurry," Riley says, swinging the rocker with his foot.

"No hurry," I tell him, taking the first bite. "No rush at all."

EVERYTHING MEANS EVERYTHING

We speak of the mysterious and hidden wisdom of God,
which He destined for our glory before time began.
—1 CORINTHIANS 2:7 (BSB)

I WAS JUST BACK AND SETTLED WHEN THE LANDSCAP-
ers came and the sound of their weedeaters cut through the
endless surf. Now I'm tossing, restless, worrying about having no
insurance or enough money in the bank for an unforseen emergency, about living an entire life missing the mark, wondering if
the uptight Christians aren't right about the State of All Things.

It's always been a sleepless fear of mine: that life's sweepstakes
are rigged for the select sure and the cruelest messages from religion are spot on. Where heaven is an exclusive club for those who
look and talk the same. And if it's an uptight heaven, I'll never
make it anyway. But would you really want to be with those who
do? How could that be good news?

Unfair, you say? What can you do about it? You're not in
charge down here. You are one among billions returning to dust.

There are middle-of-the-night anxieties you'd never even

consider in practical, waking hours. Even if the middle of your night is high noon.

My best effort to beat insomnia didn't work. One dose of melatonin did nothing, and even though the sleepytime tea was pleasant, I didn't notice any effects other than an increased urge to wake up and pee. The Snooze Water is a gimmick, I believe. I tried making sleepytime tea with Snooze Water and double crushed-up melatonin last night, and it amped my dreams up even more vividly than before.

In the nightmare, a lady called from her garage, the car running while she laid the seat back and waited for the fumes to take her away. "I can't do this anymore," she said, her words slurred and slipping. "I just can't." There was something familiar in her voice I couldn't quite place.

"Hang on, wait," I pleaded. "Don't hang up. Don't leave me."

I ran for my truck. The starter clicked. No charge. I cradled the phone on my shoulder and threw up the hood, checking cables, trying to keep her talking and awake, praying for help, for insight, for anything. The skies turned silver, missile traces streaming from the east. The woman's voice grew distant and still.

I cut across the cul-de-sac to a shortcut through the woods and into her yard. I was in her house, shouting, trying to find the garage. Never-ending stairwells took me to the same floor, and doors opened to dead-end walls while the ceiling sank lower and lower still.

My phone showed zero bars as the echo of faraway bombs shook the ground. The lights blinked twice before plunging the room into total darkness. More bombs, like the footsteps of a giant in the land. I hoped it was Jesus returning, tall as a skyscraper, to split the eastern sky. Not so meek or mild this time, finally come to set things right.

Suddenly it was quiet. A frail voice called from the other side. All the doors were locked now.

I woke up with legs thrashing, still trying to kick through the wall. I've had this dream before but never so intense. It felt like I was trapped in some end-times movie with the most suspenseful scene stuck on repeat. It felt more real than the waking world.

I click on the old videotape, watching Jake and Elwood crash past Disco Pants and Haircuts in the Dixie Square Mall, but it feels like I need to do something more productive, so I shut down the television and study Ecclesiates awhile. In strange and trying times, you can always look to Ecclesiastes. God would have to be the only Christian willing to publish King Solomon's weird, moody memoir.

Wait, is God a Christian? How does that work?

Either way, I don't know why church doesn't preach more Ecclesiastes, because Solomon got it right. It's a life of illusion and control, confusing sometimes to find balance, to try and figure out why we're all here. But if Solomon made it, maybe there's hope for the rest of us too.

I'm not very consistent with journaling, but I've actually made it through a few entries, so I pick up Tina's workbook and turn to the page with Jesus looming over Niagara Falls. It says that nothing is wasted if viewed from the right perspective. Everything working together for the good means you can't just brag on the shiny parts and hide the strange. Jesus knocks already knowing. Throw the doors open. Come clean. *Everything* means everything.

"Isn't it just like Jesus to redeem all things?" the author asks.

DAY 4

Some say there are no accidents, that we end up right where we belong. Regardless of what you believe, how have past experiences prepared you for your journey today? Write about a time when the hidden hand of God worked all things together for the good.

TUESDAY'S GONE, RIDE ON

[THEN]

You have experienced many things. Were
all those experiences wasted?
—GALATIANS 3:4 (ICB)

KKAS HAD A STANDUP DJ BOOTH AND phone lines that tied into the control board with a red light flashing to show incoming calls. With the flick of a switch the caller's voice would come over the speakers (but not the air), and you could go about your business, having a conversation through the monitors and the mike. A lot of bored, lonely people called on my overnight shift, wanting to hear their song, to talk about life for a while. I didn't have to answer unless I felt like it.

A pair of coeds called in one night, chatty and giggling, just bored, saying they were freshmen at the little Christian college over the river in Rankinville.

"I applied there after high school," I told them. "Even though I had decent grades and a letter from the preacher, they still wouldn't let me in. Admissions lady said I 'wasn't a good fit,' whatever that means."

"They like safe-and-same here," the alpha coed said. "Sounds like you might be too much fun."

"*Fun!*" cried the sillier one. "We just want to have some *fun!*"

"So what y'all do for fun?"

"Last semester we got written up for spitting off the footbridge," Silly confessed.

"Whoa. Holy Rollers gone wild."

"Oh, that was stupid," Alpha cut in. "It wasn't even like anybody got hit. And we're not Holy Rollers. You should come hang out with us sometime! If you're not too famous to hang out with regular people, that is."

"Okay, yeah. Maybe so," I said, ignoring the earlier warnings of my fellow DJs.

"Girls'll call you, sounding all flirty and sweet, wanting to meet up," Sandi Strands, our superperky drive-time DJ had cautioned me at a staff meeting the week before. "But don't do it. It's better to leave the mystique."

"One time this girl called, said she was runner-up to Miss Mississippi," Chuck Buckle chimed in. "Figured I couldn't lose. So I met her at the Sizzler for strawberry pie."

"And?" I asked our region's top-rated radio personality. (Chuck was the only DJ to use his real name. "Why change it if it's already cool?" he said.)

"Pig farmer," Sandi cut in.

"Wasn't that bad," Buckle shot back.

"Zombie pig farmer," Sandi said. "I was there."

I covered my face, peeking through my fingers. "This story is so not good."

"Actually," Buckle admitted, "she really did farm pigs. I mean, we are in the rural south."

Sandi laughed the trademark bubbly chuckle that resounded out of early-morning radios across the land. On-air she sounded as spunky and cute as Reese Witherspoon. In person she looked like Blanche from the *Golden Girls* after a six-month bender of meatball subs and Chunky Monkey while following the Grateful Dead across the Midwest.

So when the holy-rolling coeds called back and needled me into a get-together, I devised a plan. "Meet me at the intersection of Bee Balm and Jasmine at 9:05 next Thursday night," I said, trying to sound mysterious and cool. "I'll take Bee Balm. When our cars pass, flip on your dome light."

"Okay," they agreed. "Look for a shiny black Jag."

"Black Jag?" I replied. "Awesome!"

I picked two streets I knew would be dark and deserted. Driving through once alone, I made a second pass and then on the third spotted an approaching car. It was black, all right. An old LeBaron ragtop with duct tape holding the right headlight in its socket and a clawmark caked with Bondo down the side. Laughing, I flashed my brights and the LeBaron winked back.

It was a big intersection and our cars sat a good ways apart. We both pulled forward. They flipped on their dome light just before we crossed. The driver was bug-eyed but as adorable as a newborn shih tzu. The passenger-side girl had deep dimples and a head full of bouncy gold curls. The top was up with both windows down.

"Hit your light!" Dimples screamed.

I flipped it on and forgot to be cool, fumbling with my window, waving both hands, expecting pig farmers, I suppose. At the cross street I whipped the car around, opened my door, and stood in the middle of the road with arms high.

Their brake lights lit the tree leaves red as they U-turned through the boulevard. I pulled my shirt straight and leaned against the truck, trying to salvage some last bit of cool as the LeBaron approached. Instead of slowing, though, the car sped up. A hand flashed out the window followed by two red bubbles and a clear, wet wave. They smacked against me with an ice-cold shock. I sputtered and lurched back, burst water balloon skins and a Sonic Route 44 cup rolling in the street before me like a smoking gun.

The engine strained to full throttle. Screams and laughter echoed as their lights faded. The streets were suddenly cold and very still.

Now I know how Jesus feels.

Funny what you think in strange situations. I'd heard a sermon the Sunday before about how the Son of man was rejected and scorned. I'm not comparing myself to Jesus, but for just a moment, soaking wet and standing like a fool in the middle of the road, I thought I might could start to understand.

I stood a long time waiting. The summer heat dried my shirt and skin. Once the shock wore off, it was kind of invigorating. Like cold water sometimes has the power to make you feel new.

I climbed back in and drove to the station. "Little early for your shift, huh?" Chuck Buckle said, half smiling as he stroked his beard.

"Little bit," I replied. "You mind?"

"C'mon in, man. Gets lonely in here. Whatcha been up to?"

"Nothing," I told him. "Nothing at all."

It was three in the morning when the red light flashed.

"Hello?" The speakers amplified every little thing. There was a sniffle, then hard breathing for a while. Some women called to talk dirty, but that was mostly Buckle's shift. Not my thing. "You there?" I asked. "Say something, or I'ma hang up."

"Is this really the DJ?"

"This is really . . . *the DJ*," I replied in my radio tone.

"Listen, I'm just gonna tell you up front," the caller said. "I been drinkin' a little tonight."

"I'm on Sundays, midnight to six," I told her. "Everybody that calls me has been drinking."

She laughed, and we made small talk for a while. She sounded young but not dumb, a little anxious but not unsure. If that makes sense. Seemed like a pretty nice girl. "I bet it's cool having your voice go out to all those strangers," she said. "People calling, playing music through the night."

"It's all right sometimes," I said. "Got a song you wanna hear?"

"Yeah," she said. "Will you put on 'Tuesday's Gone'? I really need to hear that song tonight."

Something about the way she said it made me ask. "Why's that?"

"Because I'm tired of living this life, and that's the song I want to ride out to." She said it flat, matter-of-fact. I couldn't think of anything to say back. "Pretty messed up, huh?" she asked. "Hope I'm not freakin' you out."

"What's goin' on?"

"It's a long story. Even if I told you, it wouldn't make no sense." Her voice caught; she swallowed hard. "You get so tired, man." The rasp in her breath rustled the speakers as she let out a long exhale. "You probably wouldn't understand. You're busy."

"It's three in the morning. I'm not that busy."

"Things ain't been the same since my mama died. There's not really anybody I can trust or talk to. Takin' too many pills, drinkin', doin' stupid stuff. Money. I don't know. It's hard to explain."

"How old were you when your mom passed?"

"Thirteen. You think you get over it, but nah—stuff like that, it don't never leave you. I just feel so lost sometimes."

"Me too. Sometimes."

"Yeah? What do you do when you feel really, really bad? Like really low."

"Listen to music. Talk to my friends. I don't know. Talk to God."

"I pray sometimes, but it don't feel like it does much good. Drinking helps for a while, but all your same old problems are right there waiting when you sober up, man. Sometimes I drink and pray at the same time—pray not to have to drink so much, drink to not have to pray. I know that sounds crazy."

"Hang on a sec," I told her, switching the mike live to give a quick segue from Bob Seger into Kid Rock. "So why 'Tuesday's Gone'?" I asked.

"'Cause that's the name she gave me," she said, her voice cracking on the last words. "Tuesday's gone, baby. Train roll on."

The studio was dim, VU meters and console lights, the TriCounty color weather radar glowing from a corner screen. Twenty seconds or so passed, neither of us saying much. "I think Tuesday is a really pretty name."

"It's okay, I guess. That's my middle name. My first name is Angela."

"Mine's Jamie. Nice to meet you."

"Real name?"

"Yeah."

"Why they call you Hollywood on the radio?"

"'Cause I got crazy hair and wear sunglasses all the time."

"I bet you're one of them DJs that looks like you sound."

"I'm just the late-night guy at a small-town rock-and-roll station."

"What's Chuck Buckle look like?"

"Like a homeless Mick Fleetwood if you shot him out of a cannon into a liquor store."

"Chuck Buckle looks like the dude from Fleetwood Mac?" She laughed.

"If he was homeless, yeah. He's got that awesome radio voice, though."

"I like your voice better," she said. "It calms me down. Really, I've been wantin' to talk to you for a long time. But I was afraid to call."

"Thanks. A lot of times it feels like nobody's listening."

"Oh, yeah. We're out here. All us crazy children of the night."

"Well, I'm right here with you. Talk all you want. But instead of 'Tuesday's Gone,' I'm gonna play 'Ride On' for you. In fact, I'm gonna play it next." I flipped the far dial and cued up cut eight. "Send it out to Tuesday or Angela?"

"Angie," she said, leaving a bit of dead air between the words. "But call me Angel."

I switched the mike live. "Three thirty-five under gray skies and overnight threats of rain. Ronald Belford Scott's swan song for you right now. Sending this one out to Angel and all the children of the night, the lonely and broken, those who can't sleep, everybody just trying to hang on. Brother Bon left us with a message: it's tough sometimes, but you keep riding on. You're listening to the Home of the Rock; this is Hollywood here with you all night long."

"One day," Angel said, speak-singing the lyrics as they rolled along. "Gonna change my crazy ways." We had a ratty old couch sitting back behind the amplifiers. I walked over and sank down into it, listening to Angel breathe and talk and sing. "Sure I'm not bothering you?" she asked.

"Nah," I told her. "I'm here 'til dawn."

JAMIE, TAKE THE WHEEL

[NOW]

It's quite simple: Do what is fair and just to your
neighbor, be compassionate and loyal in your
love, and don't take yourself too seriously.
—MICAH 6:8 (THE MESSAGE)

T'S 8:08 ON A CLOUDY WEDNESDAY NIGHT, AND I'M
standing on a downtown sidewalk, staring at Lionel Richie.

A goliath Lionel posed next to an equally mammoth Sheryl
Crow with her head tilted and a come-hither look, their auras
backlit gold, and the words on the billboard declaring, *Sweet
Sounds. All Day, All Night . . . LIGHT 106.*

KKAS is still here. Sort of. The old radio station sits across
the street from city jail. I got summoned here for an evaluation a
few hours after I wrote about it in the workbook. City jail rarely
calls.

Some might call this serendipitous or a sign, but they taught
us in grad school that humans are hardwired to seek out con-
nections. We exaggerate chance and call it destiny, ignoring the
random chaos stuff. We make our own signs. We believe what we
want and need to believe.

They also taught us not to expect any parades for enlightening the public to these conditions. Behavioral psychologists spoil a lot of fun. Maybe the fact that we're hardwired to find relationships is the sign.

The elevator takes me straight from the street to the second-floor jail. A girl with carrot-colored hair, apple cheeks, and a gap between her front teeth sleeps peacefully in the front holding cell. Her tiny frame is curled into the corner, loosely secured by a lime-green safety smock.

"Miss Darla," the lady jailer says, giving her shoulder a shake.

Zzz.

"Darla!"

"Seriously?" I complain. "Next time I can't sleep, can y'all strap me in restraints and lay me on a concrete slab in the middle of booking? Save me a room. I'll stay here tonight."

"Ain't she something?" the lady jailer asks. "I'm lyin' awake half the night, and here this inmate is sleeping like a baby." She shakes her again, harder this time. Darla moans and rolls over in the flickering fluorescent light. Her clothing is dangerously askew. I turn and stare through the cell door's window.

"Darla's a sweet person. Good-hearted as all get out," the lady jailer tells me, fixing her outfit. "But when she get to drankin', girl go crazy. Caught her runnin' through traffic hollering 'bout hell is hot. Okay, she decent now. Turn around."

I turn back as the jailer pulls a pink barrette from her pocket and pins Darla's locks up out of her face. "You so pretty," she says, somehow both chiding and kind. "Listen to what this man's got to say. Do what he tell you." Then to me, "Lord, I bet you seen it all in this job."

"No, ma'am," I reply. "Ain't seen a thing."

"Yeah, right," she says, stepping outside the door. "Be out here if you need me."

Darla sits up, smacks her lips together, and rubs her eyes. She's the kind of fair-haired girl that could pass for twelve or twenty-five. "You kinda look like Jesus," she says, gesturing to my beard and hair.

"If I could just figure out how to act like him."

"Tell me 'bout it," she groans, slumped over and pressing her face to the cool surface of the cinderblock wall. "Jesus, take the wheel."

"I heard that," I tell her.

"Heard that," she sighs. "You bail bondsman?"

"Nope."

"Commissioner?"

"Un-uh."

"Preacher," she decides.

"Not quite."

One eye opens. "Then who are you?"

"Psych guy."

"Oh, shoot." She sits upright, blinking hard. "You can get me outta here. If you only knew my story, mister."

"I do know your story." Pause. This is the fun part. "That's why I'm here."

Five minutes later Darla's back in street clothes, eating a baloney-and-cheese sandwich on the front bench of booking. "All aboard," I say, passing back through from the copy machine.

"What's that?" she asks, cramming in another mouthful and rattling her shackles as she swings her short legs back and forth.

Taking a seat beside her on the bench, I point and read from her bright blue Vacation Bible School tee: *All Aboard Noah's Ark.* There are a giraffe and some balloons on the front.

"Oh, yeah," she says, dusting a litter of crumbs from her belly. "Church folk gimme this. They been letting me sleep in the back room of the thrift store."

"Where does a person sleep in the back room of a thrift store?" I ask, swinging my feet alongside hers.

"Anywhere." She shrugs. "Old couches. Pile of clothes. I was sleeping on the porch 'fore the bugs got bad. I ain't picky, though."

"Sleeping on somebody's old underwear. Huh. Passed out drunk in a side cell. Jailhouse sandwich and leg shackles. I don't mean to sound judgmental but, uh, maybe you should start being a little more picky. Y'know?"

Darla starts to speak but stops short. Her eyes flicker down, then away. "Yeah," she says in a quiet voice. "Prob'ly so."

For just an instant all the noise of convicts, two-way radios, and steel cell doors disappears, and there is only one bench and two people. We sit staring at the bars and bold-print warning signs, both of us wondering how life came to this. She offers it again, same words, different verse, a lot more somber now. "Jesus," she says, "take the wheel."

"Heard that," I reply.

If I'm on any mission, with any message, it's this: I am not above it. I'm just like you.

"Sometimes I feel like Jesus is singing that same song back, only using my name instead."

"What's that mean?" she asks.

"Like Jesus is saying, 'Jamie, son, I gave that wheel to you. Faith isn't an excuse for irresponsibility. Learn to drive.'"

"You hear Jesus singing?" Darla says.

The lull breaks. "Never mind." I smile, holding out my hand. She studies it a half second before offering a hearty shake. "Nice to meet you," I tell her. "But let's try not to meet this way again. Okay?"

"'Kay," she says, crinkling her nose when she smiles. "Hey, can I get another one of them sandwiches?"

"Jailer?" I call. "Can Miss Darla have another sandwich?"

"Girl look like she could use another sammich," the lady jailer replies. "Yeah."

"You a pretty nice guy," Darla says.

"My mama thinks I'm pretty," I reply. "Not so sure about the nice."

She breathes deep and lets the words go with a lazy peace, like blowing dandelions over a field. "Well, we all got the best and worst in us, I guess."

There's a tug in my gut, so I palm ten bucks from my pocket and pass it to her in another handshake, this one a little more awkward until she feels the bill against her fingers.

"Thanks," she whispers, coughing and sliding the money into her jeans.

"You get over to this place I'm sending you, shoot straight, and work the program, okay?" She nods, taking another bite. "And if you get in a bind," I tell her, "find me."

"Even if I mess up again?" she mumbles, sandwich crammed to the side of her mouth. "You'll still come help?"

"Even if you mess up again," I promise. "Find me."

"Okay," she says with that crinkle-nosed, gap-toothed smile. "I will."

The lady jailer escorts me back through a series of locked doors. "Ain't seen you in a while," she says. "You go to the jails a lot?"

"I spend more time in jail than a seven-foot pyromaniac wearing an *I Hate Cops* shirt and riding getaway on a Minnie Mouse Big Wheel."

"You funny," she says, slapping my arm. "We need to get you up here more often."

"Call me," I tell her. "I'll come. I used to work across the street in college."

"At the radio station?"

"Yep. The inmates used to shout down requests."

"I remember that!" she says, smacking me a second time. "Wish they'd a never changed. I used to like it when they played rock-and-roll."

"Yeah, me too," I say, stepping into the elevator. "Let me know if you got somebody, okay?"

"I'ma call you," she reminds me as the doors close. Though she can't see me, I nod. The elevator groans and starts a slow crawl down to the street. I walk to the back parking lot and sit on my hood, making the necessary calls to get Darla transferred out of jail and into treatment. Insurance companies love to put you on hold and play that awful music—not jazz, not classical, certainly not Lionel Richie or classic rock. I hit Speakerphone, turn down the volume, and lay it to the side.

From behind Light 106's billboard the old downtown looks the same—bridge lights shining off the river and a legion of one-way streets. If I stand on the bumper, I can see through the back window to the DJ booth, the ON AIR sign illuminated now.

Interesting how different things look once you get them out of your head. The stories from my past ramble just as much as my patients' do. Or maybe I've heard so many I frame my own history that way. There's insight in the ramble, though. Guess I was taking late-night crisis calls even before I was the psych guy.

And the Holy Roller coeds? My church had been leaning on me to seek out other believers so as not to be unequally yoked. Since I deejayed heathen rock radio and the hot college dance club, their concerns might have been valid. That's the reason I agreed to meet girls from the strict Baptist college. I was expecting sugar, not spice. Halos, not horns. Sweet Christian innocence, not two tricksters who would lure out some poor, desperate DJ and attack him with water balloons. Although in all fairness, I found out after the fact they'd called in on Chuck's shift and he'd put them up to the whole thing. Buckle. What a comedian.

What does it all mean? I do not have a clue. "Trust the process," the workbook says. "The Bible doesn't whitewash or edit. Neither should you."

Still on hold. Same bland song. Something about it sounds vaguely familiar. Finally, I figure it out. It's the never-ending version of "Stairway to Heaven," Muzak style. Flavorless but still somehow mesmerizing.

The river is swollen from yesterday's storm. I stare off into the distance, listening as water gushes around the supports. Soon I am traveling back in time again.

MAMA KNOWS

[THEN]

I revealed myself to those who did not ask for me;
I was found by those who did not seek me.
To a nation that did not call on my name,
I said, "Here am I, here am I."

—ISAIAH 65:1 (NIV)

I WAS DRIVING OVER THE BLACK RIVER BRIDGE ON MY way to work the midnight shift at KKAS when the swooping space-age synths from Rush's seventeen-minute opus "Overture/Temples of Syrinx" came over my radio. If you hear "Freebird," "In-A-Gadda-Da-Vida," or side one of *2112*, you can pretty much bet the DJ has gone to the bathroom or on break.

Sure enough, I turned down South Sixth and there he was: DJ Chuck Buckle, vegetarian skinny with thin, frizzy hair, in a billowy white shirt with half the buttons gone. He was sitting on the hood of his blood-orange Geo Storm, smoking and talking to the sky. I parked and walked over.

"Hey, hey, Holly Dolly," Buckle said in his classic rock-radio croak. My DJ name was J. Hollywood James, but Chuck called me Holly or

Holly Dolly or sometimes just plain HD. "What's the name'a that church you go to again?"

"The Lighthouse," I replied. Locusts swarmed the streetlights, and a sweet, sticky stink lingered in the air. "Why?"

A voice rang out from above. "Promised mama I'd go soon as I got out."

City jail sat second floor of the police station across the street. A pair of hands hung out past the barred window. I stepped back and shielded the lights. The inmate was sandy blond and shaggy, like Wooderson from *Dazed and Confused*, except sadder, further down on luck, and his eyes were really badly crossed.

"Lighthouse Full Gospel," I called up to him. "In the old furniture store under the water tower. Who's that?"

"Li'l Jay," Buckle said. "You know Li'l Jay, doncha?"

"Nice to meet you," I called again.

"That one them Holy Roller churches?" Li'l Jay asked. "What's the people like?"

"We got good and bad," I told him. "Just like anywhere's else. I go mostly Sunday nights, but come on anytime."

"What's the cover charge?" Li'l Jay joked.

"You gotta give your heart to the Lord," Buckle shot back. "That's the charge."

Li'l Jay's voice dropped low. "Mama says I need to get right."

Buckle squinted, taking a hard toke. "Mama knows."

"When you gettin' out?" I asked.

"Week from Tuesday, if I don't screw it up this time."

"Don't screw it up," Buckle advised.

"Man, it's like I *know* right," Jay drawled, "if I could just *do* right. Y'know?"

"Trust me," Buckle said, staring toward the river. "I know."

Li'l Jay and I looked to the river too, its bridge lights reflecting red against the water, a trail of taillights fading down the far span.

The Geo's radio was playing low, Rush's opus now wrapping up. "Well, fellas," I told them. "Better run."

"See ya, HD," Buckle croaked. "Rock and roll."

"Rock and roll," I replied, heading for the door.

"Hey, Hollywood," Li'l Jay shouted. "Can you play me somethin'?"

I turned back. "What's that?"

Li'l Jay gripped the bars now, the neon sign of Boogie's Bail Bonds lighting up his craggy face. When he smiled, from where I was standing, it was almost like his eyes went straight. "Can you play me, 'Mama, I'm Comin' Home'?"

"You got it, brother," I promised. "See you soon."

Inside, I grabbed Jay's song and cued it first. "Seventy-six degrees just after midnight at the Home of the Rock." I turned off the mike. There were ten seconds left in a sixteen-second intro, so I flipped it on again. "Everybody's looking for their place. We're all just trying to get back home. Jay, brother, this one's for you. Hollywood, here with you through the long night."

I rolled the volume down and pushed back from the console. The request line flashed and an automated voice came over the line. "This is a collect call from a correctional facility. Do you accept the charge?"

"Sure," I laughed. "Yes, I do."

"Hey, man," Li'l Jay said. "Just wanted to say thanks."

"You got it."

"What time you said that church was again? The night one."

"Six on Sundays."

"I'll find a way to make it, brother. If I can just get out, I'll see you there."

ONLY FAITH AND VERTIGO

[NOW]

I have woven a parachute out of everything broken.
—WILLIAM STAFFORD

I'VE GOT A REALLY NICE COUCH UPSTAIRS. IT'S OBLONG and seamless, the color of French Quarter café-au-lait. The downstairs couch is some tatty pink job, but the upstairs couch, so I'm told, was handpicked by Coco Chanel. I like to eat Cocoa Pebbles while sitting on Coco's coffee-colored couch, pondering the mysteries of God and life. We're here for a reason, right? Isn't the pinnacle of existence finding out your reason why?

I was taught that the world was a confused and selfish place. But Christians—the right sort of Christians who attend the right sort of church—have the revelation. They know their place and discern God's guiding voice above the noise. They have a firm grasp of purpose and live victorious lives rich with meaning. If you become the right kind of Christian, you can have this sort of life too.

This notion gives me great hope. Find the right switch, and

the room fills with light. Life suddenly makes sense. You can live in forward motion, sure of your steps. I am still trying to figure out the right kind of Christian to be.

Everything looks different at 4:47 a.m. Thirteen minutes until I go off call, and it all diverts to day shift. If nothing is pending, I can turn off my work phone and sleep. Sometimes the hospital will call my personal phone, though, if it's an emergency. Hospitals have a lot of emergencies.

I saw fourteen people in various stages of distress last night. I did not help them all. Some situations I likely made worse, though my intentions were good. But I helped some. I did my best. Until about 2:45 a.m. It was all fog and diesel fumes after that.

Drinking the leftover milk from a bowl of Cocoa Pebbles— maybe that's the meaning of life. All we have is now.

Usually I'm doing paperwork and follow-up until nearly 8:00 a.m., but 5:00 a.m. arrives, and all is quiet, so I brush my teeth and get into bed. When I wake up, I read Psalm 91. Before bed, it's Proverbs 3: Seek wisdom, guard clear thinking, stop trying to figure everything out. You'll lie down in peace, and your sleep will be sweet.

I stare at the lights as they twinkle, glowing and fading again. Soon enough I slip into the dream.

I'm in a shabby apartment in the worst part of town. Thieves are at the door, and when I bar it with the coffee table, they are at the window. I try to lock the windows while hands lunge through the screens, grasping for my clothes and hair. I force the windows shut, and the thieves are back rattling the flimsy door. There is a family behind me—a woman and small children huddled against the kitchen wall. "You need to hide. You need to get out," I shout.

"There is no other way out," the mother replies.

"If I wasn't so thirsty, I could fight," I tell her. She pours me grape Kool-Aid from the fridge, and I think perhaps it will regenerate me, that the Kool-Aid Man will burst through the wall so we can all escape. I drain the glass, but instead of quenching my thirst, it's salty.

"We're out of sugar," the mother cries. "Salt is all I had."

The door splinters at the hinges as windows smash. A hand thrusts through, grabbing my shirt.

This is so not good, I think.

I wake up parched with the anxiety of the dream still on me. Why do good dreams fade quickly while the memory of a nightmare lingers on?

It's eleven minutes after eight. I toss and turn until finally falling back into a fitful sleep. I am back in the shabby apartment, shoving a bookcase against the door, the family behind me larger now. The process repeats until I stumble out of bed at noon completely frustrated, telling God the sleep was not sweet as advertised and that I don't have any control over dreaming. In dreams I am helpless. Jesus needs to watch my back.

I transfer a load of clothes to the dryer and start on dishes in the sink. Chores caught up, I plug in my calm-down video and stretch out on Coco's couch. The bleach-blonde woman sings "Wind Beneath My Wings" while bratwurst sizzles and a lop-eared Rottweiler drags himself across the grass. Smoke overtakes them—and the screen flips to *Zapped!* Scott Baio might be underrated, but I'm not in the mood for silly movies, so I switch to the Gospel Channel.

"Everybody has rough parts in their story, parts that don't seem to make one bit of sense," the woman preacher with a smoker's voice says. "The question is, do you want to redeem your story? Are you willing to work with God? Or do you want to stay stuck all your life?"

She's a few minutes into the first of a seven-step plan when a heavy sleep sneaks in, sweet as Proverbs promised. Right in time for the alarm to sound and totally ruin it. It's almost like God gets me on a technicality.

There's a scripture covering that too: "Creation was subjected to frustration." Romans 8:20, take your pick of version. The Son of God came to save us from our sins but not our frustrations. They must be important somehow. Maybe if we were too content, no one would try and go to heaven. What are you going to do? Ask for your money back? It's not like God offered a satisfaction guarantee. There are no guarantees. There is only hope and faith.

I stagger downstairs, turn the chair to the sinking sun, and drain a two-liter of Diet Coke until my head starts to clear. At five after five the first crisis call comes in and another night begins.

A new patient at Charter House threw a fit and broke a bunch of furniture. Barbie's gone to a conference, Ronnie has a scratch down the side of his face, and Tina is scrambling best she can. The patient is at the end of Hall C, big bellied and burly with a bowling-ball head, spitting profanities and pacing tight circles, confused mostly and scared. "What's his name?" I ask.

"Buddy," Tina says, then whispering so only I can hear, "mentally, he's only about nine."

"Oh, good," I reply. "We've got something in common." I ease toward him. "Easy, Buddy. Easy. Let's just calm down, all right?"

A retro-future entertainment console from the eighties lies in pieces around him. He slings a plastic shard against the wall. It ricochets back, whizzing past my head. "I don't like it here," he shouts, kicking a second piece. "I want to go home and watch TV."

"Trust me," I tell him. "I wanna go home too. We all do."

He sways side to side, eyeing me with suspicion. "I don't know you."

"You do now. I'm Jamie." I reach out my hand, and he backs away, twitching and gripping a snapped leg from the console like a prison knife. "Looks like you broke our TV stand, but that's okay. We needed a new one anyway. What's your favorite show?"

"*The Simpsons*," he says, still guarded.

"Ah, I love that one too."

Buddy nods and lowers his hands a bit. "You look like Sideshow Bob," he says.

"Aw, man. Sideshow Bob's the bad guy," I grouse, bumping my fist twice against the wall. "You really think so?"

At the two-hit signal, Ronnie rushes out of a side room holding a twin mattress like a battering ram. I fall in beside him, and we pin Buddy against the wall as the nurse tech slips in and sticks twenty milligrams of Geodon into his hip. Half a minute passes. He stops fighting, drops his shank, and slides slowly to the floor.

"Sorry, Buddy," I tell him. "Didn't want you to get hurt."

"I didn't mean to hurt nobody. I just wanted to watch TV."

"We can watch all the TV you want, my man, but you gotta calm down. You almost knocked me in the head and put a pretty bad scratch on Brother Ronnie here."

"I'm sorry," Buddy says in a singsong voice, his eyelids heavy now.

"First day's pretty scary for everybody," Ronnie says. "It's all right."

We lug Buddy's drugged carcass to the front lounge, prop him on the sofa, and hand him the remote, ready to duck in case he somehow finds a second wind. He flips channels five or six times and, lo and behold, there on channel 9 is *The Simpsons*.

Miracles come in strange ways and strange times. Seems like my casual prayers are the ones that get answered best.

"Well, hallelujah," I reply.

Buddy settles in, chuckling to himself as Springfield sings the praises of the monorail. Soon he is snoring, lights out.

"Can I get some of that Geodon?" I ask the nurse tech, still wound tight from the showdown.

"Sure," she says, grabbing a second needle. "Where you wanna get sticked?"

"Not just yet," I beg off, checking my phone for the next call. "Got a long way to go, short time to get there."

"Ain't that a movie?" she asks.

"Everything's a movie," I reply.

Ronnie walks back in with an ice pack against his eye, tapping his fist against mine. "Mattress trick," I tell him. "Works every time."

"What about that night you tried to pin Big Wilda by yourself?" He laughs. "Didn't work too good that time."

"I had just gotten to where I could forget that."

"Oh, we not ever gonna let you forget," he says. "Hey, you still coming to play that show with us, right? We need to practice."

"Yeah. When is it again?" I stand up quick and get so light-headed I collapse back into the chair. The nurse tech slaps a blood pressure cuff on me.

"Ninety-eight over fifty-four," she says. "What have you eaten today?"

"Some Cocoa Pebbles?"

"You need something with more substance. Let me check. I think we got some leftover tuna casserole."

"Pass," I say, woozy at the thought of stinky fish and vertigo. "I gotta go. I'll grab something on the way."

I cut out fast, self-conscious for nearly fainting. Tina catches me at the truck, downing an energy shot. "Are you all right?" she asks.

"Sure. Just running lately."

She tilts her head, sympathetic. "God's still got you on my heart, Jamie."

"I bet he does," I shoot back. I'm bad about talking before I think. "I mean, y'know, thanks."

"Did you get a chance to look at my workbook?"

"That one you gave me? Yeah." I'm about to make fun of the picture of tightrope Jesus at the waterfall when she cuts in.

"I wrote it," she says. "To help those called to the helping profession find inspiration and rest."

"So wait . . . What? That's not your name on front."

"I used a pen name. I don't need to draw attention to myself. It's not about me."

"Oh, wow," I say, changing my tone. "I've been reading it, not every day but most days. It might take me more like forty weeks instead of forty days."

"Time means nothing to God," Tina says. "Works either way. Think about it. What's the first thing you do when you meet a client?"

"Pray?" I reply, certain that's the answer she's looking for.

"After that."

"Think of other places to put in my application?"

"No, silly," she says. "You ask people to tell you their story and help them see how it's relevant to their lives today. It can't all be outflow. You have to have water flowing both ways. So wouldn't it be helpful to work through your own stories too?"

I want to tell Tina that my stories seem pretty random so far and I can't honestly say I've ever felt called to this job. But instead I smile and say, "Huh. Maybe so."

"Trust the process," she says, squeezing me into her side hug. "Just be open to whatever comes along."

I step into the Trooper with one hand holding the door. "Jesus trusted no one," I reply.

"Jesus trusted the process," she says, drawing two fingers from her eyes to mine. "You're better at this than you think. Come see me when you finish. I'll be curious to see what you find."

My ears burn as I shut the door. "Deal," I promise, jamming the gear knob into Reverse, grinding it until I find the fit.

Ronnie flags me down at the end of the drive. "You okay?"

"Yeah, man, fine."

"Union Chapel, three weeks from Sunday night," he says, answering my earlier question.

"I'll be there. Only thing is I might have to slip out early if I get a call that can't wait."

"The call is the call, brother. It is what it is."

"Is what it is," I reply. We bump fists one last time as I swing the truck back and catch the buzzing phone.

"Got your boots on?" Squiggly asks before I can even say hello. "They're lined up waiting. You're not gonna believe what's next."

A THOUSAND NIGHTS OF DANGER AND GRACE

When anybody tells a candid story of failure or sorrow, it
tends to make the world bigger and safer for everyone.
—SANDRA TSING LOH

A SEVENTY-SIX-YEAR-OLD WOMAN IS UNDRESSING
on the highway by that billboard where the injury lawyer
poses with his Yorkies and promises swift justice. At the next
call, ten miles south, a delusional man goes wild, and the security officer unleashes pepper spray in a tiny spare bedroom with a
window fan on high. We all spill out into the grass crying while a
neighbor tries to pour milk in our eyes.

There's a mom sitting in a wrecked car in high weeds, unable
to deal with her son's diagnosis. The guy at Daly County Jail ate
some screws. I'm caught talking twenty minutes to a man with
pneumonia because I cluelessly entered the wrong room. That college freshman I trusted and let go home last Thursday left a note
that said, *Sorry, but I just can't keep going this way.*

I've got a gunmetal crucifix from when I was a kid hanging
around my rearview mirror along with a medallion that says, *God,
grant me the serenity to accept the things I cannot change.* They twist

and shine off the streetlights as I zigzag from one tragedy to the next. Sometimes I slip them around my neck to remind myself that it goes further than just, "There but for the grace of God, go I." Even if I fall, I have to believe grace is there, ready. The Bible promises that grace shadows the broken and mercy never sleeps. It's never too late. There is no such thing as too far gone.

A haggard little man with a box of matches and a trash can full of gasoline sits in a dark carport, ranting about the end of the world. "Everything kills you," he jabbers in a cackly tone. "Sunshine and frying pans, plastic bottles, telephones, aspartame."

"Yes, sir," I call over from the mailbox at the end of his drive. "Kinda scares me too." Which is true. This morning when I couldn't sleep I wrestled the same twisted thoughts. It's a strange moment when you see yourself in someone so flipped out.

"You know what fear is like?" he asks, his words unnervingly cold. "It's like that Whac-A-Mole. You hammer one down and two more come at you from the side."

He strikes a match and lets it burn to his fingers. I grab my binder and scribble his words so I won't forget.

A man with gray whiskers rides by on a banana-seat bicycle with tall handlebars. "George talkin' all crazy again?" he says, stopping beside me. "Don't pay him no mind."

"Says he's got a trash can full of gasoline."

"That ain't gas." Gray Whiskers laughs. "It's probably beer. George, he do this all the time."

Whiskers rides away. I take three steps toward the porch. The smell hits me—fresh-cut grass and gasoline—taking me back to the summers of youth. For a few long seconds, I am lost.

George rips a match down the striker strip. The flame casts shadows against his face as he starts to sing in a high, lonesome voice:

you and me, brother / in his hands
   you and me, sister / in his hands

I sing along softly as I step onto the carport. Gray Whiskers was right. It was only beer.

Teens with firecrackers prank call the suicide hotline. Some lady's cat claws me from behind and my face swells up because I'm allergic. A friend of my stepmom's can't find an antidepressant that works and didn't know who else to turn to. The shy, conservatively dressed girl who leads the contemporary song service is secretly hooked on hydrocodone. "Please don't tell," she pleads, pushing back tears. "I'll lose my job. They won't let me sing."

I pull into the library parking lot and lay the seat back, hoping to get a few minutes rest. Pastor Reddy once preached that peace precedes calling. That's how you know you are on the right path. Soon as I close my eyes, the crisis line rings. Maybe I should ask for my old job at the library back.

The police request help with an escaped mental patient in the abandoned apartments behind the bowling alley. I locate him, but the deputies have left me, moved on to another call. The patient seems volatile, possibly ready to explode. Or perhaps I'm projecting. Broken bowling pins are scattered through the grass next to a cotton-candy maker and disassembled *Bride of Pinbot* pinball machine. "I used to play that," I tell him. "All the time."

"Me too." The patient nods. "I worked here in high school. It was the best job I ever had."

I misread him. He's not angry, just sad and lost. He squats down by the candy maker. There's a scene on the glass of a circus train, monkeys juggling, and elephants standing on hind legs. "I used to spin the cotton candy," he says, covering the elephant with his hand. "It's the only thing I was ever really good at. That's why I come here. To see if maybe they'd take me back."

A hard wind sweeps between the buildings, tumbling trash scraps against my leg. The neon *OPEN* sign buzzes from the bowling alley's blacked-out side door. "I don't know about you, but I could use some caffeine," I reply. "C'mon, you can tell me more about it inside."

Here's the score: I'm working a dead-end dangerous job in the middle of the night for not much money and no place for advancement. My social circle consists of junkies and schizophrenics, inmates, suicidal housewives, cops and ER docs, and convenience store clerks on graveyard shift. In one sense I am alone in the wilderness, the best possible place to meet God. In another I am drifting too far, needing to settle down and get serious about making a life. Am I lost? Or found? I wish I knew.

Sean's mom from junior high band carpool sells weed now. A close friend from grad school has been hiding an eating disorder, and it's getting out of hand. I break up a catfight at the psych ward, and the wilder patient bites my first two fingers. Marlboro taught me never to pull away from a bite, so I tuck my palm under her chin and bounce her head off the wall until she lets go. There's a crack in the Sheetrock, and dust fills the air. The patient lies in a heap as others stare at me like I've lost my mind.

"Are you all right, Jamie?" Jackie, the charge nurse, asks.

My blood feels sluggish and my head is fever hot. I pull one last Sudafed from my pocket and chew it into bits. "Yeah," I tell her. "I'm fine."

It is not even midnight yet.

I'm sitting at Hilltop ER, a decrepit, old one-floor infirmary out in the boondocks of our new expanded-coverage area. The psychiatric hospital sent out a memo about our exciting new opportunity for growth. They're making a lot more money now and not passing a nickel of it on to me. I just have to drive farther. I don't mind driving at night.

Hilltop is deserted. There's one nurse on duty, outside for a smoke with no security on site, and the doctor is sleeping in a travel trailer parked in the field out back. My patient is a big guy with cold blue eyes and crooked sideburns, looking like a combination of heavy Elvis and hillbilly Stephen King.

I glance over the intake report: history of paranoid schizophrenia, increasingly agitated, isolating, not sleeping, not taking his meds. "For the most part," I tell him, waving the sheet, "our reports are about the same, you and me." No response. So much for breaking the ice.

His mother dumped him at the ambulance door and told the nurse to call her if he needed a ride home, but really, she'd rather we send him somewhere safe and far away for a long, long time. "Like in the old days," she said, "when they'd lock folks up for good."

It's just me and Sideburns in the back exam room. "So you been feeling pretty bad lately, huh?" I ask. His expression shifts from sorrow to rage to confusion and back again. I chew my thumbnail and fight sleep, zoned out, waiting for whatever comes next.

The exam room is claustrophobic and the instruments antique. There's a glass IV bottle on a pole next to a Roger's Farm Supply Calendar featuring the Tractor of the Month. This month is Miss Becca Mercer, Corn Fest Queen, atop a 1965 Allis Chalmers D17. A pair of wooden crutches lies crossed against the wall.

Sideburns reaches into his pocket and in one fluid motion pulls a knife.

"Pretty. Bad," he finally replies, flicking out the blade, his blue eyes glassy now.

Time really does move slower when you wonder if you are about to die. I think about all the years in psych wards and crisis response, misfit to misfit in the darkest hours, a thousand nights of danger and grace. Sometimes I truly do feel called and chosen, like I'm on some mission from God. Other times not so much.

I wonder who's going to drive my truck home, how far it is to the doctor's trailer in the field, and just what kind of doctor could they get out here anyway? If I get slashed, could I superglue myself shut and make it home to Dr. Black? I'd trust him better to stitch me up.

What if I have to take the knife and stab this guy in self-defense? Could I do it? I think so. I'd trust the country doc to sew him up. I might even help.

Short prayers, desperate. That's all there is space for now.

Sideburns turns the knife. It gleams in the exam-room lights. I can read the blade—a stag-handle Case, double XX. I keep waiting to feel something: fear, compassion, anger, adrenaline.

"That's a real nice knife," I tell him in a voice that sounds more detached than calm. "My dad collected Case. I think you might have a rare one there." He eyes the knife, confused again. "Mind if I take a look?"

Sideburns folds the knife and hands it over to me. "Really?" he says, his words thick. "You think it might be worth somethin'?"

I hold the Case in my hand, testing its weight, staring into Sideburns's sad face. "Yeah," I reply, flicking the blade out again. "I think it really might."

I study the lettering down the side, tracing my thumb lightly over the razor-sharp edge. Then I close the blade back and hold it before him. "But let's keep it in your jacket pocket. The nurse here's kinda nervous, you know? Speaking of her—" I check his pulse with my left hand while my right slides the knife into his coat. "Whoa, pretty fast," I say with concern. "Are you anxious?"

"Real bad lately," he says.

"Watch that second hand," I say, nodding to the clock. "I'll show you how to slow down your heart." As the seconds tick, I speak slower. "What's your most favorite place?"

"My bed at home. I got trash bags over the windows so the light don't come in."

"For real? I do that too. Okay. Imagine you're in that cool, dark room and everything is good. Just the way you want it to be."

Sideburns closes his eyes and takes a long, deep breath. I match mine to his. "Keep breathing," I tell him. Thirty seconds passes. Forty-five. "You can open your eyes, if you'd like. That was good. Your pulse got a lot slower. Let me run these numbers to the nurse before I forget. Would you like something to drink?"

He glances at his wrist and smiles sleepily. "Y'all got any Sprite?"

"One Sprite," I reply. "Coming up."

I lay his papers on the front desk and sign them quickly. "Bed two is good to go," I report to the nurse as I walk past the ashtray to my truck. "Already called the sheriff. Have the doc check him quick, okay? And can you get him a Sprite?"

"Can do. Thank you, baby," she says with one last drag. Her smoke is still drifting as I'm halfway down the drive and into the night.

It's after a crisis that the emotions rush in. Regret, panic, anger at the situation, imagining worse-case scenarios, angry at myself for being so careless. I slip Sideburns's knife from my pocket and flick out the blade. I'm not a mental-health clinician. I'm a failed kid magician, maybe not the master of distraction, but still capable. I am a wannabe Batman of the Adam West kind. Guess all those comics and magic books when I was growing up weren't for nothing. Every now and then things do work together for the good.

The small-time criminal I bought the Trooper from built a secret compartment under the center console. I twist the latch, open the false bottom, and drop the knife inside, where it clatters against other crisis contraband—bootleg switchblades and confiscated pill bottles, a Ruger .22. A coworker, Robert, asked me to hold his pistol because he didn't trust himself anymore. "You've heard it all before, Jamie," he said. "And you've seen enough not to judge."

Robert is one of the finest, most compassionate therapists I know. "Whatever I can do," I told him. "Let me know when you're ready to take it back."

Been over a year now. I asked him the other day. "Not just yet," he replied.

I drank all my energy shots too early tonight, so I ride with the windows down, cool air rushing through the footwells and into my face. Reaching into the console, I rummage out Sideburns's knife again. Life is full of intersections and choices. Each choice takes you down a different road. I hope God in heaven has a map where he can show us all the paths we didn't take, the end result of every choice. In that place we'll finally know the balance between choices and fate.

My phone buzzes. I click it off Silent and take the call. Squiggly starts with a rundown on the first of Westwood's two waiting patients, presenting problems and current status, social security number, insurance, date of birth. I switch to speaker and set her in the visor, staring at the knife as she talks, turning it in my hand. The wind rushes around me as I test its weight and run my fingers over the stag-handle bone. It really is rare. I wasn't lying. Probably worth a hundred bucks, at least.

I sling it out the window, watching in the mirror as it skitters and sparks down the road.

"Sorry, Jamie," Squiggly says as she finishes up. "Looks like it's one of them nights."

I get the first patient shored up quickly, but the second is determined to make it a counseling session. No matter how many times I politely redirect her, she ignores me and goes into some long-winded story of how family mistreats her and life has let her down. I know she's just old and lonely and I should suck it up and go the second mile, but I'm long past running on empty.

"Ma'am?" I say, a little more assertive now. "I need you to answer my questions. I'll be glad to set you up with a good therapist. But I'm not it."

She coils back like I'm some kind of monster and informs me what an unprofessional and compassionless individual I am. Then she crosses her arms and refuses to speak. I leave her room feeling like I've been beaten with broomhandles and dragged by horses down a muddy gravel road. But I also know what her problem is. She's sweet as pie—long as you give her what she wants. Eventually you build yourself a prison living that way.

After I make my judgment, I realize something else: I am often guilty of the same. This job really sucks sometimes.

I find Dr. Black in the back lounge examining a chartreuse spinnerbait as if it is a suspicious mole. "I can't live like this anymore," I tell him. "Something's gotta change."

"Gender reassignment's a little beyond my scope of practice," he jokes, trying to lighten the mood. "But I feel your pain."

"Seriously," I tell him. "My sleep is wrecked. I'm ready for that script."

"The natural didn't work?" Black asks. "What'd you try?"

"Benedryl, melatonin, counting blessings, chamomile tea. Hot bath. Cold room. Johnny Cash reading the New Testament. James Earl Jones reading the Old. Valerian root. Yoga. Yogurt. End-times prophecy conferences from Alabama charismatics."

I pause, blank stare, blinking.

"Lemon Balm. Old episodes of *Cosmos*," I continue. "Russian literature. Ice bath. Decoding Revelation. Rebuking Satan. Reciting the Twenty-Third Psalm. Belladonna. White willow bark. Turkey. Tart cherries. Scott Baio films."

He grabs his pad and scratches out the dose. "Start with half," he suggests, handing me a sample for tonight. "Don't take it unless you're close to bed."

"Got it," I reply. It's the first prescription I have ever had. "So this helps you, right?"

"So far," he replies.

I slip the script and sample into my pocket and head out the door, down to the red dirt hill. Daybreak hangs blue at the horizon, so I can walk through the old apartments without seeming shady. Secrets still live here, behind chipped-paint doors and pavement cracks, in windows and snapshot memories, in something so difficult to explain that calls me home. They say the past is revealed in glimpses, like childhood pictures pulled randomly from a box.

I remember that summer night Ash Braddock and I snuck down late and jumped our bikes into the apartment pool. The manager was a crabby old clown named Coneigh, who wore green-checkered pants and floppy hats. She yelled at us from her bedroom window, warning that the cops were on their way. We tore off down the street to our hideout in the trees.

The police car drove by slowly, its searchlight scanning. We laid our bikes flat and pressed against the back of the widest pin oak we could find. The cruiser stopped. I could hear the chatter of the radio, static between the noise. Flashlights danced in the branches over our heads as footsteps drew near. The beam paused on a twist of crossvine close enough to touch. My bike pedal stuck up from the brush five feet farther, its reflector ready to give us away.

"See something?" a stern voice asked. Ash grabbed my sleeve as we held our breath. The beam panned right, dazzling red as it passed my reflector.

"Nothing here," a second voice replied. "They're probably long gone by now."

The apartment pool is blackish now, the hideout trees cut back for power lines. But the big pin oak remains. There are still snarls of crossvine and the window where Coneigh beat her fist against the side of the building and squawked that we'd better not run.

"Nostalgia serves a purpose," Dr. Figgpen taught in Theories of Personality class. "When we're facing change or feel our lives are spiraling, we pull those sweet moments close, think back to when things worked out for the best. But like most sweet things, you have to be careful. Too much can make you sick."

I walk down to the oak tree and make a lap around, stopping at the place where we hid. There, in faint white marks, sit our initials, scratched with the house key Ash kept hanging on a string around her neck. I trace the letters with my finger, thinking I am still too much the same. Time is an illusion, Einstein said. There is only now.

DJ Cleavon Swan guides me back home, all the way from Memphis on the radio dial. "Fourteen minutes after five under cloudy skies and early morning rain. The Mighty Clouds of Joy reminding us all, brothers and sisters . . . if Jesus can't fix it, nobody can. So lay your burdens down and rest, my children," Swan says in a soft, low voice. "Peace. Be still."

I put off the pile of paperwork and fall into a feverish dream—

of dizzying heights and tight mazes, of calls to crisis where I never can arrive. I dream of the stag-handle knife turning in the light. As hard as I try, I cannot make it disappear. And Jesus doesn't seem to be fixing anything.

It's a tiny blue pill, smaller than a Tic Tac in my hand. Half is minuscule. I pray for guidance, peace, and mercy. Then I take it.

Within minutes my frantic mind goes silent, like helium filtering slowly into my brain, lifting it higher and higher into the night until, finally, it vanishes from sight.

Soon I am sleeping the dreamless sleep of angels.

II REVELATION

The race is not to the swift, nor the battle to the
strong, neither yet bread to the wise, nor yet riches to
men of understanding, nor yet favour to men of skill;
but time and chance happeneth to them all.
—ECCLESIASTES 9:11 (KJV)

Catastrophe can be a means of grace.
—EUGENE PETERSON

SEE YOU IN HEAVEN, FRIEND

If you must err, do so on the side of audacity.
—SUE MONK KIDD

THERE'S A CHINK IN THE SECURITY FENCE AROUND the water tower that I'm pretty sure I could squeeze through if I tried. Sure enough, with a few scrapes I'm inside, cutting across tall blue pipes and knee-high grass to stare up the massive columns that run to the two-hundred-thousand-gallon tank.

Headlights slide around the corner, and I hit the ground, hiding in the grass. It's not a cop, just an old Dodge Diplomat with a handicap placard swinging from the rearview mirror. Still, I lie low, waiting until they pass.

I feel stupid. It's like I'm on some bizarre, broken, and quite possibly pathetic late-night magical mystery reminiscence tour. *For research purposes*, I assure myself. After astronomy bombed, I considered a major in archeology. Astronomers look to distant early stars for signs of life. Archeologists dig for treasure in grains of sand and crumbling jars of clay. Psychologists study story fragments in search of the bigger picture. Past reveals future.

Everything seems legit in the name of science. Maybe this is my mission. Maybe I was born to wrestle God.

The Diplomat sits forever at the stop sign. The window is down, talk radio on, Art Bell discussing a mysterious bottomless pit on Manastash Ridge that has the power to bring dead pets back to life. I roll over and listen, intrigued, a bit disappointed when the Diplomat finally motors on.

A small-town water tower looks as big as the Statue of Liberty when you're lying right under it at night. Late one Sunday in our senior year, Elroy, CC, Shells, and I set out to climb to the high rail that surrounded the tank. Elroy wasn't his real name. It was Leroy, but one day in English III, Mrs. Kinley said he must be dyslexic, so we started calling him Elroy after that. Sometimes, when he did something really dim-witted, I'd call him Yorle, and he'd slug me in the arm.

I talked all cocky while we were making our espionage plans and driving to the tower, but once I stood on Elroy's shoulders, grabbed the skinny ladder, and climbed about twenty feet up, fear paralyzed me. The round metal rungs felt slippery, and the ground beneath me started to whirl. I pushed on another few feet and froze. That's when the chicken sounds and laughter began. I slinked down and lay back against the windshield, watching as my friends scurried to the top and spray-painted our graduation year across the tank.

That night was a source of cowardly regret for a long time to come. I did not carry the flag or help leave our mark for all to see. Word traveled quickly. Regret is a difficult cross to bear.

Later, when I started going to Lighthouse Church, I could see the tower from my pew near the back. I tried to tell myself that Jesus wouldn't be down with the whole tower-climbing graffiti thing anyway, but I never could buy all in. There's that saying about the glory of God being a man fully alive. I remembered lying there listening to the drone of passing cars and the echoes of joy as my buddies ran the rail with their cans of Krylon, looking as if they could reach out and touch the summer moon.

It was quiet in the car riding home. No one made fun of me then. Suddenly I was an outsider. They'd shared a rich experience, a secret mission, something I could never understand. My old classmates will talk of that night until their dying day: "There was that one guy too scared to climb. What was his name again? Ah, it doesn't matter now."

Chickening out or climbing—which was the less spiritual act? There are no Bible stories of teenage Jesus. Sometimes it's hard to figure out what he might think about things. Jesus walking planet Earth didn't react or reply like anyone thought he should. That's why we killed him. Sometimes I wonder if we would just kill Jesus again.

After I had been at Lighthouse Church awhile the tower was mercifully repainted. It was a town ritual. The seniors would climb up and paint the tank. A year or so later the city would put up a fresh coat so the new classes could make their mark.

I stand and stare through the circle of steel surrounding the rungs, straight up the side column, still not sure what God's opinion might be. It'd be nice to redeem myself tonight, but that three-story water tower in Bumpkin with the winding staircase and sturdy rails was one thing. I don't think I'm ready to face this much fear yet. Besides, it's right off the highway, and I'm not in high school anymore. Crisis doesn't carry that much cachet.

I slink back to the fence, stop, and take one last look at the tower. The moon sits off the high rail looking as if I could pluck it like a ripe orange from a tree. Maybe tonight I could make it thirty feet.

With no assist from Elroy's shoulders, I shimmy up the highest valve and stand on a giant iron handwheel. Still can't reach.

The yellow moon taunts me. Somewhere beyond the pines, I swear I hear a chicken cluck.

Deep breath. Jump.

The skinny rung slaps and stings my hands. I pull myself up and start to climb. My stomach flips at twenty feet, but I keep pressing on. Twenty-five. At thirty feet I stop and take slow breaths to fight the panic. The tower sits on a hill, and I can see the tiny lights down Highway 39 and the happy glowing pig sign at the Piggly Wiggly right off Main. The treeline blocks everything beyond that.

"If you ever really want to live life," the lady preacher with the smoker's voice said, "sometimes you have to do it scared."

One rung at a time, step by step, until I am a third of the way up the tower at somewhere close to forty feet. I pump my fist in victory. Quickly. Then I push back against the safety cage with my legs locked around the bars and look out over the trees. The river winds like a muddy black dragon into the night. Thomas Towers's beacon cuts across the sky. I reach out and touch the moon. Metaphorically, at least.

There's an ink pen in my pocket, so I ease it out and make small, smudged marks on the ladder—my initials and the date. The first good rain will wash it clean. But tonight I have made it this high. I feel silly. But I also feel completely alive.

Going up was the easy part. Each step coming down is death-grip terror at quarter speed . . . until the city spray truck rounds Slick Street with roof lights flashing. I scramble past the last twenty rungs, drop to the ground, and roll into hiding right as the truck pulls into the station.

Thanks be to God.

Literally, it's like I should give thanks. Or penance. Remembrance. Something.

Once the streets are sufficiently empty, I slip back through the chink and walk down to the Lighthouse Church parking lot. It's Big Betty's Bayside Tavern now, with neon beer signs in the window and motorcycles parked outside. A bright orange banner over the door says, *No Cover. Y'all Come. Everbody Welcome.* Video poker sits in the spot where my back-pew seat used to be.

One long look back to the tower. The high rail still looks like Mount Everest to me. For the first time I realize what's missing. The tank is spotless. No one has made his mark.

[THEN]

I DIDN'T THINK HE'D REALLY SHOW UP.

But there he was, leaning against the light pole at the far end of the church parking lot in what I guessed to be his best set of clothes—a worn blue dress coat, pressed jeans, and a skinny black tie—looking a little anxious and unsure.

"Jay!" I said. "Cool, you made it."

"Yeah, man," he replied, pressing his hand into mine. "Promised Mama I would."

I started second-guessing myself as we walked toward the door. My church was kind of crazy. Pastor Danny B. Sholtie was a former middle school custodian with a slight speech impediment and sea dragons tattooed down his forearms. He was a nice enough fellow but sometimes went off on nutty rants, banging the pulpit and telling us how Ezekiel's fire in the sky was actually flying saucers and the number of the beast could be found throughout Six Flags over Texas if one simply knew where to look.

Personally, I loved slam-bang conspiracy preaching, although probably for the same reasons I took side jobs announcing midget wrestling and monster truck shows. Loud and crazy was very entertaining to me. But for spiritual growth? Maybe not so good.

Jay was the first person I had ever invited to church. We shook a quick couple of hands, and I steered him to the far back pew, praying for something tamer since I'd brought a guest.

I took a look around the sanctuary after we settled in. The Lighthouse flock was made up of Holy Rollers, converts, convicts, ex-Wiccans, past and future psych ward patients, humble servants, weirdos, Jesus freaks, black sheep, broken women once loose but newly chaste, sweet old grannies who'd slip you a roll of nickles and suggest you needed more meat on your bones, big families that smelled like moth balls and moldy cheese, and previously friendly alcoholics who had sobered up but turned mean.

On second thought, maybe the Lighthouse Full Gospel Tabernacle that met in the old furniture store under the water tower was exactly the right kind of place for Li'l Jay and me. "Hey, um," I explained, half apologizing as the service started and the congregation stood. "The music's pretty good?"

Brother Henry was a blind piano player who looked like a white Ray Charles with his slicked-back silver hair and dark Ray-Bans, swaying side to side while he sang about rugged crosses and power in the blood. Brother Henry played that Pentecostal mix of hard country and rhythm and blues, and when he did "What a Friend We Have in Jesus," you felt like Jesus really was your friend, like he was God come down from heaven to lend a hand.

"This ol' dude's pretty awesome," Jay leaned in and muttered.

Henry's wife, Tilda, worked the overhead, keeping the lyrics on screen so everyone could sing along. She had long gray hair knotted in a bun and wore blue-jean jumpers and high-top white Air Jordans.

"Jesus walked on the water," Tilda said, taking the pulpit mike and wiping away tears. A few amens resounded around the room. "And Jesus raised the dead." The hallelujahs rose a little bit louder. "Je-sus"—she turned to compose herself—"gave sight . . . to the blind!" Amens rang out all over, coupled with several "Yes, Lords" and one "Come on!"

Tilda raised both hands to the low popcorn ceiling and paced a slow lap with her eyes closed tight. Then, with full conviction and fire, she proclaimed, "And I want every believer! In this church! To agree with me that Brother Henry will receive his sight back—tonight!"

"She calls her husband Brother Henry?" Li'l Jay asked, his eyes wide as the people shouted and the elders filed in around the piano.

"Uh-huh," I replied. "All the time."

"Cool," whispered Jay.

Brother Henry stopped playing and sat stone-faced while the elders prayed, his lips pursed and ear tilted toward the ceiling as the pastor took a bottle of olive oil from the pulpit shelf and slathered it around Henry's eyes.

Hands stretched forth and voices joined in, pleading for God to open blind eyes, to let Brother Henry see Tilda "one last time, Lord." I sat with head bowed and elbows across my knees. After a minute or so I peeked over. Li'l Jay was sitting tall with one hand reaching toward the front.

"Why ain't you got your hand out, man?" he asked, catching my glance. "If that old cat throws off them glasses and can see again, that'll be about the most amazing thing I ever seen."

I nodded and stretched out my hand, wondering if I shouldn't have invited Jay to First Baptist instead, or if I should have invited him to church at all. *Would he be disappointed if there wasn't a miracle? Would I?*

"Hey, Jamie?" Jay said. "If the Lord heals Brother Henry's eyes, don't you believe he might could fix mine?"

Jay's greasy blond hair was pushed hard to one side, and he had a snaggle tooth that stuck out over his bottom lip. One blue eye locked in on mine while the other stared off into the lights. He pointed to a puckered scar running down the side. "Fella sucker punched me at Folly boat dock when I was sixteen. Ain't been right ever since."

"Yeah, brother," I told him. "I believe."

The prayers rose to a fever pitch, then faded as one by one the elders filed away. Pastor Sholtie leaned down, wrapping his arms around Brother Henry before stepping back to the side.

Henry sat alone now. The church was still. His fingers touched the keys, sparse notes at first, then soulful chords, minors and sevenths— the ones that hang unfinished to make you feel the empty spaces inside. Then Henry began to sing about a place where everything good waits and there is no more loss or pain, about being homesick for a country where he'd never even been, a faraway city where time won't matter anymore.

I closed my eyes and let his ragged voice run through me. I don't know that I've ever heard someone sing with so much longing and hope. He finished the last verse, played one last bittersweet run, and spoke slowly into the microphone, "If I don't see you here again, I'll see you in heaven, friend."

Brother Henry placed his hands in his lap and lowered his head. Tilda walked slowly to his side. He stood and she led him back toward the pew. I looked over and Li'l Jay's eyes were red with tears.

"It's okay," I told him, knocking my knee against his as he turned away. "Sometimes I get choked up too."

He cleared the catch in his throat. "Really?"

"Yeah," I admitted, pausing before adding the rest. "Brother Henry and Tilda do this nearly every other week."

He nodded a long time before speaking, and when he smiled, it was almost like his eyes went straight. "Next time," Li'l Jay said, wiping his nose down the sleeve of his old blue coat, "think it'd be all right if I bring Mama too?"

Sholtie bolted to the pulpit before I could respond. "Oh, saints," the pastor crowed, smacking his hands together and rubbing them back and forth. "You're gonna want to take notes on this one. Tonight we're going to talk about trumpets and the fillment of tabernacle feats, and let me tell you, heh-heh-heh, it's close to the end of all things. I might not even make it through this sermon before we're all eating fried chicken in heaven with Abraham."

"Hang on," I told Jay. "Hold that thought."

THE END OF ALL THINGS BROKEN

[NOW]

And they were oblivious, until the flood
came and swept them all away.
—MATTHEW 24:39 (BSB)

BOMBS STREAM FROM THE SKY AS SKELETONS CLING
to chain-link fences; barren streets and turned-over school
buses, forests leveled and skyscrapers crushed, entire cities blown
to dust as another round of shock waves arrives like tsunamis of
atomic destruction.

This is not a dream. It's a video I just found online of the
Rapture movie they showed us that day at church camp when I
was nine and my friend's sister tricked me into going. The preacher
promised that God would soon split the eastern sky, this time as the
Lion and not the Lamb, tall enough to be seen from every nation,
ten thousand miles high and rising, his head and hair white like
wool and eyes a blazing fire, a name tattooed on his thigh that no
man could understand.

"Are you ready to meet him?" the preacher warned. "Are you
sure? If not, you can know without a doubt. Right here, *right* now."

The other kids were petrified and crying as adults steered them toward the altar. I stayed in my seat awestruck, certain I had witnessed the most incredibly *awesome* church service of all time. I was finally hearing about a Jesus I could not wait to meet—a giant Christ who would crack the sky and come down like lightning with fire in his eyes and a sword in his hand to bring an end to all things broken and start paradise over again.

A camp counselor approached. "Would you like to go down front?" she asked, her hand stretched out toward mine. She had hair the color of shiny pennies, pretty green eyes, and was wearing a cinched white jumpsuit with red tigers all over it. Her stick-on name tag said *MS. SUZY*.

"Oh, no, ma'am," I replied. "I'm ready."

Ms. Suzy shot me a skeptical look, perhaps because I was sporting a cutoff Sunkist shirt, prescription sunglasses, and an avalanche of unruly hair. I was the only fifth grader who looked like a weed dealer or roadie for Blue Öyster Cult. She slid into the seat next to mine, punctuating each word with a two-fingered tap against my knee. "Are you sure, now?" she asked, her fingers lingering at the last word. She leaned closer. Her breath smelled like coffee and barbecue corn chips. "I'd be happy to go down with you."

I smiled a weak defense. "Yes, ma'am," I agreed. "I'll go."

"Great!" Ms. Suzy said, eyes twinkling. "Tell you what: Sit tight. Let me grab the logbook, and we'll have ourselves a meeting with the preacher down front." She zipped off to dig beneath a side pew. And like a thief in the night I vanished, out the door and into the trees.

I slept straight from six to nearly ten this morning before the thunderstorm stirred my rapture flashbacks again. Sometimes the solution is so simple. Half a Zombien when I wake up with my mind in overdrive puts me back down for four hours of solid sleep.

"Eighty-six dollars," the pharmacist whistled when I went to pick it up. "Shame you don't have insurance."

I pulled the emergency hundred-dollar bill from my wallet and pushed it her way. "How much is sleep worth when you work crisis all night?" I replied.

I take half a tablet every other day, toughing it out on days between. At that rate, thirty pills last nearly four months. That's less than $6.00 a week—the price of Szechuan chicken and a Diet Coke at the Bok Bok Wok. In Psych 101 Dr. Stephens made a point of letting students know that sleep is a primary requirement, at the foundation of Maslow's Hierarchy of Needs, along with water and food. "Without the basics," he lectured, "we wither, lose focus, and eventually crash."

Twenty-four bucks a month to sleep better feels like a bargain to me.

The Apocalypse flick is strangely comforting. A great star falls into the ocean and the moon turns to blood. Half a pill is bitter, but the bitter is good. It signals the helium that will soon fill my brain so I can watch it fly away, sleeping without dreams, caught up and taken to a better place. It is like some small rapture from the worst of me.

It's never promising when you walk into the ER and everyone rolls their eyes. "Ugh," I reply. "What's my number?"

"Num-*bers*," says Charge Nurse Amy. "You got one in bed four, another in bed twelve, and by the time you get through with those we'll have a third waiting for you in nine."

"I'm gonna need some Valium. Where's Dr. Black?"

"Out smoking."

"Black doesn't smoke."

"Exactly," she says. "We've been slammed. We all need Valium. Wait 'til you get a load of your lady in twelve."

Better to tackle the tough ones first. I peek through bed twelve's window and reach for the door. A pale, pinched face stares back not six inches from mine. I fumble for the handle while she's turning from the other side. Pulled off balance, I stumble in. "Hi, there," I greet her, not exactly professional yet. "I mean, um . . . hey, hello." I glance at her papers. "Roslyn, is it?"

"I'm waiting for the counselor so I can get my medication and go home," Roslyn snaps back. "Are you the counselor?"

"Jehovah's Witness," I fib. "Can I interest you in a pamphlet?" Sometimes I joke at inappropriate times, mostly when I'm nervous.

Her expression turns putrid.

"Yes, ma'am," I confess. "I'm the one you're waiting for. I'm here to help."

"If you really want to be helpful, give me my medications and let me leave."

I give her a first look over. Birdlike and bony, with a mouth stretched in a thin, tight line like she's never known happiness one single day of her life. There's some kind of accent going on. "What medications would that be?" I ask.

"Percocet, ten milligrams, every four hours, and Xanax PRN," says Roslyn, raking me with her glare. "I keep trying to tell these rubes down here I have diagnosed anxiety and fibromyalgia, but no one will listen. If you don't believe me, you can call my doctor back home."

"And where is home?"

"Wisconsin." She sniffs.

I close her chart and speak with a little more certainty. "I'm not actually a counselor, but tell me what's going on and I'll see what I can do."

Roslyn rambles about idiot politicians and the oppressive

weather down South, her mother's traumatic decision to pull her out of private school in seventh grade. I finally interrupt. "Do you want to hurt anybody?"

"I'd like to kick the behind of my sister-in-law that got me into this." Her eyes turn to slits as she twists up her hands into fists. "Smack those so-called nurses out front. But no, I'm not going to hurt anyone."

"Are you seeing or hearing things?"

"I am not crazy. You try to say I'm crazy, and I'll sue this facility and I'll sue you."

"Sorry, had to ask," I reply. "Do you want to hurt yourself?"

"Of course not." She blows out her breath, disgusted. "Why don't you have a name tag? I'm going to need your name."

"Jameson Blaine, ma'am."

"Middle initial and credentials?" she demands, scribbling it down.

"Reuben. CVT. My friends call me JR."

"I'd like to speak with your supervisor, Mr. Blaine," she huffs. "They told me after I saw you I could get my medications and be on my way. That's been hours ago now."

A four-second fantasy streams through my mind—that I could somehow call Jesus into the room and say, "Look, I never signed up for this. If you've got any problems, tell this guy." I wonder, though, whether Jesus would take her side or mine.

"All right, then," I reply, tuning back in. "I can't write prescriptions, but I'll go talk to the doc."

Curses flitter like chicken feathers in a Kansas twister as I leave the room. I find Dr. Black in the hall. "Pills must be working," he says. "You don't look like *Night of the Living Dead*."

"Gee, thanks," I reply. "So, what about bed twelve?"

"Twelve," Black says, eyes shut. "Remind me."

"Wisconsin."

"That hag threatened everybody here," he says. "Throw her to the wolves."

"Pack. Of . . . wolves," I reply, reading aloud as I pretend to note it in her chart. "Stat."

"Hey, I know," he adds, as if he's thought of the most therapuetically appropriate approach. "Can you put her in jail?"

"Probably, but it wouldn't stick. Then we might be in trouble."

"Since when are we afraid of trouble?" Black asks. I drop my chin, giving him a look. "What do you want me to do?" He sighs. "Write her a script and send her home?"

"Send her home," I suggest, smiling like a crocodile. "No script."

"O-kay." Black snickers. "But you gotta come with me to deliver the news."

We walk into her room. Black clasps his hands behind his back, giving his best soap-opera doctor look of concern. "I've consulted with my colleague here, and we feel the best way we can help is to refer you to a pain management specialist."

I brace myself for more cursing, but instead she stares in disbelief. "What kind of people are you down here?" she asks, bottom lip quivering. "Don't you care that I'm in obvious pain?"

"We're bad people," Black explains. I smile pleasantly and nod along. "Now, if you'll excuse us, we've got a house full of very sick people tonight."

We exit as Wisconsin sits crying. I look back through the glass, feeling rotten.

"Jamie, sometimes you gotta be the bad guy," Black says. "I got a call from Skylark. She's already been to three ERs tonight. It wouldn't have helped any to give her more drugs."

"I know. It's hard, though. I'd rather get cursed."

"Supposed to be hard," he says. "Or else we'd be jerks all the time."

Bed four is a cut-and-dry admit, and nine's blood alcohol level comes back .285, so he'll have to wait until morning. Wisconsin is still crying when I pass back. The smartest response would be to walk on, but my stupid conscience turns me around. If I don't try to make peace, I'll stir out of sleep with the moment stuck on replay in my mind. I'll just stick my head in for a second.

"What's wrong?" I ask.

"There's always something wrong," she says, not so haughty now. "I know you're busy. I'll figure it out somehow."

I take a seat by the bed and hand her a tissue. "I'm not so busy now."

She smiles the slimmest, slightest, tiniest stiff-lip smile of all time. But still, it's a smile, so I offer one in return. Sometimes the Hallmark moment comes from the place you least expect.

"What difference does it make?" she says, honking her nose loudly before handing the tissue back. "You're not even a real counselor anyway."

"I'm 'bout to flash half the town if I don't fix myself," Stacie says, pulling at her strapless yellow sundress. "Jamie, you got that money you said we could borrow and your boss would pay you back?"

Everybody wants to stop at the convenience store before they go into treatment. You need a few last-minute supplies, some snacks, a cold drink from the cooler to help take the edge off. Now and then, if I get somebody in bad detox, I'll have to buy a half pint so they can survive the trip. Last thing I need is seizures in my truck. I let all my patients know that the hospital gives me a small expense account for such things.

At the risk of sounding petty, stopping at the store on the way to the psych ward is my favorite part. It's a fragile time, but sweet, too, being with people in their lowest moment. But I have to stay close. I've lost a few. It's no fun chasing your patient through the projects behind Killin's Fast-N-Dandy at 2:00 a.m. No fun at all.

"How much you need?" I ask Stacie, a twenty-seven-year-old divorcee addicted to pain pills, troubled men, and tanning salons. I picked her up at her friend Linda's duplex. Stacie was willing to go into rehab tonight as long as Linda could ride with us. They packed her stuff in Walmart sacks and threw on sandals and low-cut sundresses, spilling out the tops and sides.

"Four dollars?" Stacie replies.

Linda's the quieter one. "We sure hate askin'," she says.

I pass Stacie a ten and a five. She smiles so big that I can see the gap around the side where two teeth got knocked out in a bar fight, and when she staggers forward and reaches for the bills, her top starts falling again. That's when Brother Benny, my pastor from Power & Light Church, walks in.

"Heyyyyy!" I blurt out as Stacie yanks up her dress top and tucks the bills inside.

"Hey, now, brother," Benny replies, still in his preacher suit with necktie loose, lanky frame leaning back and eyes wide.

Stacie offers what's left of her smile and hangs her handbag on my arm. "Sugar," she says, "hold our purses, will ya? I gotta pee."

The girls trot off, heels clacking over the tile floor. "Brother J," Benny says, brow furrowed, in a very pastorly tone. "Who's your lady friends?"

Explanation violates confidentiality. It's a spot I am constantly in. "Friends?" I reply, looking around as if maybe he's imagining things. "Oh. Just friends. Hey, how's that new building project going? I heard you guys got approval for the pool."

There is no pool. Mental health is nine parts magician; I'll distract you with my right hand while the left makes the rabbit disappear. I am far more Houdini than Dr. Phil.

"Brother," says Benny, wincing with concern. "Is everything all right?"

"Couldn't be better," I insist, fidgeting back and forth, knocking over half a rack of Sour Cream 'n' Salsa pork rinds and spilling Slim Jims when I try to pick them up. "Whaddya mean?" I am far more Will Ferrell than Siegfried or Roy.

My lady friends come clacking back as I'm clambering across the floor with an armful of pork rind sacks and fake Kate Spade purses. There's a brief, awkward pause while everyone stares, waiting for the others to speak.

"Ladies, I am so sorry. Forgive me for being rude. I'm Benny," he introduces himself. "Pastor over at Power & Light, where Jamie goes."

"Oh!" says Stacie, pulling her top up before shaking Brother Benny's hand. "We been there before!"

"Do you know Lacey Harris?" Linda says. "She's my aunt on Momma's side."

"Sister Lacey, of course." Benny nods. "Don't know where we'd be without her. That woman is a true servant."

"She sure is," Linda says, nodding her head. "Ain't a day passes Aunt Lacey don't pray for Stacie and me."

"In college I wore these ratty old Nikes to work and school and church—'cause they were all I had." I chime in. "One day I came out of bombing this physics test, and there was a brand-new pair of Air Max on the seat of my truck with a sticky note that said, 'Let us run with endurance the race God set before us!' It was Sister Lacey. Still can't figure out how she broke into my truck."

"Sounds just like her," says Linda. "She'll get devious for the Lord."

"So how you guys know Jamie?" Brother Benny asks.

"We're eloping," I tell the preacher, straight-faced as I can. "All of us. Please don't tell my folks. Not yet."

Stacie takes her purse back and swats my sleeve. "Jamie's taking me to rehab," she says, neither proud nor shamed. "I gotta get some help. Soon as I'm out and clean, I'm gonna come get you to baptize me. If you'll do it, that is."

"Shoot, I'd be honored," Brother Benny says. "You just let me know." The pastor hands us a card with his number on it and says he'll be praying for safe travels and guidance for us all. He pays for his gas and goes his way as we wave good-bye through the front window.

"My feet are killing me," Stacie says, pulling off her sandals and handing them to me by the straps. "Jamie, I was gonna ask if I could get a beer, but I think I can make it without. You care if we buy some Gatorade and chips?"

The hospital doesn't pay me back. They quit that a long time ago. Jesus said help people covertly and without flash, understanding that soon enough, you'll be needing somebody to help you too. There's so much stuff I don't get right, can't get right, will never in this life get right. But maybe the little things really do count. Maybe love and mercy really can cover a multitude of sins.

"It's y'all's money," I tell her, handing over a fistful of spilled Slim Jims. "Get whatever you want."

"In that case, grab you something." Stacie winks, fanning the bills out of her dress. "It's on me."

There's a hollow-eyed woman holed up in the back bedroom of a run-down house, wedged between the window and the bed with a .38 derringer in her hand. Her mother called and begged me to come. The woman does not want me here.

"What can you possibly do for me?" she asks as I enter the room. "Do you really think there's something you can say that could change my mind?"

The trim is painted mailbox blue, the walls and floor bare timber. Prescription bottles and empty cans are scattered around. The ceiling fan is missing a blade. "No," I tell her. "That's your choice. There is help, though, if you want it."

A peace-sign beanbag lies next to the bed. I sink down into it. A jade-green vase sits on a shelf next to a stack of DVDs with *Lethal Weapon 2* on top. Above the urn hangs a high school graduation picture of a smiling boy with sandy hair, long over one eye. Inscribed in the photo's corner is his birthday, a dash, and the date of his death, a year to the day. The woman hangs her head.

"It's just too hard," she says.

"I can't fix it," I tell her. "But I'm here to listen to whatever you want to say."

The lopsided fan wobbles hypnotically as her story spills out in trickles and floods. With every revolution, the fixture shakes loose, flickering, darkness and light. After a long while she asks me, "What are you even doing here this time of night? Why ain't you at home with your honey, sleeping?"

The window by the bed is open, and a breeze blows through the screen. "I got no place to be. Talk all you want. Long as I'm home before the sun comes up."

She turns and looks to me. "So who are you, really, anyway?"

The air smells like dirty old clothes and frying bacon. There's a TV in the corner with the sound turned low. *The Graduate* plays on Fox's late night movie. Dustin Hoffman drifts across a pool before an infomercial flashes for Thighmaster Gold. "I'm the guy who shows up at three in the morning and listens to people with pistols who just aren't sure they can go on."

She lays her head back and rests the derringer against the sill. "Guess somebody's gotta be," she says. A scatter of crows caw, close, then farther away. She leans across the bed and hands me the gun. "Hold this for me awhile, okay?"

The pistol is mother-of-pearl and polished steel, its weight seductive. I pull the hammer back and stare at the slug. In a circle around the steel, it says, *FEDERAL 38 SPECIAL*. I shake out the bullet and roll it in my palm. "Okay," I reply.

An eighteen-wheeler passes on the highway past the field, its radio playing "Smoky Mountain Rain." We sit for a moment, listening. It segues into "Storms" before fading slowly into the night.

"Ain't heard that song in a long time," I tell her.

"Always did like that song," the woman says.

Not too much later, I help her onto the stretcher, down the drive, and into the ambulance I'd requested. Before they close the door she reaches for my hand.

"What's your name again?" she asks.

"Jamie."

"Jamie," she says, gripping tightly. "I won't forget."

The driver shuts the door. I rest my hand against the rear window and say a short prayer for peace. She raises hers in return, lies back, and closes her eyes. The flashing lights wink twice, and the ambulance slowly drives away. I stand and watch until the flashers fade from sight.

It's a long way home on a dark highway. Her pistol sits beside me on the seat. What do you say to a mom who lost her teenage son and faces financial ruin over the hospital bills? That everything happens for a reason? Heaven needed an angel and God never wastes a hurt? I wish it were that easy. I wish so many things. There are no easy answers at 3:00 a.m.

The only thing I know is to give all my attention to one person for the one brief moment we share. Something happens when I'm able to sit quietly and not obsess over trying to come up with some inspirational reply. A lot of times I can feel that person's pain. I don't mean that in some spooky telepathic sort of way. I mean that when I calm down and pay attention, I can start to understand.

This job might be killing me. Or saving me. One or the other. Maybe both.

The sun is rising by the time I turn off the highway and take the back road home. I tell God it would be fine with me if he only let the sun shine early afternoons. I tell him I wouldn't care if the sun hardly ever came up at all. Sometimes when I'm punch drunk and sleepy, God and me, we kid around.

As I pull into the driveway, the bluejays sing their mildly annoying ode to joy. I park, hide the pistol, and head upstairs to bed. Roll the credits; another night is done. Half a pill waits by the bedside, but thirty minutes later my brain is still in high gear so I swallow the second half. Black said it was okay to take a whole pill now and then. You gotta sleep, right?

I flip the Bible to a random page. "Lean not on your own understanding," King Solomon suggests, "if you want your paths to be straight."

Straight paths. That would be something. I wonder if Moses ever read the Psalms.

DAY 10

God meets us mostly in our wilderness—in the unexpected, unstructured, and unplanned moments of our life. He delights in surprises, appearing in burning bushes and tongues of fire, and in walking on stormy waters to meet us exactly where we are.

Tell of a time when God took you by surprise.

HEAVEN TONIGHT

[THEN]

God still comes to us and reveals divinity in the
common, ordinary, earthly material of our lives: loyal
dogs, faithful friends, tasty treats, foibles, sins, triumphs,
graces, adventures, and misadventures. The divine is
in the details of our lives. God still dwells in the Word
and in the world, in the stories we live out each day.
—REVEREND WILLIAM MILLER

T WAS A BRIGHT SUNDAY MORNING AT THE LIGHTHOUSE
Full Gospel Tabernacle, located in the old furniture store right next
to the water tower downtown. Harsh fluorescent lights and rows of
beat-up folding chairs sat under butcher paper taped over show-
room windows. A fat orange stripe cut across the off-white walls, and
stenciled through the faded logo for La-Z-Boy, boldface letters now
declared *VICTORY IN JESUS*. Heads were bowed, eyes closed.

"If this message spoke to you today," Pastor Sholtie said, "I want
you to raise your hand."

Sister Revell hacked into a handkerchief as the AC unit rattled to
life. Water from a leak in the ceiling dripped slowly to the tile floor.

"No one looking around," the pastor warned. "Just between you and the Lord."

Throats cleared as the preacher paced the space between the altar and the pews. "Come on, church," Sholtie pleaded. "Come on . . ."

The pastor had just preached a pretty good message about how we all fall short, about man's weakness and desperate need for God. About how we try and try and still don't get it right.

"Anyone who's struggling this morning," he said. "Anyone needing prayer. Just lift one hand in a show of faith."

I figured that pretty much covered everybody. Surely the building must be a sea of lifted hands. I try and try and don't get it right. Plus, college math was kicking my behind. So . . . what the heck. I lifted my hand too.

"Yes. Yes!" Sholtie exclaimed. "I see those hands." Brother Henry's piano swayed us, soft and slow as Tilda's soprano fluttered over his melody like a sparrow in the wind. "Move, Lord," called some unseen saint. "Move."

I lowered my hand.

The praise band joined in, and the tiny choir sang softly about walking that Jericho Road. Sholtie's voice rose above the noise. "If you had your hand lifted this morning," he said with a silvery lilt, "I want you to come down front and meet Jesus."

Do what, now?

Sholtie paced harder, his words on edge. "Come on, brother," he implored. "C'mon."

I opened my eyes. Half the church was staring. Part of me was tempted to step to the end of the row, turn, and bolt out the back door. But, instead, I walked down front and met the pastor there.

"Bless you, Jamie!" he said, pulling me close and smiling like an angler with a five-pound bass. "Bless your heart."

"Wait a minute," I whispered. "Where's everybody else?"

"Shhh, brother," the preacher said, his coarse hand heavy on the back of my neck. "It was just you."

Jules was on her back porch when I arrived, propped sideways on her thrift-store sofa, painting her toenails purple and Barbie pink. "You did *what*?" she asked.

"At church this morning," I explained, shading my eyes from the sun. "I went down front for prayer because I'm failing math, and I guess they thought I was getting saved."

"But that's crazy," she said. "It's just for math, right?"

Jules's jet-black hair was a tall, tangled mess, and she looked like a mash-up of Janis from *Mean Girls* and Joan Jett. She was a loudmouth bartender who cursed in Italian, drove the old couple next door to the grocery store every Tuesday, and always had time to listen to my silly, anxious thoughts. I climbed the steps and flopped down beside her. "You ever been baptized?" I asked.

"Sure," she said, focusing back on her toes. "When I was a kid. At least I think I was. Why?"

"Pastor says I have to go back tonight and get baptized."

"You didn't tell him it was just for math?"

"There wasn't any way to say it 'til it was too late," I told her. "Besides, you know. Math and other stuff, too, I guess."

"Can't ever hurt to get baptized," she said, reaching over to dot my thumbnail pink. "Right?"

"Guess not," I replied. "Preacher says you have to or it doesn't count."

"Really?"

"That's what the preacher says."

Jules twisted her lips and looked up to the right, like she did when she was thinking deeply. "Maybe I oughta go with you," she suggested. "Just in case I need to get baptized too."

Pastor Sholtie preached about how all of heaven rejoices when just one sinner comes clean, about the fruit of outreach and the power of God to change broken lives. Jules elbowed me in the side, talking behind her hand. "Even if you're just flunking dimwit math and stuff."

Then Sholtie pointed back and informed the congregation that I had come forth that morning, made a public proclamation, and decided to be baptized that very night.

"That's not the way you told it," Jules said.

"I know."

"Brother Jamie," Sholtie said, his hand extended to me. "If you'll go to the back, we'll help you get ready now."

"You coming?" I asked Jules.

"Sure," she said. "I'm with you."

We slipped around back and into the choir room. Deacon Johnny stood by in slip-on coveralls, wielding his mop like the Grim Reaper's blade. Next to him was a big, bossy woman with mean eyebrows, carrying a robe with a multicolored yoke and doves down the sleeve.

"How y'all doin'?" I said.

Jules lifted her hand. "Howdy, all."

"Let's go, mister," the woman urged, pushing the robe into my hands. "We gotta get you ready. Today is a very important day, one you won't ever forget."

"Hey, check out this robe," I told Jules, trying to be casual to hide my nerves. "Doves and rainbows."

"And who might you be?" the woman asked.

"Julie," Jules said. "Jamie's friend."

"Your friend needs to wait out front," the woman replied, polite but icy, quotations around the word *friend*.

"If it's, uh, okay," I said, my foot bouncing as I rocked side to side, "I'd like for her to stay." The woman cocked her carved brow, turned without a word, and walked away. Jules shot me a worried look.

"A lotta people get the Spirit when they come back up," Deacon Johnny offered, his Arkansas drawl slow as a week in a small county jail. "You'll feel cleaner and lighter. Closer too."

"Yes, sir," I replied, unsure of what else to say. "Okay. Thanks."

Johnny leaned his mop in the doorjamb and walked to the far side of the room to fetch towels. The robe lay waiting across a stack of wine-red chairs. I picked it up as the praise band began to play "Love Lifted Me."

"Well," I told Jules, taking a long breath in and out. "Here goes."

"Jamie," Jules said, "do you trust me?"

"Sure, uh—"

Before I could finish my sentence, she yanked me out the side door by the wrist and hustled me toward her Chevy SS while the choir went a cappella on the refrain. She burned tires out of the lot and into the fading sun before they even knew I was gone. At first we were quiet. Then we laughed. Then we were quiet again.

Jules piloted over the levee and turned onto the dirt road that runs by the river's shore. She parked in the bushes before the bend, threw her shoes on the floorboard, and ran toward the water.

"Come on!" she shouted.

I shucked off my boots, stashed my wallet in the glove box, and followed her in.

We were knee deep in the river under a 6:30 p.m. summer sun, long dusk with night rising through the trees. The water was warm at the surface and cooler in the deep. For five minutes or so there was absolute silence, both of us knowing something strange and sacred was taking place but unable to articulate what we felt. Then, suddenly, the sound of music.

"Hey," said Jules, eyes up and to the right. "You hear that?"

"Yeah," I told her, "but where's it comin' from?"

Like some sweet epiphany movie scene, the bow of the *Dixie Queen* slipped around the bend. We waded out farther as it drifted by and the music grew louder. There was a party on the back deck, streamers and lights twined through the rails, masked ballers dancing while a trio played "Brown-Eyed Girl."

The dancers spotted us and rushed to the rail, shouting and waving, and we waved and shouted back. A woman in black threw us her mask. I jumped to catch it and missed, but it floated nearby, glittering purple against the muddy brown. I snatched it up and gave it to Jules, and just as she pulled it over her head, the wake from the paddlewheel knocked us flat. We straggled back up, neck deep, and all the party people cheered.

As the riverboat glided into the coming night, we lifted our hands, cheering too.

"I hate that song," Jules laughed, water spitting out of her nose.

"Me too," I laughed back.

"But it's, like, my all-time favorite right now."

"Mine too."

Treading water near the middle of the stream, we watched until the *Dixie Queen* faded from sight and the waters grew still. "Hey, Jamie," Jules said. "I feel cleaner."

The river was murky and cold in the depths as the strange silence settled back in. "Lighter," I told her. "Closer too."

We lay back on the bank in wet clothes, waiting until they were dry enough to drive. The glow of the city smoldered against the clouds, and the moon sat high above, stars close and bright. "You're still majoring in astronomy, right?" Jules said.

"I am this semester," I answered. "But, you know. The, um, math thing."

"Tell me something astronomically cool."

"Gamma rays traveling at the speed of light could kill us all instantly."

"Something not scary," she said.

I pointed near the Big Dipper. "There's two stars in Ursa Major that are actually one we see twice because the gravitational mass of their galaxy warps space time."

"So, that's not science fiction? You can really warp time?"

"Einstein says there are infinite roads," I told her. "Endless possibilities running parallel to this life. He said that everything already happened. We just haven't lived it yet."

"Wow, that's pretty deep," said Jules. "We haven't gotten to Albert Einstein in any of my classes yet."

"Not Albert," I corrected. "Bobby Einstein. Assistant manager at Radio Shack."

"Che cavolo," Jules sputtered, rolling her eyes. "You got early class tomorrow?"

"Yeah, but I'm not sleepy."

"Me neither," she said.

Three Bridges Road was one turn off of the main drag, a flat piece of blacktop that cut through the fields. Five minutes from town, it felt like the middle of nowhere. The AC was on high so we could ride with the windows down. Warm air rushed in while cold blasted from the vents. We rolled in the wonder and stillness of late night on a dark country road, through narrow spaces where the treeline hugged the shoulders before opening to endless rows of cotton and grain.

At the second bridge we stopped and got out, just to check the spot where we spray-painted our names back in the spring. Jules leaned her head back and stared at the sky. "So you think it goes forever?" she asked. "It's gotta end somewhere, right?"

Some questions are better asked than answered. I gathered a handful of flat, smooth rocks and skipped them across the water beneath the bridge. Jules walked down to throw a few. We were on the shadow side, too dark to see the stream. She tossed one high and we waited, but no splash came.

"Wouldn't it be cool," she said, "if we could drive through the stars, riding until we came to that last one, to keep on driving to whatever was on the other side?"

"The faster we travel," I replied, trying to remember my professor's line, "the slower time passes by."

"What do you think heaven's really like?" she asked.

"Tell me a good memory."

Jules skipped another rock before speaking again. "Back when I worked at the pet store, I loved opening in the morning. There was a bell on the door, and the puppies would wake up and get all excited when they heard it ring. I would open their cages, and warm, sleepy puppies would rush to me, barking and jumping and pressing their cold noses to my neck. Somedays I would get there thirty minutes early just for that." She made a happy little sound—*hmm*.

"Maybe that's what heaven's like," I told her. "And you can hold it forever because we're free from time. You can live in it again and again—ten thousand agains, just as good as the first. If you want."

Jules was quiet as we walked back to the car, eyes fixed on the night sky. After the second bridge it was mile after mile of thick forest, the highway like a tunnel through the trees. "So what's your heaven like?" she asked.

You can say anything while looking out the window of a dark car. "In first grade I had to transfer to a new school, and it was scary, and I didn't like it. At the end of the day, I stood on the front steps waiting for what felt like forever. I was afraid Mama wasn't coming, that maybe she'd packed up and left while I was gone, that I might never see her again. Then she came from the other way and called my name. And when I ran to her, she swooped me in her arms and started laughing. I can still remember the way that moment felt."

For a while there was only the sound of the wind and tires against the road. The trees closed in tight, and Jules drove slower, listening.

"After my parents split, my dad would drive down on Friday nights," I said. "I used to get off the school bus, grab my suitcase, and stand on the hill in the yard, counting headlights coming down the road. It got to where I could tell his particular lights from far away. I can still feel that feeling—when I first saw his lights. When his truck pulled into the drive and I knew everything would finally be all right."

Jules notched the radio down and let the night air rush through her fingers.

"I think heaven will be like that a million times more," I told her, and the words felt true, solid as stone.

"God, I hope so, Jamie," she said low. "I really do."

Just after the third bridge the trees gave way to fields as far as the eye could see. Jules slipped in Stevie Nicks—that song about the sea of love where everyone wants to drown. Stevie was like spun gold and ragged sackcloth, like the stars and sky were a shawl you could pull around you safe and tight.

"You think maybe heaven could be a little like this too?" Jules said, her face lit blue from the dashboard lights. "Like riding in a car at night? Not really wanting to be anywhere except right where you are?"

"Hope so."

"Take the wheel," she said.

I leaned over and held the Chevy steady. "Endless roads," Jules said, her coal eyes shining. "Let's just drive to heaven tonight." She opened the sunroof and stood on the seat, arms high and eyes shut, hands dipping and swaying in the breeze.

Jesus and Einstein were right; time is just an illusion. The wind whipped through the car, stars bright. I slid behind the wheel, stuck my head out the window, and pushed the accelerator to the floor.

The Piggly Wiggly off Main had an old *Super Zaxxon* machine jammed between produce and the magazines. It was 95 degrees under the brutal southern sun and 59 inside the Pig. I was just about to blast the robot dragon when a hand rested on my shoulder. "Brother Jamie!"

It was Pastor Sholtie. The dragon spit fire, and I was dead. Sholtie pulled back and punched my arm. "How you been, man?"

"Um, pretty good, I guess."

"Hey, didn't you used to work here?" he said, shaking his finger. "I believe you might've smushed my wife's bread one time."

"You must be thinking of someone else."

"All I know is somebody mashed it good. And twisted it!" He laughed. "She probably made some huffy remark or didn't tip or something. We had to fold the ham around the bread instead of the other way around. I kind of liked it better that way."

"Reverse ham sandwiches, wow. That's something." The suspense was killing me, so I blurted it out. "Hey, about the baptism thing."

"It's okay," he said. "Sometimes we get carried away and forget that ministry is people first. Sorry if you felt pushed."

"I could've handled it better."

"We all could have. You find another church yet?"

It was like there were two Sholties. There was the pastor in the pulpit and this down-to-earth guy I was hanging out and talking easy with. I liked the down-to-earth Sholtie a lot better.

"I checked out a few," I told him. "But it's gonna be something anywhere you go."

"Churches are kinda like restaurants," he said. "You gotta go where they feed you. We'd love to have you back, if you ever want to give us another chance."

"Thanks."

"Well, I gotta get some bread." He chuckled.

"Hey, about that baptism thing?"

"Yeah?"

"I don't do crowds too good. Could we get it done just me and you?"

"Of course."

"I do have one friend I'd like to bring."

"Bring anyone you like," Sholtie said. "As few or as many as you want."

I shook his hand and got three steps away when a sudden conviction washed over me. I had to confess. "Hang on. Wait."

"Yes, sir?"

I turned back. "Preacher, it was me. I squished your wife's bread."

"I know, brother," he said, smiling, "I know."

COME AS YOU ARE

[NOW]

But it was the LORD's good plan to . . . cause him grief.
—ISAIAH 53:10 (NLT)

I T'S A GLOOMY SUNDAY EVENING BY THE TIME I PULL into the church parking lot and wait until the last stragglers slip through the door.

Lighthouse Tabernacle, First and Last Baptist, Lot Casters International, Church on the Rock, True Vine Temple, New Wine Fellowship, Highway to Hill. Been to a lot of churches. Hard to find your fit. Now I'm here at Power & Light, a modern brick catchall located midtown. Brother Benny's a good pastor. He's calm.

The crew-cut usher that used to coach football at the junior high looks both ways down the sidewalk before pulling in the welcome mats and stepping inside. That's my cue. I like to be the last of the very last stragglers. The sign out front advertises *Come As You Are*, so here I am, still hungover from sleep meds and wired on caffeine, a little burnt out but not ready to give up yet.

I thought taking a job at a big, influential church might give me a leg up into the scene, but the preacher at Six Flags Over Jesus left the same week I started, and the people left with him. So I tried joining the staff over at SuperPew next to Chuck E. Cheese, and that one folded too. Kind of a bad feeling when you sign on with two up-and-coming megachurches, and within a year attendance has plummeted, and they're talking of parceling up the property for sale to the good people at Gigatel, Inc.

I've never been very good at church stuff, but that's my testimony: I'm still here. I'm going to sit quietly in the balcony for now, though. I don't want to shut down any more churches.

The lights are low as the music rises, slow and emotional—a song about how we're battered by sin but grace is bigger, back to the start, coming home again. My tastes run more toward tried-and-true gospel, like "Power in the Blood," but I try to keep an open mind toward everything. Except the time they changed the lyrics from "Y.M.C.A." to "Why Aren't You Saved?" Or that night the praise band played "Danger Zone" to lead in Brother Benny's sermon on lust. I know it was supposed to be half joking, but the other half was spectacularly grievous, like staying awake through brain surgery to hear the bone saw rattle your skull. I ran to the south support beam to see if I could push down the building, like Samson in an illustrated sermon of sorts, but the pillar was way sturdy, and, alas, I'm no Samson.

The houselights come up as the congregation mills about to shake hands. The front pews are loosely packed with a smattering of pressed suits and silver hair. I like a church with a lot of old people. It feels solid and trustworthy, like you don't have to worry about your tithe money going to the Shiloh Dogtrack or Mad Sally's cashbox at the Chalet Bar & Grill. There are a thousand secrets in a small Southern town. I've heard a few. One of these days I'm going to get a nice, boring, mind-your-own-business job with no scandals or messy people stuff. I wonder if Moses said the same thing.

God have mercy on us all.

A stylish young lady waves to me from the floor. Clueless, I offer a quick hand back. She stands with arms out, like *Really?* Finally, I recognize her. It's Linda from the Quik-Mart, fixed up all proper and hanging with the cool kids while I'm lurking in the wings looking like some Tilt-A-Whirl carny from the Rowena, Kentucky, fair. She steps under the balcony. "How's your buddy?" I call down.

"Seven days clean!" Linda calls back, hooking arms with Aunt Lacey. "You wanna come sit with us?"

"I'm good, thanks."

I took a skills assessment in grad school once. It said I was an observer and a connector. I watch, help people get to where they need to be, then get out of the way. It felt good to see those results, like maybe things were working out the way they should.

Sure enough, just in the first few rows, there are seven people that I either brought or sent to church, three I admitted to the psych ward, and one married couple that I introduced.

Then again, the other day I took an online personality test called "Which Simpsons Character Are You?" and the results came back 96 percent Otto, that dude who drives the bus. Oh well. Guess they wouldn't build balconies and back pews unless somebody belonged here. Church would just be one long front pew.

A young mother comes to the platform to give a report on her baby's progress at Children's Hospital. Brother Benny asks us to bow our heads and remember this family in their difficult time. Swift and silent, a teenager with half-blue hair slips up and sets a neat bundle of cash at the mother's feet. As he steps away, one of the senior citizens sneaks over and does the same. They bump fists in passing; the oldster winks and sets one finger against his lips. I'm supposed to have my eyes shut, but sometimes, just for research purposes, I look.

An impeccably put-together woman takes the stage next to announce that spaces are going fast for her upcoming class series "Complete: How to Find God's Perfect Mate for You." There's a graphic of a map on the Jumbotron with a dotted line running from a cartoon resembling a Christianized Betty Rubble straight to a heart with a halo floating above.

I imagine the choir practice room crowded with women, and even a few girls, while Sister Impeccable mans the PowerPoint, flipping through pictures of the church's men. Low hisses and murmurs fill the room as my photo flashes across the screen. They've used the shot from my hospital badge—the one the HR lady snapped after an all-nighter that involved pulling an executive's hypomanic wife out of a Jacuzzi and wrestling a hallucinating bath salts abuser in the parking lot of Freeport Pawn. The one that looks like some sad mug shot after I got arrested for public intoxication and conspiracy to overthrow Mayor McCheese.

With another click a red *X* covers my face. "Stick with men who look like they could run for public office," Sister Impeccable suggests. "Or at least manage the shoe department at Sears."

Brother Benny reclaims the pulpit and starts in on his sermon series, "Patience and the Fruit of Leviticus." God bless Benny, but sometimes he tries to stretch five minutes' worth of message into a half hour. As much as I need lessons in patience, soon enough my mind begins to stray.

I think Jesus might've been sending us a secret message when he said he'd build his church on Peter. Seriously? The most temperamental, undependable apostle of the bunch? Peter, who denied Christ three times quick even when he was warned before-hand what would happen? Peter, who was fishing naked when Jesus returned, only to put his clothes back on *before* he jumped into the water to swim to shore? Peter was so unreliable God had to knock a terrorist named Paul off his horse and commission him to write two-thirds of the New Testament. Then Paul and Peter got in a fight.

No wonder Jesus asked how long he would have to put up with those guys. Makes me wonder if Jesus ever rolls his eyes and asks how long he'll have to put up with me.

I'm thankful the Bible shows Jesus in community but also as a stranger who frequently sought solitude. Jesus disappeared. I bet that really made Judas mad. He probably had the schedule planned out for maximum productivity. You know how those finance majors can be. I bet Judas had conferences booked all the way through AD 40. *Where's Jesus? Gone again? Did he at least leave a number this time?*

Every now and then they should let me preach. Just for a different take on things.

Uh-oh, Brother Benny's wrapping it up. Must have dozed off. If they could somehow compound the sedative properties of a church service, I'd never need a sleeping pill again.

"If this message touched your heart tonight, with nobody looking around . . ." As the preacher builds toward the altar call, Squiggly buzzes with a client at Skylark ER.

Sammy catches me at the side exit. He's a big, broad deacon with a prop comic's nose, slate-blue slacks, and a suit jacket the color of sunset.

"Jamie, son!" he greets me.

"What's up, Crockett?" I stop and finger his lapels.

"Sharp, huh? It's Tahiti Dusk. Got it downtown." He brushes lint from the sleeves. "Where you rushing off to? Got a call waiting?"

"Always."

"Thought you were off on Sundays."

"I'm on a mission from God." Sammy shoots up his eyebrows, impressed. "The hospital can't get anybody else to do it," I admit. "Plus, I need the cash."

"When do you sleep?"

"Not much. My doc buddy gave me a prescription and that helps some, but y'know, I hate depending on pills."

"Jamie, half the people in this church take something for anxiety, including my crazy wife. Sometimes God parts the waters, and other times he sends a boat. If anybody knows how to be careful, it's you, right?"

I should give some confirmation, but I can't get the words to come out right. Sammy holds the door open and salutes. "Carry on, soldier," he says.

Driving late—that's my altar call. Nobody listening or looking around. You can congregate in the outer courtyard, but we all meet God alone. No trickery. No hiding now.

This morning I came home, swallowed half a pill, and waited for sleep. And waited. I took the second half and finally faded, but it only lasted a few hours. So I bit off another piece. At this rate I'll run out before my refill comes due. Eighty bucks a month, and I'm still not sleeping that great.

Here's a basic truth: that which earns our living often drives us insane. But you gotta eat and pay the bills. And who's to say the difference between a living and a mission on this side of things? So you pray for change and grace and do what it takes to make it through another night and day. You keep driving on.

I walk into Skylark and everybody's bouncing off the walls, codes calling over the intercom, staff scrambling through the halls. "Let me get to my guy and I'll be outta y'all's way," I apologize.

"Sorry, Jamie," the nurse replies. "The code is your guy."

TROUBLE IS MY GAME

All who were down on their luck came around—losers and
vagrants and misfits of all sorts. David became their leader.
—1 SAMUEL 22:2 (THE MESSAGE)

SOME NIGHTS I DON'T FEEL LIKE RIDING AROUND OR
drifting aimlessly through some grocery store, so I head home
to try and relax. People sell old videotapes on eBay. Imagine that.
For $1.67, I got two cassettes packed with movies taped off late-
night cable in the eighties.

No extra footage this time, other than six episodes of *The
Golden Girls* spin-off where Sophia shares hotel cooking duties
with Cheech. It's not too bad, actually. Every time I have to adjust
tracking I feel incredibly hip, like some new-wave archeologist on
the forefront of cool. But after twenty minutes it gets to be more
trouble than it's worth.

I flip on the kitchen radio as the DJ announces it's nine forty-
five before Bon Jovi sings about going out in a glorious blaze. I've
got a big bowl of Cocoa Pebbles ready for cold milk when the crisis
line rings.

"Call for County Crisis, come back. Freebird, you got your
ears on?"

The second videotape contains the Smokey and the Bandit

trilogy. Turns out Squiggly's a big fan, so lately we've been pretending we're CB truckers hauling bootleg freight across the Georgia line. Start taking crisis too seriously and soon enough you're in crisis yourself.

"Ten-four, Squiggly-Wiggly, you got the Freebird," I bark back. "Come on."

"I got ya thirty-two-year-old male threatening suicide following breakup with significant other. Over."

I shoulder the phone, open the refrigerator, and grab the milk. "Roger. What's his handle?"

"Hershaw McCall," Squig says, in a normal voice now.

"Put him on." I pour the milk. There's a burst of hiss before the voice comes through.

"Hell-o?" the voice says, backwoods yokel as homemade shine. "Hello?"

"Anybody there?" he says.

"You got crisis. Go ahead."

"I'm gonna jump!" the caller says, suddenly frantic. "I swear I'll do it this time!"

"Whoa, partner," I say, closing the fridge door with my foot. "Ease up. Talk to me. Where you at?"

"I'm at home, man."

I stretch, roll my neck, and flop back into the chair. "Yeah, but where is home?"

"Oh," Hershaw answers. "Out south of Bumpkin." Pause. Panic again. "And I swear, that no-good hooch, Missy . . . I'm *jumpin'*! This is *good-bye*. Y'all better send somebody out here *right now*. And prob'ly all they gonna find is my dead body!"

I can picture this guy in my mind: rawboned and greasy with shoulder-length hair and a three-day beard. A fistfight scar marks his cheek and his eyes dart around like a cornered raccoon. "Okay, easy," I reply in my crisis-man-calming-you-down voice. "There's nobody on tonight but me. Now where exactly are you?"

"Out on the danged roof, man. I told ya."

"And just where is this roof?"

"You know where Hickory Road is?" Hershaw asks. "'Bout seventeen miles past where the highway splits. You'll see a body shop on the right and behind that some trailers. I'm last one in back."

"You're on the roof of a trailer?"

"Yeah, and this is *good-bye*, Missy!" he shouts away from the phone. *"Good-bye, ya ol' witch!"*

I walk from the kitchen to the stairs, giving space for the caller to settle down before I ask a very important question. "Is it a two-story trailer?"

"Naw, but it's on a ridge," he contends. "And there's a bunch of glass and car parts down there."

"Uh-huh," I reply in the dubious tone of a late-night crisis guy who didn't start yesterday, y'know.

He fumbles with the phone before speaking again, quieter now. "Listen, man, I don't know what else t' do. She's gonna take the baby and leave." One small sob breaks loose. "Will you please just come help me?"

I stare into the cereal bowl, listening to my Pebbles crackle and pop. "Kinda cool out tonight," I tell him, slipping on my worn-out sheepherder's jacket and black cowboy hat. "Might take me a while to get there. Hope you got a coat."

"Should I put one on?" he asks.

"Yeah. You should definitely put on a coat."

"Hold on," Hershaw says. He walks to the corner of his roof, just above the bedroom window. Standing at the dresser by the bed, there's a stork-legged woman with stringy hair shoving clothes into a paper bag. A fat-cheeked baby clings to her hip, chewing on an empty bottle of shampoo. Sometimes when I'm talking to people on the phone, I can see things unfold like a movie scene, just from the words and background noises I hear. It's probably speculation or magical thinking or the by-product of ten thousand late-night calls. Strange thing is, a lot of times the movie in my mind turns out to be pretty much dead-on to the truth.

"Missy!" Hershaw hollers down. "Throw me a jacket, will ya?"

My cell phone crackles as I hear her shout back. "Hershaw, yer sorry butt can freeze fer all I care!"

"Can you please hang on a second, sir?" he says to me.

"You bet."

Hershaw sets the phone down and lies flat, hanging over the roof's edge. His head pops into view at the top of the bedroom window. "Aw, come on, Missy. The crisis man sez I need a coat."

The baby perks to the sound of his voice and starts to laugh and wave. Hershaw makes a silly face, waving back.

"Oh, all right," Missy gripes. "Which one you want?"

Hershaw picks up the phone again. "She's going to get me one," he tells me. "You comin', right?"

"On my way." I grab truck keys and pull down the brim of my hat. "Just hang tight, okay?"

"Mister," Hershaw says, "I'll be right here on this roof 'til I see your lights."

It's a long drive out with plenty of time to think. On the radio, Brother Rickey Medlocke is singing his highway song about flying high and low and how, Lord, all this madness might not be crazy as it seems.

Sometimes this mission feels like I'm riding shotgun with the devil and other times shotgun with the Lord. That opening wager in the book of Job still boggles my mind. I wonder now and then if there's a poker game going between the archangels and Old

Scratch, a stack of chips on the table with my face on top. If so, I hope Jesus steps in and turns that table over too.

When you're driving late at night, it's easy to let white lines and wonder take your mind away. *Turn the tables, angels. Riding shotgun with Jesus tonight.*

Headlights split the darkness. Up ahead in the distance, there's a flickering light and a hand-painted sign that says, *Lonnie's Paint & Body.* Just behind a slanted, trash-strewn garage lies a gravel lane scattered with dilapidated trailers. At the end sits a dirty single-wide with no siding. On the roof, a shadow paces the ledge.

I pull up and park. "That you?" a voice calls out.

I step into the drive and stare up into a rough-cut but smiling face that looks exactly as I expected. Great. I have supernatural powers that do me absolutely no good.

"I didn't bring no pizzas or subpoenas," I call back. "So, yeah, I guess it's me."

A rust-eaten swimming pool slide leans against the side of the single-wide, so I grab the ladder rails and hustle up onto the roof. Hershaw pulls me into a bear hug—a little awkward at first until I give in and hug back. You only live once, they say. I don't completely buy that. I think we might well live a zillion lives. But I believe this much is true: you only live now.

"You an answer to a hard prayin' man, that's what you are," Hershaw says with a tear in his voice, emotional again. "I seen that commercial y'all got about needing help, and I tell you, I musta sat thirty minutes trying to get up the nerve to call."

"Easy, buddy," I laugh. "'Bout all I can do is listen and help folks get help."

"Yes, sir," he says, stone serious now. "That's exactly the miracle I'm needin' right now."

"Whoa, you weren't joking," I tell him, hanging on to his

elbow as we pull back and formally shake hands. "This is way up on a ridge."

"See all that busted glass way down there?" he asks, pointing with the filthy cast strapped around his left hand. "Was I lyin'? Missy, she told me wadn't nobody crazy enough to come out here this time of night, but soon as we start talking I knew you'd come."

"How's that?"

"Aw, man, I could tell you was a regular guy." He grins and scratches the cast across his beard. "Ain't no different'n me."

The screen door opens and a rail-thin woman steps into the yard. She shifts her baby from left hip to right and squints up to where we stand. "Lard, have mercy," she moans with a slow, sad shake of her head. "What in the world you doin' up there with him?"

At 1:00 a.m. I'm summoned to a blacked-out room in the top floor of an uptown boutique. Fashion-show posters are tacked to the walls, newspapers scattered on a desk. An emerald Tiffany lamp glows from a low shelf filled with books on photography and art.

A long-limbed woman sits legs crossed on the floor, older but chic. She's wearing a black dress, half-kicked-off heels, and her makeup is a smudged mess, like a paint fight between Picasso and Salvador Dalí.

I'm standing in the doorway with hall lights behind me, cowboy hat and patchwork jacket, hair twisted and wind-blown big. "Come in," Chic says. "You look fabulous."

I walk into the office and get a closer look. The dress is swanky, and what I thought was smeared lipstick is actually part nosebleed. From the top of a redneck's single-wide to elegantly wasted fashionistas. Crisis is such a trip.

"Be all things to all people," Saint Paul said in Corinthians. "Just so you might save one." The other night I bought an eye patch at Rite-Aid for $1.25, after watching *Escape from New York*. I haven't had the opportunity to wear it. Tonight would've been the night.

"Where'd you get that great jacket?" Chic asks in a scratchy voice.

"I broke down one night on a back road long way from town. It was freezing cold, and I didn't have a coat. I said this desperate prayer, and a tow-truck driver showed up out of nowhere and pulled me home. He gave me his coat."

"This might sound crazy," she says, "but I believe God sends angels at exactly the right place and time."

"What if you wait and wait and don't get your angel?"

Chic pulls three tissues from a box and blows her nose with trembling hands. Specks of blood appear. A soft laugh breaks loose but quickly turns to tears. "Then it wasn't your time," she says.

"How long has it been this bad?" I ask, already knowing.

"When I moved to New York, I'd never so much as seen a person do drugs," she says, staring through the window and raking fingers through her hair. "Second night there, I met Andy Warhol in the bathroom of Studio 54. Everything after that is a blur."

"Warhol didn't do drugs. He was in church every Sunday and volunteered in the soup kitchen."

"Now how could you possibly know that?"

"Friend of mine worked with him. Said Andy was actually pretty straitlaced."

"Actually, yeah." She smiles at remembering. "Your friend is right."

I sit cross-legged by the bookcase. "What was it like?"

"What was what like?"

"Disco. I used to DJ clubs."

"People think it was all about drugs, but that's not true," she tells me. "It was about being totally alive in the moment. Every night was like the last night of your life. We never gave one thought to what tomorrow might bring."

There's a Polaroid pinned to a corkboard of the woman from another time, in a strapless red gown and surrounded by beautiful people; her eyes sparkle like marquee lights. She catches me staring.

"But it could be empty too." She sighs. "And when you woke up in the morning, you were still your same old messed-up, lonely self. I didn't need drugs so much when times were good. It was the hard times that dragged me down."

I sneeze twice and look around the room. A gray cat is coiled around the lamp, pawing empty air. "Are you thinking about hurting yourself?" I ask.

"Yes," she confesses, both defiant and sad. "Yes, I am."

"How would you do that?"

"I would light two road flares and jump into a barrel of gasoline. At night."

"Really, now."

"If you're going, go big. Make the front page." Chic rests her head against the side of the desk, gazing at the photo again. "Some people die long before they're buried. You know that?"

There's a time to speak and a time to sit quietly and wait. The gray cat slinks down from the lamp and nudges her hand. "Pills," she admits. "I've got some saved."

"How many saved?"

"Eighty-six Lortab. Forty Halcion. Some methadone."

"That's enough," I reply. The gray cat whaps her tail against me. My collar itches, and it feels like my head is on fire.

"But I can't go back to treatment again," she says, this time more to herself. "I just can't."

The good thing about late-night crisis is you can sit in the silence and think of the right next thing to say. "If I told you what you just told me—would you leave?"

A long pause. "No," she says.

"Would you make sure I got somewhere safe?"

"Yes."

"C'mon, then," I tell her. "You know what we have to do." She follows me down the hall. In a different light she looks older and frail, but she smiles weakly and holds up a ready suitcase. "You packed?" I ask. "You knew you were going?"

"I don't want to go. I don't want to attend those stupid groups and hear those stupid doctors and counselors say the same old stupid things. But I know if I don't get help, I'm not going to make it," she says. "I'm not going to have to ride over in some stupid ambulance, am I?"

"I could get them to turn on the stupid lights," I offer. "It would be very dramatic."

"No more drama," she says, rubbing her forehead. "I just want to get some sleep."

"I'll take you in my truck," I tell her as we exit down the outer stairs. "Quicker that way."

"You don't mind?" she asks. "You won't get in trouble?"

It's 2:13 a.m., and water rushes from a fire hydrant into the street. The window above flashes red from the fortune-teller's neon hand as the beacon on Thomas Towers rolls east. I spit my gum into the sewer grate, step back, and hold out my hands. When you get the movie moment, better play it for all you can. "Trouble is my game," I reply coolly.

"Thanks," she says, laughing through the same crumpled smile. "Okay if I smoke?"

"Long as you crack the window."

We ride a mile or so, neither speaking. "Do you miss it?" she asks as we cross the river.

"Miss what?"

"Deejaying. In my day, being a DJ was the coolest job on earth."

"Yeah," I tell her. "I think about it all the time."

"If you deejay again, I've got a name for you," she says, motioning from my hat and jacket to the sky. "You should call yourself the Midnight Cowboy."

I bump open the glove box, take out the eye patch, and slip it on. Chic sits back, nods, and flicks her ashes into the night. "Fabulous," she replies.

DAY 17

Stop trying to make everything fit and make sense. God in the box is *religion*, the god we can control and understand. The living God is alive and unpredictable, often found in the last places one might expect.

Paul was blinded. David was tending sheep. Moses saw the burning bush.

When did you first hear the call?

DON'T LET THE LEFT HAND KNOW

[THEN]

To the pure, all things are pure.
—TITUS 1:15 (NIV)

I WAS COLLEGE-BOY BROKE AND NEEDED CASH, SO I applied for a part-time DJ job at the local country radio station, arriving for the interview in a cowboy hat and Tony Lama boots. After no small amount of laughter, I was informed that the position was actually for their sister station, KBJC ("God's Power in Music!"), located in a dinky portable building out back.

KBJC's program director was a cool old dude with a pompadour named Roy Macoy who told me he once played guitar for Ricky Nelson before getting saved and delivered from secular music and the love of worldly things. "We're looking for somebody on weekends, six to noon."

"Six a.m.?"

"Six at night to noon might get a little tedious," he pointed out. "Are morning shifts a problem?"

"No, sir."

"Praise the Lord, then!" Mr. Roy said. "Welcome aboard! You are familiar with Christian music, right?"

"Oh, yeah, sure," I told him. "I love gospel." Fake it 'til you make it, they say. Especially if you need the job. Besides, it was music for God. How bad could it really be?

Christian music was awful. It was syrupy and contrived. It was a Z-grade copy of popular music, stripped of soul and several years removed. It was an insult to both God and man.

I liked some of it anyway.

On weekend nights I deejayed the college dance club until two in the morning. I'd stumble in at daybreak and sign on the Christian station with smoke still in my clothes, playing some white-bread quartet singing about the devil in a phone booth dialing 911 while my head felt like it was being stomped by ogres. Then the record would end and I'd give the weather forecast and announce another song about God's everlasting power and grace.

Every week I expected to be fired. I'd drag in late, turn the live feed down, and blast Metallica in the cue. Once I accidentally played two minutes of "No Bone Movies" right in the middle of the Moody Bible Hour. Twice I forgot and left the mike on, letting a curse word slip out over the air. Mr. Roy never got mad. He had a gentle way of correcting, telling stories, and asking questions that made you come around to the truth and want to do better on your own.

Much to my surprise, he called me to his office one day and promoted me to music director. I was still an absolute reprobate, "borrowing" audio equipment for personal use, hot-rodding the station news wagon with roof flashers blazing, rigging giveaways so my friends won free Mexican dinners and gave them back to me. Still, I was determined not to let Mr. Roy down.

I had this crazy notion that KBJC might give me a show where I could play all kinds of songs and talk about how music speaks to the human condition, how we are all struggling and searching for peace, that "Landslide" or "Free Bird" could be just as much gospel as "Amazing Grace." All truth is God's truth, right? To the pure, all things are pure. Everything is gospel if you look at it right.

I proposed my idea in staff meeting and everybody grimaced like I'd just kicked a skunk. "Jamie, I don't want to discourage you," Mr. Roy said. "But the local churches sure wouldn't go for that."

KBJC introduced me to this nutty preacher named Danny B. Sholtie who did a show every Saturday at ten. Off air, he was calm, friendly—almost shy. Until I gave him the signal that he was live. Then, for twenty-six minutes, he would ramble and rage with spit flying and fists in the air about nuclear winter, alien demons, and Rambo angels in the latter days.

I would listen intently, fascinated. For about three minutes. Then I'd go to Control Room B and do homework. Sholtie could see me through a partial window, head down, working, and thought I was studying with him every step of the way.

"Brother, you don't know how much you encourage me," he said, gripping my shoulder and nearly coming to tears. "I can't see the people out there, and sometimes I wonder if I'm wasting my breath. But then I look over, and there you are following along and hanging on every word!"

I wasn't following along. I was writing some term paper on Tesla. But I didn't have the heart to tell him that. Reverend Sholtie never asked for money and paid for airtime out of his own pocket. For a radio preacher, I thought he was a pretty decent guy.

One Saturday Sholtie kept giving me peculiar looks during his on-air rant about Ezekiel and Planet X titled "Good News about the Destruction of All Mankind." When the show was over, he pulled me to the side and in a kind voice said, "I think God has something special for you, brother. But he says you'll never get there with a selfish attitude."

"Uh, okay," I said, a little shook. "Wow."

Just the previous morning I'd been in Professor Van Cleef's sociology class. "How many firstborns do we have?" he'd asked. "Anyone grow up primarily as an only child?" A few hands went up. I lifted mine quickly before doodling in my notebook again.

"Firstborns and onlys often wrestle with self-centered traits," Van Cleef lectured. "Do you see these attributes in yourself? Be honest. Most of you have matured past that stage by now, but some find it difficult to embrace change."

The Tuesday before, I'd lied and told a classmate I didn't have enough gas to give him a ride home. Another day some Girl Scouts were selling cookies in front of Piggly Wiggly, and I walked to the far door to avoid them. I won four tickets to the Joy Twin Cinema, and instead of inviting friends, I went all four times by myself. Jules found out, stuck her head out the window while we were driving down Main, and shouted, "Jamie's *so* stingy!"

Now, I wondered if she wasn't somehow in cahoots with this telepathic preacher. I tuned back in as he recited a scripture about barns of plenty and vats of new wine, if only we were willing to be givers and live with open hands.

"Like, even gum?" I asked, a piece of Trident hidden in my cheek so I wouldn't have to share.

"Little is much when God is in it," he replied, adding that the only time the Bible dares us to test God is in generosity, guaranteeing that we couldn't outgive him. "Try it, Jamie," he declared, "and I will promise you this: the giving life is the most full-of-joy, fun life you will ever live."

I never was one to back down from a dare. So I decided to take Brother Sholtie's challenge and test God. I decided to try giving things away.

I stood in the club's DJ booth that night looking over the crowd and thinking about the reverend's advice. If I gave something away, it would just mean less for me. Minus couldn't mean more. College kids had to be frugal. But Sholtie was saying not only could I give things away and be happier—somehow I wouldn't do without. Also, he said not to wait. That I should start looking for opportunities to be a giver right away.

As the DJ, I could theoretically give drinks to anyone I wanted. But officially, on the books, I could buy them for a buck. Sholtie said true giving was sacrificial, that it has to cost us something. Inspiration flashed like a strobe light over my head as I remembered a Bible verse I'd read commanding us to give beer and wine to those with troubled hearts.

"Start where you are," Sholtie had suggested. "Just give whatever you have to give."

So I started paying people's tabs. Covertly, because Sholtie said that was one of the conditions. You couldn't blow your trumpet about generosity because then everyone crows over you and you've got your reward. You had to be top secret and not let your left hand know what the right was doing.

Jules was tending bar, so I had to tell her something. But I was vague about it and didn't say anything about Jesus or the ESP preacher from gospel radio.

If you looked especially sad or lonely, your drink was miraculously free. Zinfandel, maybe, or a Long Island Iced Tea. Say you lost your job? Girlfriend dumped you? Some mystery philanthropist covered your bill. It's not like I was planning to testify on air about the blessedness of giving away Alabama Slammers to the brokenhearted. Besides, I was still half Catholic. Catholics believe that when Jesus changed water to wine, it was God's way of saying, "Life is tough, so relax responsibly and enjoy each other's company now and then, all right?"

Look, the Bible says Jesus went to churches and Jesus went to the roadhouses and taverns where sinners and roughnecks live. You don't ever hear a story about Jesus turning over tables in a tavern, though, do you?

Right at peak time, two pretty girls rolled into the club with a frumpy third-wheel girl trailing behind. They took a table just off the dance floor, carrying on like a pair of cheerleaders-turned-stewardesses while their coworker/cousin/roommate sat in the corner looking like Peyton Manning in drag.

I watched third-wheel girl for a while—shy and self-conscious, the expression on her face like some sad, old bulldog dragged to a fireworks show. Then I flagged Jules down. "What's, like, our most romantic drink?"

"Flirty Fizz," she shot back, smacking on the piece of Big Red I'd given her earlier.

"Uh, second most."

"Doggie Kisses," she offered.

"Third."

"I don't know," Jules said. "A Sweet Southern Belle?"

"What's that?"

"Merlot, Fresca, and pineapple juice."

"Perfect," I replied. "See that girl over there?"

"C'mon, Jamie, don't be mean."

"No, I'm for real. Send one over. Remember, don't tell, don't even hint who sent it."

Jules reached over, unlatched the half door, and stepped inside the booth. "All right," she snapped. "What's up?"

"What's up with what?" I asked.

"You know what," she said, that sort of evasive circular questioning between close friends when one of them is trying to hide something.

I focused on the board, adjusting my faders. "What?"

Jules leaned in until her face was about two inches from mine, scowling with her Elvis-y pout and Egyptian eyes. My give-it-away smile makes me a terrible liar. So I decided to tell her straight. "I was reading that part in the Bible where Jesus says we should be givers, so I'd, um, like to try and do better."

Sometimes, on Sunday mornings, Jules would put on her flower-print dress, and we'd sit in the back pew of her parents' Southern Baptist church. When her mother was looking, she'd make me hold her hand. Jules was a straight shooter, but she wasn't ready to tell her parents that much truth just yet.

"Jamie, baby," Jules said, hugging me from the side, "listen to the Lord."

She delivered the Sweet Southern Belle. Confused, the girl pulled out her purse and offered some cash. Jules shook her head and pushed the girl's money back, once and then again before walking away. From the way Jules fanned out her hand I could tell she was saying something like: "Honey, sometimes a guy sends something over just to be nice. Enjoy, okay?"

Third-Wheel Girl looked uneasy, and for a moment I feared I was only making things worse. But then, when she thought no one was watching, she took a sip and smiled, and a rush of happiness fizzed up through me like my heart had been carbonated and given a vigorous shake. The nutty radio preacher was right: giving is fun.

Jules passed the booth and snagged my left headphone. "She's a sweetie. Now if you really want to do something nice, go ask her to dance." We stared each other down for a second. Jules cupped her hands around my ear. "I *dare* you," she said.

I unlatched the door and let her in. "Your next song is cued and ready," I told her. "Just give me a minute to get to the floor."

I cut a path around back and up from the side. The girl slow-sipped and swayed to the beat, watching her friends sashay across the dance floor. I slipped in beside her. "Hey, whatcha doing?" I asked.

"Oh gosh, sorry!" she said, bumping back and spilling her Southern Belle. "Is this table saved?" She had on an LSU sweatshirt, gold granny glasses, and a top ponytail. When she stood up, I was eye to eye with Mike the Tiger. That's how tall she was.

"No, no," I explained. "I mean, why aren't you dancing?"

She blushed, smiled sweetly, and the happy fizz rushed through me again. "Come on," I said, taking her sweaty hands and leading her to the floor. Her friends circled around us and cheered, "Sa-rah! Sa-rah!"

But Jules didn't play the song I had cued up next—a mid-tempo number, nice and safe. She played Marvin Gaye's "Let's Get It On," with its saucy guitar lick and suggestive lyrics talking about sensitive people and how sweet and wonderful life can be. I glanced over the crowd, and Jules was on her toes, pointing my way. "Go Ja-mee!!!" she cried out over the mike.

"Jamie! Jamie!" Sarah's friends joined in.

Shoulder to shoulder, we danced with hands in the air, and as I looked around, every person in the club was grooving. Jules's blue-black Mohawk bobbing in the booth. The side stragglers and the bouncer at the door. I could even see people in the parking lot getting down. It felt like the whole world was dancing. For just a moment, we were all in one accord.

Sarah leaned in, one hand on my wrist. "Did you send me that drink?"

Don't let the left hand know. "Wasn't me," I replied, giving it away with my smile.

"I love you!" she shouted.

"I love everybody!" Jules sang loudly, suddenly dancing beside us.

"Hey!" I said, gesturing to the booth.

"You got two minutes." She winked. "Your next record is cued and ready."

As a hundred sweaty faces bounced all around, I took back my DJ booth and turned up the mike. "If you love somebody tonight," I told the peoples, every hand up and waving side to side, "be sure to let 'em know."

A club is so quiet once it's shut down. Jules and I were cleaning up. "How much I owe you?" I asked.

She pulled a tab from the cash drawer and figured it quick. "Twenty-six straight," she said.

"Okay, hang on." On a busy night I might make that in my tip jar. "That'd be a pretty good miracle," I told her while walking to the booth, "if God made it where I'd break even."

"Yeah," Jules said, wiping down the bottles. "That'd be really all right."

I had a big plastic pickle jar sitting by the half door of the DJ booth. Jules had colored it opaque with a purple Magic Marker, covered the opening with duct tape, and cut a slit in the top to slip the tips through. I grabbed the jar and peeled the duct tape back.

It was stuffed with cash.

I carried it back to the counter and dumped the money out.

"Whoa!" Jules gushed.

"You tell anybody it was me?"

"No, buddy," she said, counting bills into stacks. "I swear."

I felt a different kind of fizzy now. Spooky, almost. Truth is I was sort of daring God back. Okay, fine, show up at church where people on their best behavior wear suits and put money in baskets that everyone can see. But will you show up in a dive bar, Jesus? Will you show up in a situation that's not so neat and clean? Are you truly willing to meet me exactly where I am?

"Seventy-eight dollars," said Jules. We stared at each other, shaking our heads.

"Guess it's true," I admitted. "You really can't outgive God."

"See, Jamie?" Jules said, twisting her lips into a grin. "You should listen to Jesus from now on."

I split the money and handed her half. "You know," I told her, "it really is more fun to give."

That next Saturday I told Brother Sholtie the whole story. Alabama Slammers and Peyton Manning in drag. Eye to eye with Mike the Tiger and everybody's hands in the air. The purple tip jar stuffed with cash. Okay, maybe I left out the part about "Let's Get It On."

He listened intently until I was through. "Little brother," Sholtie said, shaking my shoulder with his big preacher hand, "we all start where we are."

I met Jules the next morning at First Baptist on Main. She was wearing a dress with big magnolias on the front, and her hair was plastered flat. We slipped into the far back pew and sat there in the Sunday-morning light like lizards in the sun. The pastor bid us to stand and greet a neighbor. Jules's parents bounded over like I was Saint Peter at the gate on Judgment Day.

"*Mom*," Jules said with a heavy sigh.

"Oh, Julie," her mother chirped, shooing her over and sliding in tight beside us. Jules eased her hand into mine. I cut my eyes.

"Shut up and hold it," she hissed, giving my knuckles a quick crush. I yelped dramatically; half the church turned to look. Her mother winked and shushed us.

We stood in the far back pew, fingers platonically laced, singing along to the first and third verses of "Just as I Am." Jules's elbow met my ribs as she flapped the hem of her dress. "Listen to Jesus," she said.

KBJC's top-ranked DJ led police on a high-speed chase and wrecked his Pontiac into Suds-N-Stuff, and behold! I was promoted to his afternoon drive-time slot. With the new position came new responsibilities. Artist interviews, live remotes, public appearances. Since I was the local voice of Christian radio, I thought it might be helpful if I actually attended a church of my own.

I tried to be theologically cool and analytical, but truth was I hoped the Holy Roller take on spirituality was true. I wasn't that interested in the notion of a God who would simply be there in hard times. Friends and family could do that. Or for that matter, Miller Lite, motivational sayings, peanut M&Ms, Ray Charles records, romance novels, or reruns of *Three's Company*. Plenty of things could help a person get through troubled times. That's not supernatural. A God who would *fix* trouble? Here and now? That's something else entirely.

Blind people in the Bible weren't consoled. They got their eyesight back. Jesus didn't tell that crippled guy, "Cheer up, brother. This too shall pass." He said, "Get up and walk." When the tax goons were breathing down Peter's neck, he made money materialize in a fish's mouth, and even when his mom's friend ran into a problem—not pain or death, just embarrassment because her party ran out of wine— Jesus didn't say, "Gosh, I'm sorry, Mrs. Nelson. You want me to run to the store?" Even though he knew it would cause much future consternation among the religious, he turned water into wine.

Jesus didn't offer a lot of platitudes or consolation in biblical times. He fixed things.

I didn't want to hear all that stuff about hearts being changed either. I could watch *Titanic* and feel a change of heart. Hearts are most deceitful. Jesus' ministry wasn't marked by subjective change. If there's no food for miles and you suddenly feed five thousand, that's a marked and observable change. The dead rising and fig trees dying before your eyes—those things are above scrutiny. So when I saw a church that advertised a Jesus who was still in the business of fixing things? That got my attention for sure.

My buddy Danny Sholtie pastored the Lighthouse Full Gospel Tabernacle, and they were one of KBJC's biggest sponsors to boot. So I started going there.

I was welcomed like a celebrity due to my radio status. The Lighthouse elders had big plans for me as well. Leadership, outreach, playing in the church band.

"Sure, why not?" I agreed. I'd always felt some vague and mysterious call to a higher purpose. Maybe this was the first open door. New-member class was required for all ministry positions, so I dutifully signed up.

We met in an upstairs office that smelled like sweat and Scotchgard mixed with frankincense and myrrh. I liked it. It seemed like a ladder between heaven and earth, the sacred and mundane. I imagined it must have been the way Jesus smelled.

On the first night Sholtie rambled in a style slightly less erratic than his radio show, fists still pumping, a little spit flying as he assured the class that God loved us and had a wonderful plan for each and every one of our lives.

"But what about that part in the Bible that says God loved Jacob but hated Esau?" I asked. "What if it's my lot in life to be an Esau? I mean, Esau didn't even seem like that bad of a guy."

I didn't have a lot of church experience, but I thought a new member class was probably something like college and the most important thing you could do was read ahead in the textbook, ask questions, and be honest about the stuff you didn't understand.

"And how about that Jeremiah guy?" I continued. "His plan looked pretty rough to me."

The tiny room got silent.

I thought these were exactly the sort of things people would and should be discussing in church, so I pressed on. "I mean, geez, Preacher, none of us got to vote on being born. So how accountable can we really be?"

There were six other members in class. They stared at me like I'd proposed a churchwide Streak-a-thon down Riverside Drive to lay aside differences and bring together the many shades of faith.

"I mean, I was, uh, just reading the Bible and wondering and stuff," I fumbled to explain.

Sholtie gave me a look somewhere between sympathy and exasperation. "Just trust the Lord," he suggested, "and let him do the work."

Trust? I thought. *Trust means fifty different things to fifty different people. And is God's plan really to let us off the hook from the work?*

I didn't say any of the things running through my head. Instead, I nodded. "I'll give it my best. Just seems kinda hard to figure sometimes. That's all."

"Well, brother," Sholtie said in a tone that indicated our discussion had come to a close, "that's why we've got to have faith."

Despite prophecies saying KBJC would bring unity and prosperity to our town, we came in dead last in the ratings, and the format was switched to sports talk. Or maybe the prophecies were right after all.

I took a job as the late-night guy on the classic-rock radio station across town, playing music for shift workers and the lonely, broken people who couldn't sleep. Sometimes they would call the request line just to talk, asking me to play their favorite songs—the ones that gave them hope and helped them feel not so alone.

TRY TO ENJOY THE RIDE

[NOW]

Let's go.

—JESUS (LUKE 8:22 NCV)

SIX THIRTY-FIVE FINDS ME AT CHARTER HOUSE AGAIN. No crisis tonight. Barbie's back from her conference and has twisted my arm into stopping by for their Halloween party. It's a pretty cool scene, residents in homemade costumes—pirates and princesses and cowboys and clowns. They're not all cliché. Wesley's dressed like a taco-weenie dog. Buddy is Charlie Brown with a zigzag shirt and squiggle drawn on his big, bald head. And Elsie has two long strips of black cardboard stuck to the front of her blouse and a plug hanging from her back pocket. "What are you supposed to be?" I ask.

"A toaster, silly!" she replies.

This is why everybody loves Halloween.

"You came to our party and didn't wear a costume?" Barbie cackles, jabbing me with her magic wand.

"I'm working."

"So am I," she says, cinching a belt around the waist of my

jacket and handing me a tin foil sword. "Now. You're Inigo Montoya."

"As you wish," I reply.

"Wrong guy," she says.

At first I thought it was part of her witch outfit, but looking closer, I can tell that her flaxen, flowing hair is not a wig. She's slimmer, and her face looks sandblasted smooth. Also, there's some sort of permanent cosmetic thing going on.

Brother Benny once preached that when in doubt we should always say the kindest possible thing.

"Exactly what kind of conference was it you went to, again?" I ask.

"Zip it," Barbie says, clamping her fingers tight. "You should really be nice to me today."

"Why's that?"

She spins me around as Tina and Neta burst from the kitchen carrying an orange-and-black cake with lit candles on top. I'm totally bewildered until I see *HAPPY BIRTHDAY JAMIE* on top and everybody begins to sing. "Because," says Barbie, dragging her finger through the icing to paint me a black mustache, "I got you a cake."

I start to play the scene off with wisecracks but instead zip it as requested. Thirty severely disabled group-home patients singing a careening, off-key version of "Happy Birthday" while wearing handmade costumes is a moment to just experience and take in. I'm not a huge fan of birthdays or parties or cake, but sometimes life catches you by surprise.

They finish the song on a high and cringeworthy note, and I blow out the candles while everybody claps. Tina cuts me the first piece.

"Red velvet," she says. "Fat-free."

"How'd you know that's my favorite? How'd you even know this week's my birthday?"

"Knowing's my job," she says.

"Oh, man," I gush, one bite in. "This cake is goo-od."

"The residents made it," Barbie says, low in my ear. I can't tell if she's joking. "Fat-free, maybe, but packed with love."

I eat three pieces of cake and receive a hundred and seventy-four hugs, but even though it feels like these are my people, crowds and attention make me anxious, so eventually I gravitate toward the back and talk to Ronnie about our next gig. They asked me to join their band. Seven black brothers and one bedraggled guitarist of questionable pedigree. I've come to the decision that life should be a bit absurd.

"All right, next show," he says, brushing beaded braids from his face, "we want you to pick one and sing."

It's a little hard to take him seriously when he's dressed as Rick James. "I don't know about that. I do better on the side."

"Just let the Lord lead you," Ronnie says, gold foil shining off his front tooth. "He didn't give us a spirit of fear. You gotta step out there sometimes."

Ronnie tells me to pray about it and glides off to manage a punch spill as Tina slides over decked out as full-on Raggedy Ann. "Hey, don't worry," she says. "I made the cake."

"Figured," I reply. "Thanks."

"So how's the journey?" she asks, referring to her workbook, I guess.

"Strange," I reply. "When's it supposed to start making sense?"

"Life is not TV, Jamie," Raggedy Tina says with one finger pointed to the sky. "But God is good, and my hope is not tied to this life."

I pause a beat and ask again. "When's it start making sense?"

"I'm still waiting," she says.

With birthday wishes complete and spiritual encouragement from the unlikely duo of Rick James and Raggedy Ann, I slip from the party to the parking lot. An elephant trumpets from over the fence and another calls back across the way. I stand on the picnic table to try to catch a glimpse of their trunks rising in the night. Not quite. But if I push the table over a few feet I could jump up, grab that limb, and climb on top of the shed.

Sure enough, a little higher and I can see over the whole back forty, from the petting zoo to the monkey house, the train station to the secret island where I'd sail out and spend my days doing research for the psych department in graduate school.

After months of persistence, I'd made a breakthrough. Trixie, my most gifted monkey, was able to differentiate shapes to obtain reward. I was looking for that missing link, the lost chord, the connection between reason and faith, certain I could be the one to finally articulate it in a manner that seemed insightful and right. With lemurs seeking candy on a secret island? "Don't despise the day of small beginnings," Zechariah said.

I crunched numbers and recorded my findings, wrestling for a way to make it all fit. My grad school notebook was kept in two parts: one for thoughts on faith, another for behavior, and sometimes the sections bled together in a mix. That afternoon at the zoo I wrote something like this:

> Psychology encourages caution in matters of faith, the symptoms of religion and delusion being much the same. My professors assure me that good questions are crucial, saying it's important to challenge one's assumptions and that feelings lie. Feelings are contingent upon hormones, heredity, sleep habits, what we eat or drink. The research is consistent: humans are flaky, prone to finding ways to believe what we so badly want and need to believe.
>
> Spiritual mentors caution that to be led only by the empirical is to risk a bleak and cynical view. The righteous walk by

faith, not sight, fixing one's vision on the unseen eternal, entertaining angels unaware. But if all your spirituality is based on
feelings, it's going to be a rambling, chaotic run.

Then again, how many Bible characters rambled? Moses
and all God's children zigzagged forty years. The great man
of faith Elijah fled for his life, pausing under a broom tree and
praying to die. Even Jesus' family were certain in the moment
that he had lost his mind. Isn't the Bible in many ways a textbook study on human behavior and the epic frustrations of man?

Here's what faith should do: make you a better person.
Deeper, truer, stronger in storms. If your faith makes you mean
and crazy, it's probably best to check your beliefs.

Herein lies the real-world problem: sometimes I am stronger,
other times I'm just crazy and mean. And the deeper truth is
this: what makes me crazy, in some strange way, also makes me
strong. Every strength is wrapped in weakness, a person's best
asset often their biggest liability as well.

The Bible speaks of that paradox—power perfected in
flaws. I wonder if faith and behavior aren't more like muscle or
bone, intricately beautiful in the way they work, but messy and
bloody if you try to separate the parts. Maybe, in some sense,
God is the original psychologist, that one true research expert
on behavior and the nature of all things.

There was a tug at my shorts while I was writing. It was Trixie.
I'd been ignoring her now that revelation appeared. She studied
me with her wide yellow eyes, long arms reaching. I clapped my
hands and she scampered up, nestling into me, purring content.
That's when I realized my rookie mistake. Trixie had not learned
to differentiate shapes. She'd learned to read my face for nonverbal
clues. All my little monkey wanted was to make me happy and get
some treats. Emphasis on treats.

I dropped the notebook and scratched behind her ears. So much for Mr. Grad Student's hotshot hypothesis. Back to square one.

We climbed into the boat and set sail, stopping to pick up Trixie's baby goat buddy, Sweet Jenny, along the way. It was the most perfect spring day—74 degrees with a sea of lilies in bloom and the zoo train carrying a load of waving third graders. We ran parallel down the river until the train shot over the bridge and ducked into a tunnel that was curvy and dark. The kids screamed in the tunnel and laughed with hands high when it came out the other side. Mr. Ricky lifted his conductor's hat and blew the train's whistle. We sounded our foghorn in return as they split off and headed for home.

I steered the Congo boat gently through the cove, Sweet Jenny softly bleating and Trixie chattering and picking my pockets for leftover Skittles. Somewhere on the ride, with the wind in my hair and tiny lemur hands clinging, I got the insight, just a little: everything is messy. Every living thing dies if you dissect it too much. We're all trying to hold the good and minimize the damage down here. We are all trying to survive life.

So maybe in a sense I was God's monkey, not so perceptive and poorly evolved, too shortsighted for anything much beyond chattering, clinging, and searching for easy rewards. And maybe God's message to me was, "Hey, that's all right. Just hang on. Try to enjoy the ride."

It was ironic, I suppose, standing there as a promising young researcher in one of America's top programs, knowing that any psychologist worth his or her salt would have diagnosed such thinking as irrationally magical, the anxious brain's attempt to paint a hopeful picture that makes sense. But there's value in the irrational. Good research always leaves room for the desperate unknown.

Ah, to be young, naïve, and in college.

Then again, here I am today, sugar-buzzed and standing on a shed behind the group home for the severely mentally impaired, dressed as a pirate from *The Princess Bride* and holding a tin foil sword. There's probably some kind of insight to faith and reason right there.

I raise my rickety saber to the night and pledge to stay forever young and hopeful, to never stop fighting, learning, or trying to figure out why, to—

How am I going to get back down now?

Barbie appears on the patio while my sword is lifted high. "Birthday boy, have you been drinking?" she cracks.

EVERYTHING YOU LOST

For here we have no lasting city, but we
seek the city that is to come.
—HEBREWS 13:14 (ESV)

THE CITY IS QUIET AT 11:00 P.M. NO STARS, NO MOON, no traffic, no lights. Rain coming later but still miles away. No calls. Not one. That's what hooks me on crisis work. These empty pockets of time where I can get lost. I understand why Jesus had to disappear now and then.

There's a Laundromat out by the college—a seedy little hole in the wall between Payday Loans and LaDonna's Beauty Supply. I had to wash clothes here one afternoon when I was a sophomore and thought it was the most depressing place on earth. Grimy floors and concrete walls, box fans churning swirls of damp heat. There is nothing sadder and more lonesome than a desolate Laundromat on a Sunday afternoon.

But everything changes after the sun goes down. What's sad and depressing during the day is strangely calm at night. The ebb and flow from a row of washing machines, the steady drone of industrial dryers. Someone asked the other day if I had an office. "I got offices all over town," I bragged.

I've been journaling in Tina's workbook like a mopey

sophomore whose boyfriend dumped her at Midwinter Ball. Wow. On page 122, there's a picture of Jesus in the door of a prop plane with his hand on the skydiver's back. Not an actual photograph, just a drawing. I wonder if Jesus is encouraging or pushing him out. I'll have to ask Tina about that.

Sure, her book's a little goofy, but it's well intentioned. I'm goofy but well intentioned. Mental health is goofy but well intentioned. Church is often goofy but well intentioned. Eden's long gone. It's a fallen world. You gotta start somewhere. We are all trying to get back home.

An hour passes before the phone rings. Most of my calls come from dispatch, but sometimes people call the helpline directly to talk. Especially late. I guess there are some things you can only tell a stranger.

A local weather girl says that even though she's twenty-six and successful, she still lives at home with her mother, who won't let her date or pick out her own clothes. "I don't think I'm too ugly, not like some beast or something. Have you ever seen TV-7 News?"

"No, ma'am," I lie, because she's actually quite lovely and it feels like the truth would complicate things. "Never seen it, I'm afraid."

Once one call breaks loose, it's usually back to back for a spell. There's a lieutenant on the take and a twisted list of carnal misconducts I try to scrub quickly from my memory banks. "I'm just trying to find the guts to keep going or end it all," a CEO at Gigatel confides as heart-dotted socks in a dryer hypnotize me with their endless spin. "Anything but being stuck between."

"How long you been stuck?" I ask.

"Ten years now," he says softly. "Too long."

Sometimes I'm glad people call. It's good to have one safe place to speak about your struggles, to just tell the truth about the way you feel. It helps to keep me straight and not feel so crazy to know there's an undercurrent of dysfunction unbiased to age, class, color, or creed. Madness runs rampant, even in a sleepy Bible-belt town. And God in all his wisdom entrusted me to be the keeper of secrets. Life is so bizarre.

A bipolar lady self-medicating with street drugs lost her kids last March and wants to clean up and try to get them back before Christmas. I agree to meet her somewhere public, and when I do, she's still coming down, crying and trying not to crash, confessing all the mistakes she's made along the way.

"Made a few myself," I tell her. And then, because it's late and I'm loopy from not sleeping, I share a couple of the worst.

It feels safe telling secrets to a stranger in the night, especially at one forty-five in the parking lot of the Quik-Stop off Riverside. Then, just because I like her, because I slammed a sugar-free Red Bull way too fast and the weight of my spoken mistakes feels as scratchy as a fiberglass sweater against my skin, I break the silence by singing the first few lines of "Amazing Grace."

"Oh, goodness, yes, yes," she says, eyes closed and one hand high. "You don't even know, honey. 'Amazing Grace,' that's my *jam*."

I transport her to the hospital and get her checked in. She cries and says, "Thank you, thank you," at least twenty times. "I'm gonna get my kids back," she swears. "This is a new start for me."

"Yes, ma'am," I tell her. "I'll pray new beginnings. For everybody."

"Please," she begs, squeezing my hands. "Please do."

I try to learn something from every person, especially someone who has been through much struggle and pain. Jesus said the broken show us heaven. Then again, we are all so busted down here. Maybe we show each other the way.

"Hey, let me ask you a question," I say. "Do you think God

would send somebody to do something they didn't really want to do and weren't much good at, even if it wracked their nerves?"

She clicks her bright orange nails against the desk. "That's a tough one. I used to make my son take out the trash because he needed to learn responsibility. But I wouldn't force him to be a garbage man. Not unless he wanted to."

"Good way to put it."

"Then again, sometimes it's hard to know," she adds. "The Bible says the king's heart is like a watercourse. And he guides it whatever way he wants it to go."

Jackie's swamped and the unit is understaffed, so I hang around to help with a new patient arriving from four counties away. I open the door, and it's a girl in her late teens sobbing and shivering, barefoot in a tank top and flimsy shorts. The deputies stand behind her leering and laughing like she's beneath their contempt.

"You couldn't get her some clothes?" I ask. "Or at least shoes?"

The tall one with his hat down tight doesn't take to being questioned. "Not our problem, bud," he cuts back. The other snorts in agreement as they turn their cold eyes on me.

"When's the last time you ate?" I ask the girl.

She shakes her head and shrinks back, so I ask again, calmer. "Sometime yesterday," she whimpers. "I don't know."

I swing the door back and she starts to panic and gulp for breath. The shorter deputy pushes her forward with his nightstick. I sweep her inside and close the door against them. "Hey!" he says, jamming his stick in the door.

"Sorry, guys. Confidentiality. Only staff and patients allowed."

"Sez who?" the tall deputy growls.

"Says me. That's the rule. You can radio your chief." I point as if he's standing right behind them. They glance back and I slam the door.

"Hang tight, okay?" I tell the girl, leaving her secure in the corridor. The hospital keeps a closet full of clothes left behind by former patients. I dig until I find sweatpants and a shirt from the university along with a pair of socks that smell decently clean. "What's your name?" I ask after she pulls them on over her nightclothes.

"Emily," she says, shaky as I walk her back.

"Jamie." I offer my hand. "What happened?"

"My parents found this note I wrote, and next thing I know, the doctor says I have to go to some mental place. I guess they thought I was going to hurt myself."

"Were you?"

"I don't know," she says, avoiding my eyes. "Maybe so."

"Give me a minute and I'll find you some shoes and food."

Jackie passes through, checking vitals and making self-deprecating cracks until she gets the girl to smile. I return with a pair of Sketchers and a sackful of junk food as Jackie heads off again. "What size you wear?"

"Six and a half," Emily says.

"These are sevens," I tell her. "But they're brand-new."

"How'd you manage that?"

I dump out a pile of Fun Pak–size cereal boxes on the card table, along with cartons of chocolate milk. "I'm magic," I reply, pouring one bowl for her and another for myself. "Plus, I've spent about a thousand nights in this place. Started 'bout your age. I'm just helping out now, though. I don't work in the hospital anymore."

"What do you do now?"

"Go around and talk to people in trouble," I say. "Some I send here and others somewhere else. Just try to help, I guess."

"Like suicide and stuff?" she asks, spoon to mouth.

"Something like that."

"Mmm," Emily says, eyes shut to savor the taste. "Forgot how good Apple Jacks can be."

"Never underestimate the therapeutic properties of Apple Jacks and milk."

We crunch and slurp the sludge. I pick up the cards and deal five each.

"Weird," she says, showing her hand. "I got both jokers."

"Really?" I turn my cards around. "Me too."

"There's four jokers?"

"It's a psych ward deck. Every other card's a joker."

She laughs out of sympathy at my silly sleight of hand, and we set the cards facedown. "Better watch your back," Emily says through a mouthful of Jacks. "I think you made those cops mad."

"Ah, forget them. I got their chief out of a jam one night. He owes me one."

"They told me everybody's scared of this place. That the high school kids dare each other to run up and ring the bell."

"Yeah, like twice a year, maybe."

"They said the hospital was built on Indian burial grounds, that it's haunted."

"Not true. I don't think. That's *Poltergeist*."

"They said you throw patients in a steel room and strap them down. That people go crazy in here and scream and cut themselves. That's why you lock them in that room." She rests her spoon in the milk and watches me cautiously, waiting.

"If you want," I tell her, "I'll show you the room."

I walk Emily down a dark and deserted hall to the last room on the left. The carpet is stained, and a fluorescent tube sputters on and off. "Only the door is steel. It's just a regular room." I slide back the latch. She steadies herself and walks inside.

The room is empty except for a hospital bed bolted to the

center of the floor with a sequence of long leather straps and buckled cuffs from bottom to top. An observation mirror is mounted high in the corner with a camera inside. The walls are soft pink, and there's one grimy window half covered with a sheet that looks out to thick woods, tree branches reaching to strangle the night. Emily covers her mouth like she's going to be sick or cry.

"Sorry," I say. "I always show it to anyone who asks."

"How many people have you locked in here?"

"Me personally?"

"Yeah."

"Too many," I decide. "One night when it was slow I had this other tech put me in the restraints. I changed out of my clothes into a paper gown and everything."

"Why would you even want to do something like that?"

"Figured I ought to know what it was like. You treat people different once you've walked in their shoes."

"Tell me about it," she says.

"Heather was the tech, and she was a softball jock from the college, so I knew she'd latch the straps up good and tight. Then I told her to leave me and walk a lap around the hospital. A lap took about ten minutes, if you didn't stop. By the time she came back I was sitting in the hall out of breath and trying to calm down. I couldn't take it."

"How'd you get out?"

"Let's just say I was really into Houdini when I was a kid. Heather was supercompetitive, so she made me lock her up and walk a lap. When I got back, she was hysterical, just losing it. Heather never cried. She played state championships with broken ribs. She was the toughest girl I ever knew. What I didn't know was she used to be a patient here."

Lightning flashes, turning our faces ghostly white. Emily

runs her hand over the strap and touches the buckle like it's delicate glass. "What happened to her?" she says as the low rumble of thunder follows behind.

"Heather's gone."

The branches sway against the coming storm, shadows thrashing across the wall. "Like gone, gone?" Emily asks. "She didn't . . ."

"No. She just moved."

"I thought maybe . . ."

"Not that."

"I lost a really close friend that way."

"Me too."

"How close?"

I cross my first two fingers.

"You can't help but blame yourself," Emily says. "But then some days you understand."

"Didn't mean to bring all that up."

"It's okay." She pulls the sheet back from the window. "I guess it makes sense, why you do what you do."

"What do you mean?" I ask.

"You know," Emily says. "What you do."

Doc Roberts, our head psychiatrist, ambles in as I'm leaving. With his Western-cut suit and matching Stetson, he reminds me a little of JR from Southfork Ranch. "What's your thoughts on Zombien?" I ask.

"I reckon it's safe," he replies. "Why? You taking it?"

"Yes, sir."

Roberts waves me into his office and opens a tall shelf packed with samples. "Help yourself, my boy," he tells me in his South

Texas twang. "Just be careful. They're killer with a glass of brandy, but you might wake up in El Paso wearing chaps."

He's kidding, I think.

"Will do," I reply, taking five packs of two.

Roberts fills a sack to the brim with pills and purple pens with the Zombien logo on the side. "The drug reps'll bring this much more again tomorrow," he says. "Take all you need."

"What's the most you'd prescribe a patient in a night?"

Roberts looks me over before replying. "No more than a couple," he says. "If you get in a fix, call me, all right?"

I nod and walk to my truck, taking the back roads down Chester to St. Marie. There's a field behind the church with rows of stone and a statue of Mary at the gate. I have never been beyond it. But a big magnolia grows across the road with branches low enough to climb, and sometimes I sit in the first bend and think about the place where all the infinite roads convene and everything you ever lost comes back for good. Closure is the ghost that leads us home. We don't get much closure down here. We take what we can get and keep moving on.

I should've been a better friend.

There are far too many should've beens.

Dawn breaks as the rain comes down. I drive home, park, slip through the back and up the spiral stairs. My mind is racing, troubled thoughts and scenes. "Save me, O God, for the waters are up to my neck," says Psalm 69.

I split the blister pack and place one pill beneath my tongue. It is bitter as it melts. The troubled scenes blur as thoughts go still. A woman on TV sings "Wind Beneath My Wings." Smoke covers the screen and everything fades to black.

THE DESERT

He speaks in dreams, in visions of the night.
—JOB 33:15 (NLT)

T HE CRISIS CALL STIRS ME FROM MY STUPOR. "'LO?" I wheeze, grappling for the phone. The line is crackly and the voice far away, familiar, but nothing I can place. Static obliterates the call—"Wait!"—and the line goes dead. I race for the truck, but the motor won't crank.

Brainstorm. Run, quick.

I explode from the brush and barrel down the sidewalk on my bike, ramping from curb to asphalt, gunning it as fast as I can. I recognize that voice. The caller isn't far away.

The streets are choked with traffic, and suddenly I realize I am pedaling down North Eleventh in tiger-striped bike shorts and a *Cuckoo for Cocoa Puffs* shirt with the sleeves cut. My mind blanks, and I'm lost on familiar ground, the street signs a snarl of misdirection, missing my turn by three streets back.

I cut through the Sonic parking lot, and there's a group of hooligan teens sitting on the hoods of cars. They laugh as I pass, hurling taunts my way. "Look at this guy . . . hey, where you goin'? Come on back, Tiger Stripes . . . what're you, scared or something?"

The hill on Twelfth slows me. I stand on the pedals and lean in. The crisis line rings.

I know this number.

The hill seems endless, a long, long way to the top. A harsh wind tears through me, and the lights of town are far below. The ringing echoes louder, from the trees, the streets, the night. I hit the brakes and slide sideways at the peak. The silence is heavy as the city sleeps. I missed my turn again.

The alarm pings, and I'm comatose. Stupid dreaming. I hate dreams. Especially the ones that seem so real, where you wake up not trusting reality, wondering if you are still even now stuck in a dream.

I reach for the cooler by the bed. The ice I put in before sleep is half thawed, but the Red Bull is nice and cold. I press the can to my forehead before popping the top and downing it quickly in bed. Morning affirmation courtesy of Psalm 91: "I will tread upon the lion and the cobra. I will not fear the terror of the night."

Clearer now, I reach for the second can, get up, and pull on my clothes.

Six back-to-back calls. A lonely, overweight computer programmer who smokes pounds of homegrown weed while watching *Blade Runner* and old cartoons. A sweet kid on an athletic scholarship suffering bouts of anxiety so crippling she has to drop out of school. An addict with no desire to quit, whose parents blame me for not being able to use my psychological powers to change his mind. Two scheming chicken-plant workers looking for a paid vacation to the psych ward like it's some sort of Alaskan cruise. And now a woman suffering postpartum depression sits in bed seven with Rotel breath and a bedazzled Philippians 4:13 hat.

I'm feeling pretty fuzzy, but she seems sympathetic, so I tell her straight. "Been having a hard time sleeping lately."

"Just give it all to Jesus," Sister Philippians suggests. "That's what I do."

I'm signing papers at the front desk when the social worker comes over and flips through a folder. "Bed sixteen requests a minister," she says to no one in particular. "But the one we usually call is gone." A nurse joins her. "This old guy's a war vet, and I don't think he's got much in the way of family," the social worker explains. "I hate to just do nothing for him."

You do it, God says.

I remind God that I'm not only a behavioral psych major but also the crisis intervention guy, and I've seen an army of people who swore they were hearing his voice, many while teetering at sanity's edge. Most times, when we think we hear God speaking, it's really our own guilt or ego or good old wishful thinking instead. I also tell him I'm not feeling very inspirational tonight.

Thanks for the nice psychology lesson, Jamie, God replies. *I hear you. Now go help.*

I stall a few more moments until the nurse finally throws up her hands and says, "We're out of options. He'll just have to wait."

"I'll do it," I offer. "If you can't find anyone else."

"You sure, Jamie?" the social worker asks.

"Yeah. I think so. How long's he got?"

"Few weeks." She shakes her head. "Maybe less. But you've been in these situations before, right?"

"Time or two," I reply. "I'll give it my best."

The war vet's stationed at the end of the hall in a windowless room with no machines or monitors bleeping. A voice, gruff but weak, rises from the dark. "You the chaplain?"

I make my way over as my vision adjusts to the light. He's pale and unshaven, eyes jaundiced, looking like a military-grade Clint

Eastwood, only sicker and more severe. I start to explain that the minister is out, that I'm just the psych guy passing through, trying to help. But instead I shake his hand and answer, "Yes, sir." His grip is shaky and his palm feverish and dry. Sometimes it's easier not to explain.

"You seem young," he grunts.

"Sorry."

"Doesn't matter now," he says. "Reverend, I need to tell you something."

Confession? One last lashing out? I pull a chair to the edge of the bed. "Call me Jamie," I reply.

"Thomas," he reports back. "Thomas Stratton, sir."

"Well, Mr. Thomas," I tell him, smelling his Old Spice after-shave and the butch wax in his hair, "I'm here to listen to whatever you need to say."

There's a pause as he searches for the words to begin. "I'm dying," he says, as a first matter of establishing facts. "But I imagine it's not uncommon for you to speak with someone in my position."

"Not too uncommon, no, sir."

It comes in spurts, confession. I didn't read *Moby Dick* for American Lit, but I remember that one part that said the crew might scramble, but a true fisherman strikes from silence and rest. So I wait until he speaks again. "I saw a nineteen-year-old kid die in combat once. He asked me to say the Lord's Prayer with him, and I did, even though I considered myself more a man of action than religious routines. You know what he told me before he died?"

I nod and he continues. "Kid looks at me and says, 'I didn't get enough, sir.' Here I am four times older, and I didn't get enough either. Anybody says they've got no regrets, they haven't lived much. I've got plenty."

"Me too."

"You're a preacher. You gotta tell the truth. I never have been much of a believer. Least not the churchgoing kind." Stratton checks to make sure I follow before soldiering on. "I've seen a lot of terrible things," he says. "Murder, treason. Slaughter of innocents. Things that make it difficult for me to believe there's anybody minding the store."

Stratton's got an air about him that tells me he doesn't suffer fools—the discipline of a career military man, one whose rank carried serious weight.

Great time to playact, Jamie. It'll all be so comical when they court-martial you. Keep quiet. Nod. Just keep saying "sir."

"Yes, sir." I nod.

"I didn't just see terrible things. I did things too. So if there's anyone up there, I didn't figure they'd have much time for someone like me." He looks away, as if steeling himself to dig out a bullet with a pocket knife. "But I saw him the other night, and I don't think it was a dream."

The air in the room suddenly becomes thin. "Saw who?" I ask.

Stratton locks eyes with mine. "Him."

I lean in closer to the rails. "I'm listening."

Thomas sits straighter, shifting the sheets. His skin is marked with splotches and jagged white scars. "I woke up dizzy in the middle of the night, and it was taking every effort just to breathe. I don't scare easy, but I was thinking all sorts of crazy things, wondering what really happens when you die, does anybody care? Next thing I know I was walking down a dark road that seemed like it went forever. I was burning hot but cold at the same time, if that makes sense."

"The desert," I say.

"The desert," he agrees. "I walked for what felt like a long time, thinking back over life and the mistakes I'd made, the way

I never let anybody close, not even my own family. I wasted it, sir. That was the feeling. A lot of the things I thought were so important didn't matter much when all was said and done."

He coughs and rubs the steel-gray stubble on his face. I can see that it pains him to be so weak, to be unshaven and unsure.

"Then, way in the distance, I could see the faintest light," he continues. "So I walked a little faster. Eventually I could hear the sound of an engine, and that one light split into two. Finally, those lights were right over the hill. Then he pulled up beside me."

There is some measure of reverence in my voice. I want to believe. "The Lord?" I reply.

"You'll think I was seeing things."

"Try me."

Stratton sizes me up before pressing on. "He was driving a black Monte Carlo with silver trim," he says in the voice of a Pentagon reconnaissance report. "The window lowered, and I could see him."

"What's he look like?"

"Like the pictures, I suppose. Beard. Long hair. You're familiar with the rock band ZZ Top?"

"God looks like ZZ Top?"

"Similar to that, yes," he says. "Except brighter, like if ZZ Top was really clean and glowing inside." He fidgets with his IV and pulls at the neck of the gown. "Look, I don't know how to say this where it doesn't sound like I've lost my mind."

If Stratton only knew how many nights I felt like I'd walked a parallel road, hot and cold, wasting time, wondering if I'd ever find my way. Just because you believe, that doesn't mean you don't struggle. But every now and then, it seems like the road takes me someplace I belong. All that's hard to put into words, though, so I tap my fist lightly against his arm and say, "Sounds pretty awesome to me."

"Yes, sir, it was," he replies. "He sat there on the shoulder of the road, and we stared at each other for a long while. Then he said, 'Come on, Tommy. Get in. Time to go home.'"

He looks from his hands to the wall, then back to me again. "Only people ever called me Tommy were my mom and daddy."

"Whoa."

"I got in the car, and we set off down that desert road . . . window down with his elbow hanging out and the wind blowing through his hair. He reached over to the console and rolled down my window too. That cold wind blew right through me, and he said, 'Tommy, son, let it go.'"

A second *whoa* would be one too many, but I'm at a loss for words, so I pause to acknowledge the weight before speaking again. "What happened then?"

"We drove all night, and right at dawn he topped a bluff and I could see the lights of a city spread out beneath us. And for the first time in a lot of years, I felt at peace."

The room is quiet. Thomas clears his throat. "It's okay if you don't believe what I'm saying. I just needed to tell it to somebody who might understand."

I nod, eyes on the floor. "What's God's car like?" I ask.

"Nice," he says. "Real nice."

I slide in close. "How about the city?"

"That city is so big." Stratton grips my hand at the rail. "You oughta see it."

"Hope someday I do."

"You will," he assures me. "You're the minister here, right?"

I'm heading down the hall to see my next client when Amy rounds the corner running full speed with Dr. Black close behind.

He catches my sleeve as they pass, and we dash outside. An old sedan sits idling in the ER's drive, a woman pounding the hood and screaming for help. Black rips open the passenger door. A morbidly obese man is slumped against the dash. Amy drags in the stretcher and we grab his arms, but he's much too heavy to move. She climbs over and pushes from the other side. I wedge in behind him, trying to use my legs for leverage. The car smells like motor oil and cracked vinyl seats. There's a kid in the back—five, maybe—watching without a sound.

"It's okay," I promise. "We got him."

The woman beats her fists against me, shouting. Black squeezes in. "On three," he says, counting fast. With one concerted effort, we heave the man onto the stretcher. Amy jumps on top, compressing his chest as we rush inside. The intercom calls Code Blue. Suddenly the room is full.

"Clear!" warns Black as we shift out between defibrillator paddles and CPR. A doctor I've never seen suggests we're wasting our time. "Keep trying," says Black.

Thirty minutes pass, and we're still working. He finally waves us off and lets the man go in peace. Everyone is silent as the room clears.

The woman waits at the end of the hall with the boy in her arms. Black and I look to each other, then away. "I'll do it," I tell him.

"Thanks, Jamie," he says. "It's my job, though."

I scrub my hands and walk into my last patient's room. It is packed with upset family members hammering me with angry looks. A woman I surmise to be the client sits bedside with legs crossed, shaking her foot impatiently.

"It's about time," she says, staring me up and down. "Can you please explain why this is taking so long?"

I calm the family, get the woman situated, then cut through the ER parking lot and down the red dirt hill. It's too late, too early, too everything. I need one still place to rearrange my thoughts.

The path veers left through the trees, and Chance Creek looks as ominous as ever—steep, craggy walls with exposed roots and a host of broken toasters, shattered glass, and sickly black water below. I can still feel the summer heat and harsh scrape of regret, the way words can make you feel so small. Sometimes it's easier to live with consequences than fear. Strange what you remember, the way seemingly insignificant things can stay with you so long.

[THEN]

I'D SLIPPED MY BIKE OUT AFTER SUPPER AND SAT ON the hill staring at the muddy canyon beyond the ramp. The sun was sinking through the sycamore trees, shadows stretched across the rail. I took a deep breath for courage and gunned it toward the creek. The ramp came quickly. Just before I hit the plywood I jerked the bars sideways and smacked face-first in the dirt, skidding toward the edge, grabbing a tree branch before I slid into the waist-deep water. A black snake slithered downstream, iridescent in the dying light. I pulled myself up, raced back home, and parked my bike under the stairs.

Twenty minutes or so later, my best buddy, Ash, tapped at the kitchen window. Sometimes, after dark, we'd ride through the rich neighborhood behind the apartments, talking about everything and nothing at all.

"Why's your face all scratched up?" she asked as we weaved through the sprinklers down Buckingham Drive.

Truth is easier once the sun goes down. "Stupid creek."

There was nothing but the sound of chains spinning in sprockets, the *ch-ch-ch-ch* of sprinklers soaking manicured lawns, dogs and mail trucks far away. "Long way across," she said, whistling through her Bugs Bunny teeth to note the distance. "But you could make it."

"You think?"

"Betcha," she replied.

[NOW]

Back home, I fall into an agitated sleep. I dream of the morbidly obese man slumped against the dash and the woman in the hall holding the kid, smoothing his hair and promising everything will be all right. The snake in the creek rises higher. I fight back and try again to sleep. It's like my brain is stuck on a tickertape of breaking news, chaos, dread, impending doom, superbugs, economic crash, rampant crime, killer hurricanes charging toward the coast, and everybody in some way or another is losing their mind. The world is held together with masking tape until the rider on a pale horse comes.

I imagine dragging these burdens up the scarred dirt path to Golgotha and handing them to Jesus in a giant trash bag. But soon enough they're right back in my hands. Paul prayed, but the thorn remained. So if God sent the mission, then maybe he sent medication to help. No spiritual journey is easy. It's a long, hard walk to the cross.

One blue pill beneath the tongue. Then another half. They melt into a bitter mess. But then the bitter fades and only sweet remains. And sleep comes like a thief.

THE CITY OF TOWERING LIGHT

Every one, without exception, who calls on
the name of the Lord shall be saved.
—ROMANS 10:13 (WNT)

THE CALL COMES IN FROM SPRING HILL, A BOON-
dock town in Rose County, thirty miles up the road. "Kin ya
hurry?" the deputy pleads. "I think this one tried to hurt hisself
for real."

"Yeah, sure," I assure him. "I kin hurry." Just for kicks, I hit
the city limits doing eighty-eight in a thirty-five, waiting for a
siren and flashing lights, for the space-time continuum to crack
and hurtle me back to the past. Nothing. Only dust in the headlights and distant trains.

I pull into the grass lot by Jimmy's Seed & Feed and walk over
to the jail. A wind cuts through the sally port as I tuck down into
my jacket and wait for the deputy to buzz me through the gate. At
the end of the corridor lies a row of four cells. I open the first door,
and there's a ragged little man strapped into the restraint chair,
wearing Hamburglar coveralls and orange canvas shoes, his hair
white and sprouting in wild shocks.

"Mr. Banks," I greet him, my voice ricocheting, the tiny cell reeking of bleach and sour sweat.

"You the doctor?" Banks asks in a damaged rasp.

"Something like that," I reply, shaking his hand through the restraints. I motion to his throat, banded by a rivulet of purple-black bruises. "So what happened here?"

Banks starts in on the story of his wife, who had taken their children and run off with the gypsy gun nut. She had sworn to stay true while Banks served out his sentence for armed robbery.

"Would've been simple theft," he explains. "But I had an old jackknife in my jeans."

His drunken daddy disowned him long ago, and lately his deceased mother appeared in his cell and told him he'd be better off to give up and join her on the other side. He fought the notion, knowing she would never say such, but still spent each night in his bunk braiding the rope.

"Made it from strips of blankets I slipped out of the laundry. While I worked, I'd read that Gideon Bible until sleep overtook me. Some nights sleep never came. Finally, the rope was long enough, and Mama kept calling me to come. So I did," he says, his voice cracking and tears streaming into his beard. "Mister, I wasn't even at my own mama's funeral. I was in jail."

I wave in the deputy. "Cut my man loose an arm, if you don't mind."

"Whatever you say, doc," the officer replies, pulling keys and loosening the straps at the inmate's right wrist before ducking back out the door. I hand Banks a washcloth and water in a paper cone cup.

"I'm not really a doctor," I confess.

He presses the rag against his face. "You're a Christian man, though, aren't you?"

"Only by grace."

"You might not believe this, " he says, "but I was raised up in church." He looks past me, through the window lined with iron bars, over the river and into the hills. "Reading that Bible the other night, I came across something. Can I ask you a question? Won't nobody else answer it for me."

"I can try."

"Where was Jesus when Judas tied the noose?"

The question hangs, bouncing off the cinderblock, filling the room with its weight. Banks continues. "Seems Judas needed him the most."

"Don't know, Mr. Banks." I clear my throat. "But I gotta believe he was there."

"Judas, he was the money man, right?"

"Think so. Yeah."

"Let me hold the money, I'd a messed everything up just as bad or worse," Banks says.

"I'm totally capable of pulling a Judas," I admit, tapping my chest. "If there's no mercy for Judas, there's none for me." I lean in closer, one hand on his bound wrist. "But sometimes living with yourself, that's the hardest part."

Banks draws a long breath, tears welling up again. "I don't wanna die, son," he says, slicking his hair back and looking me over. "If there's any way you can help me, I'd be much obliged. I'll work it off, wash cars, cook. Just whatever y'all need me to do."

"You got experience cooking?"

"Ah, no, sir. I worked some at a fried-chicken joint in high school, but I was only there about a week."

"How about washing cars?"

"No, sir. Not professionally, at least."

"What're you good at?"

Banks hangs his finger in his bottom lip, looking down. "Not too much good, I guess."

I hold the answer and let him wait. But then he quietly says, "Please?" And it kind of breaks me.

"How about we send you to the hospital for a while? I got some friends there'll help you stop seeing and hearing things, and we can work on payback down the road."

He throws his head back and blows out a grateful breath. "Thank you, God, thank you. Bless you so much for this. I mean it."

"No problem. Anything else I can do for you?"

"Little more of that water before you go?"

I move to the faucet and fill his cup again. "You hungry?"

"Sure could eat something," he says.

I slip around the corner, grab a honey bun from a discarded tray, and hand it to him with the water. He places the bun in his mouth, breaks it with his free hand, and gives half to me. I sit, and we eat without speaking. The air is thick with weird and wonderful thoughts mixed with the old priest's homily I heard long ago:

This is my body, my blood. God with us in this cell, in communion and fellowship, brokenness and joy, in the still small spaces of the night. For what is communion but remembrance and thanks, knowing the only righteous privilege is to help another up and along, knowing we may well need the same help soon? Maybe this is why Jesus drew near to the poor in spirit and had only harsh words for those so sure their hearts were pure. Sometimes you give the living water, other times you drink from another's cup. We are all as different as we are the same and all in need of the same things. To offer grace, hope and love. And receive the same.

"Good honey bun," Banks mutters, crumbs scattering into the straggles of his beard.

"The best," I tell him, holding the moment longer before standing to button my coat. "Hang tight. We'll get you dressed back and ready to go soon."

"I'm ready," Banks says, pointing to his orange slippers and jail-striped coveralls. "This here's all I got."

I slip off my jacket and hand it to him. "Oh, no, sir," he says. "I can't."

"Someone gave it to me when I needed one. Take it. Preacher once told me you gotta be willing to turn stuff loose."

Banks takes the coat, holding it like a baby in his arms. "Good and bad both," he says. "Yes, sir. I heard that sermon too."

It's colder out, but I ride with the windows down, glaze from the honey bun sticking my fingers to the wheel. Judas asked, "Why this waste?" Rahab marked her faith by hiding the spies. We see through a dark glass in this life. What if I couldn't stop drinking or had a hard time controlling my mind? What if I were the prodigal, dragging back home for the umpteenth time?

"Just one new command I'll give you," Christ said. "Love each other. The way I loved you."

At the red light a shabby fellow in a stocking cap pushes a grocery cart across the street. He pauses in front of my truck to tie his shoe. The cart carries some ragtag clothes, trash bags, and a big stuffed bear with one missing eye. There's a handmade sign on the side of the cart that says, *Jesus is coming soon.*

As the light turns green, he fumbles with the strings on his shoes. I bleat my horn and wait for his face. He stands with hands up and an apologetic look. "Hey," I call. He walks to my open window. "Can you tell Jesus to hurry? I'm ready."

"Son," Shabby says, leaning in close with a laid-back, toothless smile, "he's already here if you know where to look."

I stop at a two-pump Chevron just past the county line. A *V* of charcoal geese glides across the clouds as locusts choke the pump lights.

The cooler inside is full of dirt-cheap energy drinks. I take out a thirty-two-ounce SkullZap and press it against my neck. The cashier blows her nail polish dry as giant pretzels turn slowly on a wheel. Powerball's at $280 million, the LED sign says. Just a dollar and a dream. I slide the SkullZap back in the case. I'm burnt. Enough caffiene for today. I grab some almonds and head for home.

It's a long, dark road through hills and barren fields. The temperature drops, and I catch a chill, rolling up the windows and turning on the heater. My headlights push softly through the darkness while white lines slip below me, and there is only the low drone of tires on asphalt, mile after mile.

A skyscraper appears in the distance, a massive gray building rising into the night. Then another. Towering spires line each side of the highway, slim needles of sparkling light.

I wonder if I am driving into the city of God, if I have taken some fortuitous turn through the rip in space-time and finally arrived, if the secret is that with a little hope and faith, you could drive yourself to heaven in a night. I wonder if my earthly self will simply vanish and God himself will walk out past the gates to meet me, just to ride together for that last mile home.

I lean into the gas, astonished as the city climbs higher, gilded structures rising around me as a figure in white waits in the distance, standing beneath the speed-limit sign, hazy but getting clearer the closer I get.

The young will see visions, the older dream dreams.

Visions and dreams, towers spiraling into the stars. An emerald pillar looms, blue lights twinkling around the peak. The figure in the distance lifts his hand.

Hello, old friend, he says, his voice like the rushing of a mighty wind. *Good to see you again.*

I am bewildered, amazed, and excited to arrive. It is as if the city glows with life, growing before my eyes, buzzing with energy, welcoming and safe. It is as if the city is calling me home.

BRRCKCKCKCKCKCKCKCKCK!

The grinding racket of tires on the rumble strip shocks me back. I jerk the wheel left, then pull to the shoulder and slap my face three times hard. The gravel crunches beneath my feet as I try to shake off the dream.

I walk out onto the highway and stand between the lines, looking one way, then the other. Everything is dark and still. There is no city. There is nothing here but empty fields.

My eyes adjust to the night. Cicadas sing from deep in the trees as a ghost owl watches from the power lines. The coast is clear, so I lie flat in the center of the road. Orion's bright arm stretches across the moonless sky, the blacktop warm against my back. Music drifts in on the wind, like a lullaby.

I know that song. It's "People Are Strange," the version for putting babies to sleep. The one that plays when Squiggly calls.

"Jamie?" she asks when I answer.

"Yeah."

"You finished yet?"

"Uh-huh."

"There's trouble downtown," she says. "Jumper off Third."

The owl takes flight as a white-hot star falls over the ridge.

"At least you're going home," she says.

"Going home," I reply.

"You okay? You don't sound like yourself."

"Yeah, Squig. Fine."

"You sure?"

I pocket my phone, staring down the road. The asphalt hums as the wind gusts harder. Far away, headlights appear.

III GENESIS AGAIN

Now the earth was formless and empty, darkness
covered the surface of the watery depths, and the Spirit
of God was hovering over the surface of the waters.
—GENESIS 1:2 (HCSB)

Every passing minute is another chance to turn it all around.
—CAMERON CROWE

DAY 29

Think back to your teenage years. This time, marked by a tangle of hormones and drama, is likely where we wrestled with God in his truest form, when we were hungry and burning with life, spiritually, mentally, and physically a jumble of highs and lows.

Write about the hand of God through these earlier times.

THEN THERE WAS THAT TIME I FOUND GOD AND BLEW UP THE GIRLS' GYM

The only true currency in this bankrupt world is what
you share with someone else when you're uncool.
—LESTER BANGS

SEVEN FORTY-FIVE ON A THURSDAY NIGHT FINDS ME
sitting on the bluff behind Highland High, trying to come up
with some redeeming story from my teenage years. Brother Benny
says we should be like Jesus. The Bible skips his high school years.
Maybe I should skip mine.

I call Charter House on a whim, and sure enough, Tina picks
up the phone. "Why are you still there, mad woman? Go home."

"Home is when I die," she says. "Everything here is temporary."

"I know better than to argue with an evangelical. Okay, I'm
stuck on twenty-nine. High school. What's the deal with that?"

"Watching my own two teens," she tells me. "They drove me
nuts. But then again, I remember how crazy high school was for
me. More happened in those four years than any other time in life."

"Hard to imagine you wild."

"Are you kidding? I was dancing to 'Brick House' on the tops of cars in the Howard Brothers parking lot."

"Can't picture it. You're just trying to impress me."

"But at the same time," she adds, "me and my friends would have these really deep conversations about God. He was pulling at me even back then."

"Trying to get you down off those people's cars."

"Funny guy," she says. "What were you like in high school?"

"Mostly awful," I reply, climbing on the roof of my Trooper to feel in league with Tina's wild side. "Halfway decent now and then. Just like everybody else. We were all pretty good and pretty bad."

"Everybody?"

"Rob Dyson was star quarterback, honor roll student, and president of FCA. Always looked like he just stepped out of the JCPenney sales paper. I caught him drinking vodka out of his locker before school one day and I was like, 'Why would you want to drink at seven a.m.?'"

"FCA?" Tina asks. "Is that the farmer thing?"

"Nah, it's some Christian athlete club."

"Well, that's sad. What'd he say?"

"He shook his head and was like, 'Blaine, you don't even know. When I went to bed last night my parents were fighting, and when I woke up they were at it again. And these Friday night football games? It's just a matter of who's the most messed up.' That was a news flash. You forget high school can be so weird that way."

"Where's Rob Dyson now?"

"City council, I think."

"Figures. So how about you? Were you spiritual back then?"

"Sure. In some ways more than now. Especially after I stole that Bible from a motel in Jackson."

Tina pauses to laugh or sigh, I can't tell which. "Sounds to me like you got plenty of material," she says. "Just have fun with it,

Jamie. Grab a thread and see where it takes you. There's not really any rules here, you know."

"There's always rules."

"Okay, then, let's say the boundaries are wide. You still got that stolen Bible?"

"Still got it."

"Read it again. God loves outrageous stories. That's what makes it all so good."

"Thanks, mad woman," I say.

"Go home," she teases.

The bluff is the highest point in the town. Standing on the truck top, I can see the moon glittering down Black River and the beacon from Thomas Towers piercing the sky. "I am home," I tell her. "At least for now."

I hang up and sit on the edge of the truck cab with my legs sprawled over the windshield. They tore the old school down after I graduated and built a big, sleek, soulless building that looks like a prison or a garment factory. The only thing left standing is the girls' gym. Guess I'll start there.

[THEN]

THE SEMIANNUAL HIGHLAND HIGH STUDENT COUNCIL Talent Show fell on a Thursday night, and I banded together with the only two other shaggy musicians in school to play a medley of metal classics.

The guys were out back sipping the one hot Heineken Tony McMony managed to smuggle from his dad's garage while I stayed inside with a break dancer and a chubby redhead in a tan three-piece suit. The cheerleaders ran the show, and the talent waited in the gymnastics room, stage right. It smelled like sweetness and dirty socks, girl sweat and drugstore perfume. It could've been sort of adorable, except for the red-haired kid pacing the floor and looking like he was about to lose his mind.

"Hey, Big Red," I called over. "Calm down. It'll be all right."

"I can't help it," Red said. "I'm just so nervous."

"Dude," I answered. "It's a high school talent show. Have fun."

I was wearing pleather flares and a stretchy black shirt from junior miss, unbuttoned to the waist. A long scrap of pirate flag was tied around my head, and my hair was teased up high and lacquered with Aqua Net. "Whoa," Bill Shermy told me when the band picked me up. "You look like Redneck Hendrix in a hurricane."

Big Red laid his hands on the pommel horse and hung his head. "Those people are *really* gonna hate me now," he moaned. Sweat seeped through his threadbare suit, the coat too tight and slacks too high. I didn't know him but had heard he lived out on Purvis Road, a dusty passage running parallel to the tracks, packed tightly with trashy houses where drugs were sold from porches and bikers fought in front yards and there were almost always police lights pinging the street. Some kids at school would make fun of Red, saying he smelled like rotten eggs, that he didn't have no daddy, that his mama was a Jesus freak who scrubbed commodes for money.

"They'll hate me," he said again.

"Why would they do that?" I asked.

"Because I'm going to preach."

I stepped closer. "Do what, now?"

"Preach," he repeated, straightening his tie and patting a thick black Bible, the pages gold leafed. "It says to go ye into *all* the world and *proclaim* the gospel. This is something I have to do."

Teenage John Candy. That's who he reminded me of. With a touch of young Jerry Falwell thrown in. "If that's what you came to do, go out there and make sure they know—What's your name again?"

He held up the Bible so I could see his name stamped in cursive across the front. "Clifford Weems," he said.

I slung my arm across his shoulders. "You go out there and make sure everybody from front row to back knows that *Clifford Weems* showed up tonight. Whether they love or hate you, make sure they hear what you got to say."

Clifford gave me a look like a drowning man eyeing the shore, like he had been waiting his whole life to hear those words. "Do you really think?" he asked. "Really?"

"Sure. Why not?"

"Hallelujah, brother." He nodded like an Uncle Buck bobblehead doll, excited and shy at the same time. "Halle-*lu*-jah. This is so great that you've found Jesus now."

"What're you talking about?"

"Everybody says your family doesn't even go to church."

"What's that got to do with it?"

He pulled back, quiet. "I'm just telling you what everybody says."

Before I could respond Mindy Reese appeared in the doorway with a clipboard. When Clifford said, "Everybody says," I figured it was people like Mindy, a cinnamon-skinned cheerleader with a turned-up nose and Daddy's money—the kind of dark-eyed Southern beauty who didn't think much of ragtag boys who didn't wear the right clothes, join the right clubs, or go to Firstpark Church like the popular kids did. We were kickball cocaptains in third grade. Our paths never crossed again. Until the talent show.

"Weems?" she read. "You're up." She turned and pointed her pen to me. "Okay, now, you guys. Where are your guys?"

"Outside," I told her. "Tuning."

"Why aren't you tuning?" she asked, politically nice but plastic.

"I'm already tuned."

Clifford took hold of my fingers with his big, hot hands. "Would you mind praying with me?" he asked, his round face close to mine.

Mindy walked over by the balance beam to talk to the dancer. I'd chugged a few ounces of Dr. Tichenor's Mouthwash before the show because Shermy said it was good for butterflies, and now the room seemed suffocatingly tight. I was sweating as bad as Clifford, stage makeup running down my face.

"Uh, okay," I replied. "I guess."

Mindy scribbled on her clipboard, then dangled the pen just inside her mouth, watching and chewing the cap. "Oh, Jeez-us," Clifford began, his voice soft and high. "Prepare the people's hearts, Lord. Give them sight that they should see."

I cracked one eye open. The break dancer flicked out his fingers as he morphed into a moonwalking robot. Mindy slipped the clipboard under her arm and clapped.

"Okay, Jamal," she said. "Bust your move after Weems, then Blaine's group can go last." At the door she called back to Clifford. "Ready?"

He squared his shoulders and strode toward the stage, as jolly as the Polka King from *Home Alone*. "Give it to 'em, Clifford!" I shouted behind him.

"Oh, yes, sir!" he called back. "I will."

Mindy announced Clifford as the next act. I could see half the stage and part of the crowd through the window in the door. The people applauded respectfully as she handed him the mike.

Feedback screeched as the teen preacher began. "Do you *know* where you would go if you died *tonight*?" he boomed. "*Straight* is the way, and *narrow* is the gate and few . . . few . . . few . . ." He galloped into view, Bible high, his face contorted and scorched with righteous fury. "*Few* are those who inherit eternal life!"

At first there was laughter, then confusion, and then the booing began. I turned from the window and flopped into the foam pit, feeling a little responsible for it all.

Jamal rehearsed his steps, pivoting effortlessly in a hot-pink tee and brilliant white jeans. For a quick instant, our eyes met. Clifford's roar cut through the building like a buzz saw through a megaphone: "*Hell* is hot, but *God* is good!" Then softer, fading as he walked, "And he loves *you* and *you* and *you* . . ."

"Amen," Jamal said in a sweet falsetto, hands lifted as he glided across the floor. "Heard that."

The boys returned and we were a band, guitars and drumsticks, a last-minute review of plans to totally rock the Highland High girls' gym. Clifford met us coming down the stage steps.

"They *hated* me!" he bragged. "But I did just like you said, and brother, you were right."

My bandmates shot me a look before moving on. I slapped Clifford's back as we passed, lingering behind. "Sometimes they hated Jesus too." It was the only thing I could think of to say. We shook hands and he walked away. "You did good, Cliff," I called, just before he stepped out the side doors to the parking lot.

A beat-to-pieces jalopy with a tailpipe dragging sparks sputtered up to where he stood. He bopped the car roof with the flat of his hand, his mouth moving, preaching again. The gray-haired woman at the wheel reached over and unlocked his door. He slid into the seat, and she pulled him close, pressing her cheek to his. Clifford sat back, telling the story as she slowly drove away.

I turned to climb the stairs. Mindy stood at the top, looking on. I lowered my head to pass, face on fire, sweat and eyeliner smudged.

"Wait," she said, catching my sleeve. She pulled a pencil from her bag and worked around my eyes. The silence was tense. I looked away. She steered my head back straight. "You had it all wrong, anyway," Mindy told me, holding a mirror so I could see.

Her cheerleader uniform was pin perfect, and she had a matching ribbon in her hair. I looked like K-Mart Mötley Crüe and smelled like mouthwash. In the mirror, our faces were side by side.

"Wow," I told her. "It's like we're twins or somethin' now."

"Yeah, my sister's got that same shirt," Mindy cracked, pushing me backward while she laughed. "Hold tight and I'll go announce your band."

"Your preacher buddy thinks we play gospel," Tony said as I tuned to his guitar.

"It's all gospel," Shermy said, twirling his sticks. "Least that's what my old man says."

Mindy ducked back and stood beside me while we waited for the curtain to rise. "Heard y'all at sound check," she said. "It was pretty good."

"Well," I apologized, low so the boys wouldn't hear, "I know it's not really your thing."

"So I have a thing?" she said, making air marks around *thing* with her fingers. "I can't just like whatever I want? Am I not cool enough, Mr. Too-Cool-to-Care?"

"No. I mean, yeah. I dunno." I clomped my distortion pedal on and off again and said half joking, "Guess I thought you were kinda stuck up now."

"I puke my guts out before every pep rally," she announced. "And most Saturday nights I'm home studying or playing Scrabble with my folks."

"I love board games," I said, swapping confessions. "And I can make really good grades, when I try."

"I guess!" Mindy shot back. "You were the smartest kid third grade."

"You remember that?"

"Then you moved off, came back, and never talked to me again."

"You stopped talking to me!"

Our voices had grown louder. My bandmates stared like a penguin was waltzing with a porcupine. "So what happened?" I asked.

The lights went down. Our Peavey stacks sizzled as Tony's A-minor split the air. Mindy leaned over and shouted in my ear as the curtain began to rise. "What are you doing Sunday night?"

"Nothing," I replied, the wall of sound growing louder. "Why?"

Shermy lit the entire sack of smoke powder we'd lifted from chemistry lab, and the stage vanished in a caustic green haze. An ominous fog billowed over the first few rows, and the mass of peers and parents roared, fists in the air as we charged into song.

In our dreams.

In reality, everybody sat with hands pressed to the sides of their heads until smoke obliterated the gym and they all fled gagging, skin burning, tears streaming from their eyes. The back doors were propped open. Children wailed. In the distance I could see the fire truck's flashing red lights.

"Thank you!" I mumbled into the mike, coughing as we crushed the final chord. "Good night!"

Mindy's dad paid me thirty bucks to deejay the Fairpark Charity Cakewalk that Sunday, and when it was over, they let me eat an entire pan of Mississippi Mud nobody claimed.

"Look what I found," Mindy said, tossing a photo from the third-grade playground onto the table. We were hanging upside down from the monkey bars, smiling big and squinting in the midday sun. "Buddies, huh?"

She grabbed a spatula with *Property of Fairpark* marked down the blade and dug through the crust to where the mud was thick. "What happened?"

I stared at the blurry faces of our carefree former selves. "Guess everything changes," I told her.

She slid the picture closer. "Not everything."

That Monday at school Clifford and I exchanged nods between third and fourth hall. Mindy smiled when we passed each other after lunch. I turned back to speak, but it was too late. She was already gone.

I pulled out of the back parking lot that afternoon thinking how ridiculous and wasted all this space between us seemed, like surely this wasn't God's intention when he knocked down Babel. Like we ought to be doing better by now.

Clifford stood at the bus stop, away from the others, head down. I wheeled in beside him and unlocked the door.

TOMORROW CAN
WORRY ABOUT ITSELF

[NOW]

Pain is a mysterious planet, but if you reach your hands out
in the darkness, you will see there are others just like you.
—ERIN VAN VUREN

T IS DARK AND COLD, AND I AM UNDERWATER.
*I believe in Jesus Christ, his only Son, our Lord, who was con-
ceived by the Holy Spirit, born of the Virgin Mary . . .*

I pull my head up from the icy water and take a breath. My
blood is thick, and my brain feels stuffed with fuzzy yarn, so I
duck back under and pray some more.

*He suffered under Pontius Pilate, was crucified, died, and was
buried; he descended to the dead.*

SkullZap makes a king-size can with a five-hundred-milligram
cluster-bomb of caffeine, ginseng, and kerosene, I think, for maximum kick. It tastes like rancid lemons in acid rain. I drain the can
and collapse into the downstairs couch with a towel over my face,
waiting for the bomb to bring me back to life. It is winter-dark

out. It was dark when I went to sleep. I slump to the side and close my eyes.

The phone wakes me at a quarter after five. "H'lo?"

"Help, I'm hooked on Zombien," the caller says.

"Go away, Squig."

"I did get a call like that, but it wasn't for your area. Just giving you a hard time."

"How many were they taking?"

"Like two or three at once."

"Two or three?"

"Maybe it was more," she says.

Squiggly passes on the night's first assignment and says to "take care and be careful, now." One at Skylark, two at Westwood ER. I grunt thanks and good-bye while pulling on clothes.

This afternoon I finally had a good dream, one that wasn't scary or too bizarre. I was in the Goodwill off St. John when a woman with mousy brown hair came by pushing a cart, combing the bins for toys and shoes. She was wearing a white sweatshirt and saggy mom jeans. The clock over the registers said two twenty, the calendar December 17. We passed and she looked at me with pleading eyes.

I woke up hopeful. The mission was specific: I had to help this woman make a better Christmas for her kids. *How much better?* I prayed.

A hundred bucks. Not a lot. A lot for me. A lot for any single mom anxiously shopping Goodwill eight days before Christmas. I folded five twenties into the book of Daniel (for God gave Daniel wisdom and insight into dreams) and circled the day on my calendar before crashing back for a few more hours of sleep.

It's been a few days since I checked the mailbox, so I walk down before heading to the ER. There's a stack of student-loan statements and a postcard from Marlboro. Says he finally got his ninety-day sobriety chip and no more outbursts or lockdowns. He might be home for Christmas. Might not.

Appreciate you, my friend, he says in closing. *Be careful. Take care.*

If two people say it in a day, must be a sign.

The trees down Park are barren and the skies at twilight crimson red. I step into the street and breathe in the late November air.

Happy Deep South Thanksgiving. It's 78 degrees.

The lady officer takes me to a girl living in an abandoned building over by the houseboat district downtown. No electricity, no heat or air, four months pregnant with a six-year-old son currently staying with the friend of a cousin who might be on drugs.

She's got one little corner fixed up with candles and books and torn-out pages from a devotional calendar stuck to the walls over her pallet. "God never puts more on us than we can handle," I read from one page. "Remember his promise and look up." I peek toward the ceiling. It is a smash of cobwebs, falling plaster, and busted pipes.

The girl reaches to touch the page. "If it wasn't for Jesus, I don't know how I'd make it through."

I shoot a quick message to Jesus, saying it doesn't seem like she's making it very well to me, that maybe a person in his position ought to be helping a little more. Also, that I looked up and unless there was a skylight lined with gold somewhere, things didn't appear to be too promising. Then I tried to think something different 'cause I didn't want Jesus mad at me. Wonder if he gets weary of hearing every secret thought.

The officer and I exchange glances. The girl is breaking the law. She isn't mentally unstable or addicted, so I can't send her in. The factory is dangerous. She's pregnant. Government agencies are notoriously inept. Sometimes your best attempt to help only makes things worse. When I worked at the library and the night-club, I almost always knew what to do. Here? Ninety-nine percent of the time, I don't have a clue.

The officer nods to let me know she's putting the ball in my court. I don't want the ball, so I nod back. She motions me to the side. "How much cash you got on you?" she asks.

"Twenty or so. Why?"

"I know the manager over at Texas Motel. She'll put her in a room for thirty and let her check out late. I'll go halves."

I hand her my twenty. "Wait, that's not half."

She stacks her Jackson next to mine. "She's gotta eat, right?"

"How far's ten bucks gonna take her?"

She eyes my wallet. I open it back. "Never had to give up my wallet when I deejayed at Fatt Sherry's."

"You were the DJ at Fatt's?" she asks. "Me and my girlfriends used to go dancing there all the time."

"Still be there, if I was smart," I grumble, handing over my last few dollar bills. "So what about tomorrow night?"

"Tonight's tonight," the lady officer says. "Tomorrow can worry about itself."

Driving away it hits me.

See? Jesus says.

It's not even seven, and I already feel sick, like my batteries are corroded and weak, like someone kicked the plug out and all the caffeine in the world won't make a difference. But food might.

I stop at the psych ward to sign some papers and raid the fridge. Jackie asks me to watch the floor while she helps with the mayhem on geriatric wing. *Geriatric mayhem* don't seem like words that should go together, but it's white-haired anarchy over there every night. I refuse to set foot in the place. I'm not wrestling somebody's psychotic granny. Everybody has their limits.

Soon as Jackie leaves, two patients start bickering and another rubs a raw spot over her eyebrow with a pencil eraser. I parse out the group leader, a mild-mannered tire shop manager named Rusty, and pull him in for backup to settle the argument. Then I grab a shoelace from contraband and tie it from Eraserhead's belt loop to mine.

"You're stone crazy, you know that?" she asks, cackling up a storm. "What you gonna do when I gotta go to the bathroom?"

"I don't know all the tricks," I tell her, "but I know a few."

By the time Jackie comes back I'm eating a chicken sandwich and playing Uno with Rusty and Eraserhead, a chain of laces trailing from my belt loop to hers.

"Just like old times," Jackie says.

On the way out I pass Brother Ponder, the psych ward volunteer preacher, giving his testimony to a small group in the dining hall for a special holiday service. I raise my hand to him and he returns the salute. "Hold on," he says, stopping the service. "I feel like we need to pray for Jamie tonight. Everybody pray, just the best you know how, and if you're not sure what you believe, pray anyway. God hears us all."

I take a few steps in and bow my head. Ponder's voice goes deep. Some patients pray silently, others out loud. For a moment it seems as if my batteries have been recharged, and by the time I lift my head, I almost feel nearly new.

"We love and appreciate you, brother," Ponder says. "Don't forget that, okay?"

Thanksgiving night is crazy. Most holidays are. People hang on through the festivities, but then family and expectations are too much and they lose it. We all lose it sometimes.

"Ooh, Jamie, something stinks like wet dog in your truck."

This is the third time I've driven Matilda to rehab. She looks like a Matilda. A brokenhearted partier from Galveston who never can seem to figure out a way to do life straight. I can relate. Is that a bad thing?

"Yeah," I tell her, my words blurring as fatigue settles in. "I've done, like, nineteen crises tonight. It's me."

I've got a morning ritual now. I'll drag up the stairs with my head feeling like the exhaust pipe of a demolition derby Ford. No worries. Crank down the air, park myself in front of the heater, chew up two sleeping pills, and wait for the plane to arrive. I am a speck in the sky, fading. Medication saves lives.

In junior high this guy named Darren from a halfway house came to talk to our class from the Scared Straight program. "People will tell you that drugs are bad," Darren said. "But I'm not here to lie. The first time you use drugs, you won't think they're evil. You'll think they're the answer to every problem you ever had. Because drugs are like McNuggets or hot apple pies. It's a lot easier to quit if you never start."

The McDonald's reference was bizarre, but we all shook our heads, both scared and straight. A fat kid named Doris butted in.

"What if you already started?" he snorted.

It wasn't because Doris was overweight and had a girl's name that the class despised him. It was because he was so obnoxiously snide.

Darren paced and ratted his hair. "Kid, I ain't telling nobody how to live their life. But drugs or McNuggets, either one—what starts out sweet will kill you in the end."

I sleep a few hours and wake again. Bits of the Goodwill

dream linger. Perhaps I'm starting to discern God's voice above the noise. I hover in the space between sleeping and awake, scenes from the dream replaying. Finally, I stir for good and trudge downstairs.

Someone broke into my house. There's an empty Cocoa Pebbles box lying sideways on the table, milk and cereal bits strewn across the kitchen.

I scramble, looking for evidence of other theft and find my jeans in the freezer. Folded neat and placed on top of ice trays. My hat's in there too.

What is this, some trickster? A psych patient bent on revenge? I check the closet. No trickster. No psych patient. Nothing in the closet but guitars.

There can be only one explanation: I ate the entire box of cereal. I put my clothes in the freezer. I don't remember doing those things. Why would I need a cold hat and jeans?

No time to process this now. I jump through the shower and grab my guitar. Squiggly's juggling calls to give me a window. We've got a show tonight.

The Greater Faith Church of God in Christ sits in a gutted-out old gas station with lemon-yellow trim and block letters over the door proclaiming: *FIRE BAPTIZED & SPIRIT FILLED!*

"Whoa," I say.

"Just you wait," Ronnie replies.

There's a room tacked onto the back where we tune and change into our suits. I peek through the curtain, and the sanctuary sits jam-packed, seven sets of short pews on each side of the room, bare concrete floor and the smell of motor oil and olive oil, tires and gardenias in the air. A row of men stands silent along the back while women sit clustered and close to the front, clutching hands and fancy handkerchiefs, their dresses and hats fabulous.

A fellow strides to the platform, tall as a center for the Knicks, looking like a cross between Chris Rock and Don Knotts, wearing a coffee-colored suit with gold loafers and a lavender pocket square. He looks out over the crowd from the pulpit, his face like flint, serious as Moses coming down the mount.

"Who's that dude?" I ask.

"Bishop Sam," Ronnie replies.

The bishop lifts his hands, and a hush falls over the room. "God is good?" he calls.

"All the time," the people respond.

"May the Lord bless and keep you. May he make his face to shine upon you and give you peace. And all the people said . . . ?"

"Amen," the people reply.

"Amen and amen, again," says Bishop Sam. "Reach out and touch somebody's hand, neighbor. Tell a friend you're glad Jesus is in the house tonight."

We gather in a circle backstage, heads bowed, arms across shoulders. "Father," Ronnie begins.

"Father," we repeat.

"Be with us," he prays.

"Yes, Lord," we agree.

"Ladies and gentlemen," Bishop Sam announces, "let's please make welcome the Southern Travelers."

I drank half a SkullZap and took two Excedrin before I came in but still feel like a slug in fancy clothes. Slinging my silver-and-black Strat over my shoulder, I smile friendly and make my way to the stage. Leon counts us off. The electricity is hot-wired in and our amplifiers override the circuits. With every downbeat the lights flicker while voices twine together in five-part harmony about leaving every burden with the Lord.

Big-legged women get slain in the Spirit, sprawled out and covered with shawls while skinny old men in purple neckties dance around them and speak in tongues as we lay into a groove that sounds like "Kashmir" by way of Kool & the Gang. It swells up in me starting from my boots, like a fistful of sparks and lightning striking the beehive, a mystery beyond caffeine or pills. "Just let the Lord lead you," Ronnie says as I bend and shake my guitar strings.

Just is the word, it occurs to me. If I could only grasp the power of *just*. Just a closer walk, just as I am. The lights dim as the groove digs deeper.

The congregation cries and grips the backs of hardwood pews, swaying in one accord, falling out and walking the aisle, walking on knees and shaking tambourines. An hour slips by like twenty seconds, it seems.

"Come on, Jamie," Ronnie calls. He pulls me close to center mike and asks the congregation, "Are you glad to see Jamie in the house tonight?"

"Amen," they reply. "Yes, Lord."

Ronnie tilts his head, one hand lifted and the other to his ear. "I said, are you *glad* to see Brother Jamie Blaine in the house of God tonight?"

"Amen! Yes, Lord!"

"We're gonna let him start this one off for you." I strum the first chord. The lights flicker. Every hand is stretched toward me now. "It's about a long train comin' . . ."

"Hallelujah!"

". . . and all you need is faith to get on board."

"Help us, Lord!"

"Take your time, brother," Leon says, wiping the sweat from his forehead as the band joins in. "No rush."

There's a fan from Baker Brothers' Funeral Home in the back

of every pew, Jesus on one side, Martin Luther King on the other. Solemn Jesus. Martin's brow creased. The people fan faster, and the faces blur into one—Jesus and King, somber, searching for the dream.

An ancient woman with chocolate skin and fire in her eyes stands in the first pew. "That's right, baby," she says, waving me with her fan. "Just you take your time."

The church is a furnace. Bishop Sam props open the front and back doors. A car sits on the far side of the street. Shirtless young men lean against the hood, listening, their cigarettes glowing against the night. A wind rushes down the aisle like the breath of God as the lights go dim.

That's when I begin to sing.

SOME KIND OF MIRACLE

He is able to deal gently with those who are ignorant
and misguided, since he himself is beset by weakness.
—HEBREWS 5:2 (BSB)

I T'S THAT WEIRD BARREN STRETCH BETWEEN THANKS-
giving and Christmas, warm one day and chilly the next,
bittersweet and sentimental, like a long road trip between places,
caught in the middle of all that's left behind and lies ahead. It's
hard to explain.

The old Southern Bakery is a four-story building crowned
with a rooftop water tower in the far corner, a rusty rocket-shaped
tank featuring their slogan, *Fresh Baked Daily!*, in faded white letters down the side.

A short set of stairs leads to a rail around the tank. There's
graffiti on all sides. Some felonious zealot tagged the border with
a boldface exhortation to *Follow Christ*. Nice to see Bob Seger still
has die-hard fans in the tri-city. *Shan loves Jay*. Maddie G. made
the climb with purple spray paint and dotted her *i* with a heart.

A haphazard show of devotion to Slayer sits next to an artsy
streak of calligraphy that simply says *God's Favorite Dog*.

You know you're in the Deep South when 90 percent of graffiti centers around Jesus and classic rock. Sweet notion, though.

I'd like to be God's favorite dog, the one he lets ride along to the grocery store when he runs out for bread and milk at ten on a Tuesday night, that pound mutt watching the doors with paws on the dash, waiting for God to come back to the car. That'd be a happy life.

Jesus climbed high places to meet God and beat the devil, looking out over the city to pray and think about the ever-falling state of man. Perhaps I am following Christ after all.

My brain feels like a cage full of monkeys snorting Ritalin. I slept four hours today and it was broken, troubled sleep, nothing of quality, just crumbs. And that was with pills. Thankfully, I had one quick call at the start of my shift and it's been quiet since.

If I inch over to the ledge side of the tank, I can lie flat, stick my head out past the railing, and look down to the street. Adrenaline is a good stimulant. Fear is not the worst thing we can feel. Better fear than apathy.

When I was about seven, I rode the double Ferris wheel with some older kids. At the top one of the boys started rocking the car to tease the girls. The seats were slick plastic and the sides open to the floor. I remember the brightly striped tops of carnival barker booths, machinery grinding just out of the lights, a family eating elephant ears, the hard dirt of the fairground far, far away.

It had been a year of confusion, the sudden death of two close friends, moving, changing schools, that first serious concussion after the baseball bat slipped out of Troy Terry's hands. You push down all that stuff you can't understand when you're a kid. But when the Ferris wheel car shook, every buried fear shook too.

I grabbed onto the older girl, even though I didn't know her. She was a tough-looking blonde in a blue windbreaker with moles on the side of her neck. "Cut it out, Desario." She laughed, smacking the guy's arm. "Can't you see the kid's scared?"

Every time I got close to falling asleep that night, I would feel the car tipping and the start of an endless slow-motion fall. I remembered hearing a revival preacher once say that God is a very present help in times of trouble, that just the mention of his name makes everything right. So I called out.

"If you call on God and he doesn't answer?" the preacher said in a voice that was stern and sure. "Then that's on you, my friend. You'd best examine yourself."

But childhood fears were simple. Fear of the dark, of heights or storms or snakes or monsters under the bed. Grown-up fears are much more complex and difficult to face. Failure, abandonment, terminal illness, the feeling that you will never ever find your place.

A scurry of clouds drift past the rooftops as wind gusts rock the tank. Looking six stories down to Fourth Avenue, I can still feel that same Ferris wheel panic clutching my throat, the slick plastic seats and Tough Girl's windbreaker sliding through my hands, the way she headlocked me and tousled my hair, saying, "Don't worry, little man. I ain't gonna let you fall."

The railing grate cuts into my chest. A taxi passes below, the service light bright against the monochrome city. It pulls into a lot, and the light goes out. A little person in a hat and yellow slicker crosses the street to meet a slender man.

The Bible says, cast your bread upon the waters. I slide three dollars from my pocket and drop them over the rail. They twist and flutter in the draft between buildings. The little person stops and points to the sky. I roll in close to the tank, the serrated grip of catwalk biting my back. The moon is low and golden, the eye of God on watch.

When you face your childhood fears, it makes you feel stronger. Like maybe confronting kid fears might help you grow up to face the harder ones too. The rush of panic drowns out every emotion. Once you conquer it, there is peace. There is no calm like peace.

At least for a little while. At least for now.

The seventeenth is a dusky December afternoon, Christmas in the air. I park and enter the Goodwill at ten after two, taking a spot in back past the toy aisles, looking over their collection of vintage LPs. The store is packed, shoppers on every aisle. Are there seriously this many people broke at Christmas? I don't want to know.

How will I approach my mousy dream woman and be mindful of her dignity without letting the left hand know what the right is doing? I run a number of options before deciding to press the money into her hand with a simple, "God bless. Merry Christmas," and be gone like lightning out the door. But what if she thinks I'm some freak and won't take the money? What if others are watching nearby?

The logistics of low-key helping can be complicated. But you can't let that keep you from trying. I fold the twenties into my front pocket for fast access and thumb through the stacks of old vinyl. Would God bless my obedience with a Beatles "butcher" cover, still wrapped? The unrevised *Appetite*? I keep one eye on the records and the other on the clock, finding nothing but John Denver, the Commodores, and a copy of the Singing Cookes *Lookin' for a City!* with a KBJC sticker on back. Your past is ever-present in a tiny Southern town. Everything's connected somehow.

Two twenty arrives, and I scan the store, fully expecting to see my dream woman close by. No white sweatshirt back in the toys. I wander the aisles, searching. There's mousy hair everywhere, but none of it matches the picture in my mind. I pass each shopper, checking their baskets, their eyes. Maybe the dream was a little off. Does anyone look hungry? Is there one sad woman in the store who seems like she might be shopping for kids?

There is not. I watch the door, waiting, flipping through more old records before moving on to cassettes. An hour passes. Thirty minutes more. Not one desperate woman enters the store. My faith in the mission is slipping now. Did I miss the date? Should I come back every afternoon from here to Christmas? Was the dream just another mixed-up dream?

I pay two bucks for *Snoopy, Come Home* and walk out of Goodwill back into the chill. Headlights line the boulevard, nightfall coming fast. A guy down the sidewalk stands beside a kettle ringing a tiny silver bell. He's beady-eyed and bearded, bald on top and chewing a fat cigar. "Good way to spend the holidays," I tell him, walking over. "Nice that you volunteer."

"Yeah, my ex-wife's suing me, and I got laid off," he replies. "Gotta make it through Christmas somehow."

"Oh." I slip the twenties into the pot. "God bless, then."

"You know what they say," he says, shifting the cigar while keeping steady rhythm with the bell. "God helps those who help themselves."

ONE PALE STAR

For unto us a child is born, unto us a son is given:
and the government shall be upon his shoulder.
—ISAIAH 9:6 (KJV)

THERE'S ANOTHER SIDE TO CHRISTMAS, HARDER TO market, not quite as suitable for cards or carols or commercials for department stores. The lonelier side, of loss and longing, the knowing that another year has passed and we are still so far away. Regardless of what you believe, there is a sense at Christmas that the answer must come from somewhere beyond ourselves. Even unbelievers sing of heavenly peace.

I like working a lot during the holidays. There isn't much pressure to be joyful and triumphant working crisis psych. It's a victory if you just make it through the night.

It's ten 'til seven, and I'm in another nondescript economy apartment on some forgotten side street in the old part of town. My client's name is Annie and she's wiry with tight gray curls, faded jeans, and a somewhat inappropriate T-shirt from Daytona Beach Bike Week.

Annie tells me that her second husband ran off with some "two-bit Alabama trash that come into some money," and she was all tore up but eventually a good friend became a boyfriend and things got better. Then he got bad sick summer before last, but she took care of him through the worst, all the way to the end. Then she completely fell to pieces and couldn't seem to get the pieces back together no matter how hard she tried.

Trying is strange science. Once you get past the inspirational sayings and well-meaning advice, what do you actually get up and do differently tomorrow that you didn't do today? What if nothing you try works?

The only thing that seemed to help Annie was Xanax in the morning and red wine at night. Soon enough it was Xanax and wine together, morning and night. Then it was Xanax and wine all the time. A neighbor finally convinced her to call for help.

"Everything hard is just harder at Christmas," Annie says, as she cries and wipes her face with her sleeve. I can see her pulse pounding at the wrist, and her eyes look yellow and sick. I don't mean to sound spooky, but it's all too easy for me to feel what that other person is going through. Seems I am never able to reach down. I can only reach out. This really makes me want to quit mental health sometimes.

"Yes, ma'am," I agree.

The sink's piled with dirty dishes, and dog food is scattered over the kitchen floor. On top of the table sits a ten-inch plastic Christmas tree with a baby angel on top and a sticker at the base that says, *Happy Birthday, Jesus!* A floppy little sheepdog badly in need of a bath lies in the corner with his head between his paws. Maybe he's taking on her pain. They say pets do that, you know. I crouch down and hold out the back of my hand.

"Henry ain't too friendly, and he's nearly blind," Annie says. "But he won't bite."

Henry sighs. But then the sigh turns into a happy little whine as his tail thumps the wall and his nose finds my hand.

"So what do we need to do?" I ask Annie. It's better if you let the client say.

There's a clock in the kitchen with a rooster on top and golden eggs swinging below. She stares as they click back and forth. "I can't do it myself," she says. "I'm gonna need some help."

"Then we have to go now." I ease up and sit beside her. "That's how it works."

"Shoot," she says. "Pam next door can probably see after Henry, but she's working graveyard and I promised to ring the bell for the Salvation Army tonight."

"Where at?" I ask.

"Rite-Aid on Ninth. Been volunteering nearly every night. Preacher said I need to try and get my mind off myself."

"What preacher?"

"One on TV late Sunday night. He said best way to get through a tough Christmas is go do something for somebody else." As if on cue, the hour strikes and the rooster crows. "I gotta ring that bell, Jamie. Ain't nobody else I can get this late to fill in."

I tap the table, thinking. Henry's nose nudges my hand. "Okay," I tell her. "Maybe we can come up with some sort of plan."

This is my plan: Annie's in detox and I'm parked in front of the Ninth Street Rite-Aid. Before I left her in rehab, she told me that Shelby, the night manager, would give me everything I need and to watch for a guy named God Bless John. "Says 'God bless' coming and going," Annie explained. "Shows up near closing time with hot chocolate. It's good chocolate, if that's what you like."

"Will do," I agreed. "Thanks."

"What did I do but mess up your night right here at Christmas?" she asked. "You work on commission or something?"

"There's all kinds of commission," I replied.

"Guess so," she said, leaning her bony frame against me. Hugs are against rehab rules, but I didn't have the heart to turn her down. "Merry Christmas, baby," Annie said. "You take care."

I make my way through the blustery night into the warm and sterile lights of Rite-Aid. A woman leans against the register wearing a baggy black shirt with the store's logo across the chest. "You must be Shelby," I say.

"How'd you know my name?" she asks.

"I'm smart like that," I tell her. "Plus, your tag says, 'Shelby.'"

"Duh," she says, smacking her forehead. "Something I can help ya with?"

I tell a vague version of Annie's story, careful not to compromise her confidence. Basically that I was sent over from the Salvation Army higher-ups to help. Which is true, sort of.

Shelby rummages under the counter and hands over the apron, kettle, a tall silver handbell, and a red Santa hat.

"I have to wear a hat?"

"I don't suppose you *have* to," she says. "But everybody else does."

"Give it here," I grouse.

The bell is crazy loud, way more *clank* than the subdued *ring-a-ling* I was expecting. "Don't you have one of those little bells?"

Shelby rocks her head back and rolls her eyes. "Are you gonna complain about everything? C'mon, man, it's Christmas."

Defeated by cheer, I gather the gear and haul it outside. There's an archway in front of the door that offers shelter from the rain, so I hang the kettle there, tie on the apron, and start ringing the bell. It's bitter cold, and traffic is slow, a few straggling shoppers tossing in leftover change. I did not dress appropriately to stand around in freezing weather, so I stick the bell handle in my pocket and bounce up and down to get warm, blowing into my hands, walking quick laps around the kettle.

A guy with a nose red as Rudolph's staggers in to buy a fifth and throws six bucks in the pot. Two jolly women with bright scarves wish me well but offer no donation. A couple crosses all the way to the other sidewalk so they don't have to pass near me. At first I slink back to give them plenty of space. But then I think, *I'm a second-hand stand-in for the Xanax biker lady I sent to rehab tonight. What the heck do I have to lose?* I bounce in closer and clang the bell, wishing them "Happy Jesus Birthday!" in an especially exuberant voice that, maybe to a stranger, sounds a little developmentally delayed.

"Christ, man!" the guy exclaims, hustling his lady through the door. I retreat to the far wall and watch them through the glass. They make their way to Family Planning and stare at the home pregnancy tests. First they argue, then she cries. He digs into his pockets and hangs his head. I notice now that the clothes and coats they wear are ragged. Back in the parking lot, I spot a sad white hatchback with a garbage sack taped over the side window.

Good job, O great and insightful psychotherapist, I think. *You should really be proud.*

She picks a kit from the shelf and they read the back panel with heads close. He reaches to take her hand. They share a quick kiss on the way to the register.

I step back as they're leaving and give the bell a rest. The girl is still tearful as she slides a dollar into the kettle's slot. "Merry Christmas," she says.

"Merry Christmas," I reply.

The wind picks up, and the night gets colder. My ears are frozen, so I unfold the Santa hat and pull it down tight.

I wonder how Joseph felt pulling that donkey through the cold desert night, on the run from Nazareth to Bethlehem with a very pregnant wife he had not yet known intimately. The angel dream had said to trust Mary. I bet Joseph wrestled with angels too. I wonder if he had any idea what their story would someday become.

A pickup parks at the curb, and a rough old codger wearing coveralls and an AMVETS cap hobbles over with a thermos and two Styrofoam cups. "Where's Miss Annie?" he asks, pouring from the thermos to the cups.

"Sick tonight. I'm filling in."

"God bless you for helping out on a night like this," he says, offering the cup. "Coldest yet, I do believe."

"Sure enough." I point to the white flecks falling through the night. "It's snowing."

John stares up into the Rite-Aid sign. "Rain's startin' to freeze," he says, shaking his head. "Just looks like snow in the lights."

A woman rushes up carrying a child, head ducked and huddled close. John steps over and holds the door. "Christmas is tough on a lot of people," he says. "It's a lonely time."

I blow the steam from my cup and take a careful sip, nodding agreement.

"My wife, she passed two years ago, so I try and stay busy." He takes a long pull from his chocolate. "She loved Christmas."

I wait before speaking. "Glad you showed up tonight. Annie told me you'd come."

John's eyes stay on the lights while the slightest smile slips across his face. "Any friend of Annie's is a friend of mine."

We stand against the wall drinking chocolate, watching cars slide past until our cups are empty and the conversation lags. "Best be going," John says, extending a calloused hand. "Tell Annie I'm praying for her tonight."

"Will do," I promise.

John stacks my cup inside his and heads for his truck. "Merry Christmas, Jamie," he calls, revving the engine to warm the heater. "God bless."

I lift a hand as he drives away. The woman pushes back out the door and stops beside me. The child is pressed tight against her, but she stretches out her hand. "Carly wants to give you something," the mother says. Carly opens her fingers, and there are two quarters, three nickels, and a dime. Her mother holds her over the kettle, and she drops the money inside. Her nose is running, and her hair is tied in tiny tight braids.

"Thank you, Carly," I tell her. "God bless."

"Are you an elf?" she asks.

"As a matter of fact, I am."

"Really?" she says with a dubious squint.

"Well," I admit, "maybe just for tonight."

Carly looks back over her mother's shoulder as they walk to their car and waves one gloved finger good-bye. "God bless, mister," she says.

The Rite-Aid sign goes dark, and the last of the store lights dim. I untie the apron and take the kettle down. Shelby cracks the door, and I pass it all inside.

"You wore the hat?" she asks. "I was kidding. Nobody wears the hat."

"What the heck?" I tell her. "It's Christmas."

She laughs, wishes her best, and locks the door. I linger in the dark of the archway, waiting. The rain stops and snow begins to fall.

I drive back over to Annie's apartment and let myself in. The hall light shines through the transom's frosted pane. I pour out food and water for Henry's bowl. There's a broom in the corner, so I sweep the kitchen, then sit in the same chair I sat in a few hours before. A switch on the back of the plastic tree makes the branches twinkle while a music box plays "The First Noel."

Henry crawls from beneath the table and presses his nose to the back of my hand. Snow flurries outside the window, piling on windshields at the car lot down the road. Through a break in the clouds one pale star shines.

"Happy birthday," I reply.

DAY 31

Remember those moments you felt most alive? Likely, they weren't anything expected. God loves to catch us unguarded. Write about one of those moments without worrying about what someone might think if they stumbled upon your words.

Write like you are free.

AND THAT'S HOW I GOT THE NICKNAME "TACOS" BLAINE

[THEN]

> Yet as I read the birth stories about Jesus I cannot help but conclude that though the world may be tilted toward the rich and powerful, God is tilted toward the underdog.
> —PHILIP YANCEY

MY MOM AND I MOVED BACK TO TOWN THE YEAR I started junior high, and it was a pretty big culture shock for me. Kids in the country weren't worried about how you styled your hair or whether or not you had trendy clothes and took a shower every day. We were all scruffy. But at my new school, the girls all looked like *Sassy* magazine models and the boys had MTV haircuts and wore cologne. I was the shy kid with tattered pants and mismatched shirts who sat in the back and talked like a plowboy. So it was probably a joke when somebody in homeroom nominated me for class president.

The week before elections all the other candidates put up fancy posters with glittery stars and witty sayings, and Jeanette Beckett's optometrist dad drove her to school in his Corvette convertible so she could give out SweeTARTS at the bus stop. She sat tall on the trunk with her feet between the bucket seats, the morning sun glinting off her braces as her dad cruised slow circles through the drop-off lane and schoolkids chased the Corvette with outstretched hands.

"Can I have some?" I asked.

"Of course," Jeanette said, smiling down on me like a vision, her voice tinged with the mix of kindness and pity that up-and-coming tweens show classmates who are far behind.

I reached up. She handed me a pack. "Don't forget, vote for Jeanette!" she sang, flashing the victory sign. Not a clue I was running against her.

I stood in the lane shoving tarts into my mouth, watching as they drove away, Jeanette waving, kids reaching, her dad's vanity plate reading *EYESONU*. I hadn't even told my parents I was running. I wasn't doing anything to try and get votes.

The school bus screeched up behind me, and I jumped and spilled my SweeTARTS across the road. "Move it, Gomer," the driver said, laying on the horn. "Or you're gonna get squooshed."

The election was first thing Friday morning, and Thursday afternoon we had to make a speech after the pep rally. The gym was packed. My fellow contenders were dressed like the stars of *Saved by the Bell* while I looked like Screech's cousin from *Hee Haw* wearing Plain Pockets jeans and a hand-me-down Twitty City *Hello Darlin'* tour jersey. Nobody had told me about the speech.

The candidates were seated in the front row. One by one, we stepped up to the stage to give a two-minute campaign as to why we should represent our class. I was sitting between Jeanette and Holly Free, close enough for our hips and elbows to touch, though they didn't because they both bit their thumbnails and leaned far as possible to the other side. The girls smelled like honeysuckle and strawberry Pop-Tarts, the glorious scent of teenage heaven. I'd played sixteen rounds of Red Rover during lunch recess. I smelled like a sweat sock full of Funyuns.

God, please just let this be okay, and help me not embarrass myself too bad, I prayed, my nervous sweat shading Conway's lusty sneer. Like most teens, I could be deeply and desperately religious in crisis situations. *If you get me through this, I'll say the Lord's Prayer fifty times.*

It was the only spiritual leverage I could remember from my limited exposure to church. If you needed God to do something, you could haggle with rote prayers. It didn't make much sense, but since when was religion ever sensical?

Jeanette stepped over me, the fragrance of flowers and strawberries filling her wake. The student body cheered as she took the stage. *Make it a hundred, Lord,* I pleaded. *Plus, I'll throw in prayers for all my friends and even my enemies too.*

One by one the seven other candidates made their case. Seriously focused, civically connected, a history of athletic leadership and academic success. Finally, the principal called my name.

The gym was silent as I walked center aisle and climbed the stage steps. I had a pair of blue Zips sneakers, and the right front tread was coming loose, squeaking against the hardwood floor and flapping like an alligator's mouth with every step. I shuffled my right foot so the sole wouldn't flop, but when I topped the last step, my Zips caught the stage lip and sent me sprawling.

The students erupted. For a long few seconds I lay on my back and stared at the rigging lights. There was a shiny balloon stuck in the very top of the steel, fluttering against the vents. *Jeanette Is The Best*, it said.

Thanks a lot, God, I replied.

I staggered up and over to the microphone. It shocked my lips and screeched feedback as the students winced and clasped their ears. "Step back a little," the principal suggested, smiling and nodding me on. I gulped a big breath and started again.

"I, uh, don't belong to any clubs," I confessed to my classmates.

"Not yet." I cupped the mike to bring it lower. "And I know I don't play sports or nothin', and I'm new here, but at my old school we had Taco Tuesdays, and it was something to look forward to in that sucky first part of the week. So if I win, I'd like to try and get Taco Tuesdays here too."

My voice sounded deeper and more sure over the speakers. I liked it. Maybe I could even try telling a joke?

"You smell like taco!" some bright young student or perhaps a faculty member shrieked.

"Um, okay, thanks," I muttered, looking back to the principal. He clicked his pen, nodded toward the steps, and I shuffled off stage.

The next morning I tried faking a fever, but Mama made me go to school anyway. I hid in the bathroom until the last minute and tried to slip unnoticed into class. The announcements began. At the end, they revealed results for class president. In third place, Sloane Farley. Second place, Jeanette Beckett. And in first place, the winner and new class president . . . Jamie Blaine.

My classmates gathered around, applauding and slapping me on the back. For a moment I was too stunned to speak. "But why'd y'all vote for me?" I asked.

The chants began. "Tacos! Tacos!"

"Those other guys are *so* boring!" Cyndi, the cutest girl in class said. "You're a total trip!"

The whole rest of the day seemed like a dream—teachers and kids rallying around me, saying nice things. When I got home and told Mama, she took me to Sears and bought me two new shirts, some shoes, and name-brand jeans.

"You stink, boy," Mama told me in her own tactful way. "You're not in elementary anymore, you know. Time to start taking a shower every day." She handed me a plastic grocery sack with two bars of Irish Spring inside.

I'd never had my own personal soap before. I smelled it over and over again. After a good lathering up with Mountain Stream and whistling the Irish Spring theme song, I put on my new clothes so I could go to the school dance. With Cyndi. She asked me.

"You mismatched your buttons, boy," Mama said, shaking her head. She was a lot younger than the other moms, and I think that was weird for her sometimes. But I could tell, in her own way, she was proud.

Jeanette Beckett cornered me when I walked into the dance. "I want my SweeTARTS back," she demanded. Her face was real serious at first, but she couldn't hold it and cracked a smile. "Nah, congratulations," she said, shaking my hand. "I think you'll do really good! If you need any help, just let me know."

I was still too self-conscious to dance with Cyndi (and nobody dances much at junior high dances anyway), but she turned out to be just as awkward and gawky as me. So, for the most part, we sat on the bleachers by the back door and made each other laugh. Toward the end of the night, DJ Rudy Gaines announced the last slow song, and Cyndi said, "Hey, come on, we should at least dance one."

She hooked her finger through mine and led me toward the floor. Along the way, we picked up others. Sloane, Sean Sherman. Jeanette joined in—all of us swaying in slow circles beneath the basketball goal while the disco ball showered us with sparkles of light.

You wouldn't think that slow dancing with the cutest girls in school would be the time to think about God, but that's what I was doing—staring up in the rafters at Jeanette's balloon, with one arm around her shoulders and the other holding Cyndi's waist, wondering just how he'd pulled this one off. I wasn't real familiar with the Bible, but the stories I'd heard seemed to suggest God had his own strange way of doing things. Strange twists of fate, strange characters, losers rallying from behind to do all right.

Who knows? Maybe God likes to root for the underdog too.

The final song of the night came to a sweeping close as our little group pressed in tight. Jeanette leaned over, her nose at my neck. "Mmm," she said. "You smell good."

Later that night I lay in bed, thinking how completely bizarre life can be, how in the space of a day everything can change. I told God, *Thanks, I guess?* I mean, I prayed not to be embarrassed, and that whole falling-on-stage thing was embarrassing really bad. But it turned out okay in the end. So, yeah, I guess you'd have to call that answered prayer.

A deal was a deal. I owed God a hundred rote prayers. I made mark one in my notebook, but before I started in, I talked to God casual-like, telling him that I didn't understand how he kept up with all the crazy stuff going on in the world and still had time to be interested in seventh-grade elections and school dances, but I sure was glad he did.

God's pretty easy to talk to like a friend. Before I could even start on my hundred prayers, I fell asleep.

Jeanette was wrong. I did not make a good class president. I wasn't any good at groups or meetings. I asked the wrong questions and still hung out with the wrong, unpopular crowd sometimes. I was too sarcastic, too silly, too serious about insignificant things. I still liked to play Red Rover at recess now and then. It's like there was a set of unspoken rules that I was always clueless about. Politics and social climbing were not in my blood.

The head lunch lady shot down Taco Tuesdays quick. "Honey, we can't be deviating from the county's plan," she said. Once the kids saw my taco proposal wouldn't fly, I fell from grace. I didn't have much to offer other than tacos and pratfalls. I tried falling more—down stairs, up stairs, out windows, over desks—but eventually it got to where the students didn't laugh much anymore.

I thought a lot about that night at the dance with the disco ball spinning, smelling like Mountain Stream, swaying between two of the most popular girls in school. If life were like a teenage movie, you could roll the credits, play a perky theme song, and have your happy ending right there. But life keeps rambling on after the credits roll.

By the end of the school year they stopped inviting me to meetings, and nobody mentioned class president much anymore. The next year they elected Greg Lambert. He was focused, well connected, and an academic and athletic success. I told Greg congratulations and wished him well when he won. He really was a nice guy.

My last role as president was to help organize the year-end dance. I thought maybe I'd play an important part—something I was good at for a change. But when I got there, they had assigned everybody else the cool jobs, and I got stuck watching coats and keeping the concession stand stocked with ice.

I sat at the side stage exit near the fuse boxes and curtain draws, watching Cyndi dance with some other guy and listening to the ice maker grind. Just then a voice, deep and full, came out of the light. Not God. DJ Rudy Gaines.

"My man," he said. "You busy?"

"Not really."

"My cousin usually helps out, but he went and got himself grounded. You got a minute to give me a hand?"

"Yeah," I replied. "Sure."

Soon enough I was triggering flash pots, firing off fog machines, helping pick songs to set the mood. "You're pretty good at this," Rudy said. "Ever think about deejaying? If you want, I can show you how."

I lay awake that night, my ears ringing and halos burning behind my eyes from all the lights, thinking maybe God still speaks and moves in mysterious ways, a little stranger than we could ever understand.

Burning bushes, whirlwinds, and still, soft voices. Donkeys and strange angels. Even through DJs at the junior high dance.

I said every last one of those hundred rote prayers. It took a long time.

LIFE IS NOT FOREVER, LOVE

[NOW]

Even the darkness will not be dark to you.
—PSALM 139:12 (NIV)

THE FRONT DESK CLERK AT SKYLARK SAYS WORKING in mental health must be hard and depressing sometimes. I tell her sure, it's difficult, but mostly it feels like a privilege. She's biting on a Romans 8:28 ink pen, and there are Bible verses printed all over her purse. Since she's a believer, I feel pretty safe letting her in on the secret: that I truly believe when I walk with busted-up people through the worst of times, I am walking with Jesus and looking into the face of God. I tell her that you can learn so much about life from the broken.

"Whatever gets you through," she says, tapping the pen against the back of her hand. "I just know I sure couldn't do it."

I'm trying to think of some semispiritual response when the crisis line rings. "Guess where you get to go?" Squiggly asks, not waiting for my prediction. "Easy Living trailer park."

"Sleazy Livin'?" I reply, stepping outside to take the call. "The one out past the mill?"

"*Ding, ding, ding!*" she says, like I've solved the final puzzle on *Wheel of Fortune* and won ten thousand bucks. "Already told 'em we're sending our top man."

"I'm the only man."

"Exactly." She laughs before the line goes dead. I glare at the desk clerk through the front glass. Scowl, even. She never looks back, so I get in my truck and go.

If they ever make a movie of my life, there'll have to be a scene in some hard-luck trailer park on the rough side of town. Just like this one. A few rutted-up gravel roads that cut through angled rows of blandly identical single-wides. Cars on blocks and blue tarps stretched over holes in the roof. At the last road there's a neighborhood watch sign riddled with bullet holes from a .22. Somebody spray-painted *Trust Jesus* over the sign, and tacked to a fence post across the street is a stenciled sheet of plywood that warns, SLOW DOWN CHILDREN. Next to that, my client's mobile home.

I knock against the screen door, and he motions me in. He looks like John Belushi, if Belushi had quit drugs and settled into a life of blue-collar jobs and hard drinking. His narrow trailer is littered with pizza boxes, fast-food sacks, and about a thousand crushed empties of Coors Light. He's pretty shaky but sweet as can be and keeps saying "I'm sorry" and "Thank you" over and over again, and I keep reassuring him that it's all right, that I've been in a lot of old trailers on a lot of nights, and, really, this is probably God's way of keeping me straight and sober too.

"I hear you, buddy," he says. "Hey, you want some of this pizza? I got plenty enough to share."

"No, sir," I reply. "Thanks for offering, though."

We throw together a quick suitcase while I point out all the things he can and cannot bring, like aftershave, shoelaces, or belts. "Guess this ain't no *Love Boat*," Sweet Belushi says.

"We'll hope not," I reply.

A few miles down the road, he starts sweating and shaking bad. I assumed with all the empty cans that he'd been drinking all day, but turns out he tried to quit before going into treatment. Should have checked him better before we left. Rookie mistake. Never assume anything. "You crashing on me?" I ask.

"Sorry," he replies. "Didn't want to be a burden on nobody, I swear."

"'S all right, buddy," I tell him, wheeling into the Fil-A Sak. "Small steps. We'll get there. I'm pretty crashed out too."

I duck in, grab a SkullZap, and ask the cashier for a half pint of Crow. She shoots me a curious look while sliding the items into a paper bag, like maybe I'm foolish enough to mix the two.

"It's not for me."

A rehab graduate once told me you're always losing when you have to explain. God should plant angels everywhere to talk you through life's crossroads. I've always felt like there's a contingent of believers whose path is straight and plain while mine is forever splitting like some choose-your-own-adventure book. "It's for my brother," I explain.

The cashier is one of those women in her forties who could pass for sixty-five—sun-damaged skin and tired eyes, reading glasses hanging on a chain around her neck. There's a crucifix wrapped in thorns tattooed on her wrist, and farther up sits a faded heart with wings and words in a circle: *Rest in Peace, Rebecca Lynn. Life Is Not Forever, Love.*

"None of my business who it's for," she says with a shrug. She punches buttons, and the drawer opens with a *ch-ching*. When she hands over my change, I catch the rest of her tattoo. *Life Is Not Forever, Love Is.*

"Seen a lot of tattoos in my line of work," I tell her. "That's a good one."

"That thing is so old," she says, glancing it over. "Still feels like yesterday, though. What kinda work you do?"

"Tattoo artist."

"Never seen a tattoo artist with no tattoos."

"Just kidding. I ride around at night helping people. That's probably the easiest way to put it. Got a guy detoxing, and I don't want him to code in my truck. Bad for resale value."

"So you work for some kind of outreach or something?"

I say it straight-faced, unsmiling. "I'm on a mission. From God." The cashier raises her eyebrows and looks to the bag. "Mysterious ways," I remind her, pointing toward the sky.

"Wish I'd have done something better with my life instead of being stuck behind this register all night."

"Bet you do more than you realize."

"How you figure?"

"How many pass your way in a night? How many thirty-second conversations like this do you have?"

She doesn't seem convinced. I try to think of a way to tell her that she's with real people, in a real place, and the words we exchange in those places are often far more powerful than the ones that fall under official outreach. There's no reason a convenience-store counter couldn't be some sort of pulpit or station of the cross, especially at night. But I can't find a way to say all that where it doesn't feel dumb. And in some sense, I'm probably trying to convince myself.

"Just a hunch," I offer. "When you're the guy who rides around at night helping people, sometimes you just know things." I grab the paper sack and head for the door.

"Hey, mister?" the cashier calls.

"Yeah?"

"Say a prayer for ol' Janice at the Fil-A-Sak tonight, okay? Things been kinda crazy lately. Just if you remember to."

"I will," I tell her. "Promise." Halfway out I turn back. "Hey, Janice?"

"Uh-huh?"

"Say one for me too. If you remember."

"Promise," she says. "I will."

I climb in and steady my patient's hand to check his pulse. He takes one shaky sip as I shift into second and turn onto the highway. "Sorry, Jamie," he says, settling back. "Didn't wanna be no burden."

"Don't worry, brother," I tell him. "We're on our way."

The morning sun is cruel and blinding. I block it with a blanket over the stairwell, roll the exercise ball next to the heater, perch on top, and let the tablets dissolve under my tongue. Just as prescribed by a qualified and caring physician. Sounds better that way.

The gospel TV station's got a preacher on from eight to nine, and he talks like he's talking to just one person about mercy and patience and how we all need help to make it through. I listen and wait for the Zombien.

"There's a woman in Texarkana just called," he says. "And she's having a hard time. Let's pray God will help her, 'cause truth be told, I'm going through a hard time lately too. So let's believe for all those struggling today as they travel life's path and seek his everlasting hand."

Life's path as of today: psychiatric crisis seven nights a week, unable to sleep, sitting on a giant silver ball with the windows blacked out, waiting for the pills to kick in. So did I pick life's path, is it all in God's hand, or is the plan some strange fusion of the two?

"I set before you life and death," Deuteronomy says. "Therefore choose life."

But we see this life through a dark window, and if there's mercy, there must be mercy for the mistakes we make while trying to do our best, when faith is simply hope for something better coming our way.

My mind is still whirling. The meds aren't working as well.

"You can call anytime," the TV preacher says, his voice easy and slow. "No one will ask for money. Someone is waiting to listen and pray."

I stare at the numbers on the screen before punching them into my phone. It's only fair. A person should be on both sides. It's a lot easier to offer help than ask for it.

The line rings seven times before the preacher himself picks up. "God's got an answer," he says, sounding more tired than he does on-air.

"I'll take one," I tell him. "I can't sleep."

"The Lord knows, brother," he answers back. "I struggle with insomnia too."

"What do you do?"

"Best I can," he replies. "But I'm still believing and holding on. What's your name?"

"Jamie."

"Take heart, Jamie," he says. "Listeners all over the South are praying for you."

The heater is warm, and my hands grow heavy. I pray for mercy and patience, for sweet Belushi who didn't want to be a burden, and Janice at the Fil-A-Sak, for the TV preacher and the woman in Texarkana, for all the crisis people last night and the ones that lie ahead. For sleep and pleasant dreams, that God has been there every step, all along, even now.

DAY 35

Have you ever really thought about how strange an era childhood is? Reach back and remember those moments from your youth, the anxious wonder and simple presence of God, the way he showed up outside the limits of religion, before you learned to filter how you feel. Think back to the memories you've long since buried, when the world was a place where anything could happen. Write about a time when anything did.

YOUR MOST FANTASTIC HEAVEN

[THEN]

For we have sinned and grown old, and
our Father is younger than we.
—G. K. CHESTERTON

I T WAS A COLD JANUARY MORNING WHEN I CLIMBED off the bus, a bandage wrapped around my head from the blow with a baseball bat two days before. I was out five minutes or so and hadn't felt right since waking up, like the whole world was on TV and I was watching from the bottom of the midnight sea.

The playground was two hundred yards to the fence that separated school from the farmland next door. I told God that if he was still with me, I needed some sort of sign. I told him I would walk to the fence to give him time, and if he didn't show up by then, that would be my way of knowing. One way or another, I would have my sign.

The wind pierced my thin denim jacket as I set out across the school yard. I slowed my pace as the fence grew closer. No God. I stepped between the barbwire and headed toward the woods across the field.

All right, I told God. *The trees.*

I charged on, waiting for a teacher to yell or some fellow student to rat me out. No voice came. Just before the trees, I started running, faster and deeper into the woods. A cluster of blackbirds exploded from the brush, and I fell backward to the ground. The sky was ash gray over the treetops as the wind howled through the branches. I caught my breath, stood, and started walking back to school. As I crossed the fence, the rain set in.

Our class was in a portable metal building kept warm by a small gas heater set into the wall. Mrs. Stewart made me sit on the farthermost side with the other misfit kids she didn't like. My feet were wet and freezing. She called us to attention with a *thwack* of her ruler and passed out a pop quiz in math.

Okay, God, I told him. *I guess we're done.*

Later that night, I lay in bed and wondered if the blackbirds might have been the sign.

Lunch recess was preempted once a week for religious studies, and only true heathens with a permission slip from home were allowed to skip and experience the joys of unstructured play. We could see them out the windows. There were only a handful, but they had the playground to themselves. I begged my mother to let me cut, but she refused.

Time crawled in a cruel fashion, but on page 9 of our Bible Basics handbook ($5.00 deposit), there was a picture of God. It showed Earth in dark space with the universe unfolding and *THE LORD GOD JEHOVAH* looming over it all, so tall you could not see his face. He was wearing a sparkly white robe trimmed in gold, and there was a triangle symbol of the Trinity on his chest. His hands were reaching with upturned palms. Earth was a marble next to God's hand.

For forty-five minutes every Wednesday afternoon, I would stare at God's picture, mesmerized. God was a million miles high and rising, bigger than space and time, tall enough to see both beginning and end of all things. I thought maybe if I kept his picture close at night, I wouldn't have any more bad dreams. The eyes of God never sleep.

I was tempted to tear out the page but afraid that even for a person on the outs with God, that might be a pretty serious crime. So I laid a piece of notebook paper over the picture and tried to draw his outline. Father Grimmig rapped his pencil against my ear.

"*Nein*, James," he warned in his thick German accent. "God is not something ve trace."

I slid low and stared out the window of my grandmother's Monza as it sped through the countryside toward Lulu's Corner Grocery. Tall cornstalks and sweet potato farms, shotgun houses sprouting in a field. Lulu kept a metal chest by the counter full of half-melted ice, and I was hoping to pull a slushy Sunkist from the bottom and drink it while waiting in the store.

We stopped at the crossing for a slow-moving train, cattle cars and cotton creeping by. I saw him from a distance, standing in an open boxcar, leaning against the door in a white V-neck T-shirt stained with rust and red dirt. Just before he reached us the train squealed to a stop.

My grandmother cursed and drummed the steering wheel. The drifter's gaze met mine. His face was leathery, but his eyes were pale as ice. He took a long pull from his cigarette and with a flourish of his right hand made it disappear. His left hand made a fist; he placed it to his mouth, and silver smoke rings filled the air. With a wink he waved the smoke away. The train shook and rattled to life, and the look on his face was pure peace. It was like catching a glimpse into the secret face of God.

"See that old bum?" Grandma teased. "That'll be you someday, if you don't straighten up."

The drifter nodded as he faded from sight. I laid my hand against the door handle, imagining for a minute I might run along the tracks and jump an empty car, that it would take me to whatever magical place it was that trains go. To find the drifter's peace and disappear.

The last car passed, and the crossing bar lifted. My grandmother punched the gas.

The bell tied to Lulu's door jingled. His store smelled like sawdust and smoked brisket. The old folks spoke in a language I could not understand. For a long moment I stood listening. Then I plunged my hand deep into the frosty metal chest.

One dull and endless Sunday afternoon my buddy Frankie's Bible-thumping big sister lured us to the youth revival with a promise of free pizza. But when we got there, it was thin-crust from the grocery store, already soggy and cold. "Shh," she shushed, hustling us into the sanctuary. "There'll be more when church is done."

She made us sit down front, and I slumped with arms folded while the evangelist assured us that in heaven there would be no more night, that eternity would be one gloriously bright and sunny morning all of the time. This did not come as good news to me. The preacher also promised, with great assurance, that heaven would be like 24/7 church. This made me want to smash through a stained-glass window to escape.

We raced to the rec hall after the last amen, but the lights were out and the tables folded and propped against the wall. "Would you two stop whining?" Frankie's sister snapped. "What's more important? Pizza or Jesus Christ?"

She slid the seat forward, and I squeezed into the backseat of her candy-apple red Camaro Z. Half the reason I'd gone was to ride in her car anyway.

The stoners in the Dairy Queen parking lot ogled as we motored slowly down Main. "Did you enjoy the service, Jamie?" she asked.

"No, ma'am." Frankie's sister was older, like closer to my mom's age. "Not really." When it came to spiritual matters, I thought the best one could do was tell the truth.

"Not even the music?" she said, knowing I was an attention-deficit drummer who spent his allowance at the record store.

"The music was the worst part," I replied.

After some measure of silence, she eyed me in the rearview mirror as if I might be first cousin to the devil himself. The message was beginning to sink in. In matters of religion, it's better to be polite than honest.

A month or so later Frankie's sister gave it another shot, taking us to Johnnie Jay's for a fourteen-inch Kitchen Buster with double cheese before a Wednesday-night get-together for the kids. The minister dressed in regular-people clothes and seemed pretty easygoing for a man of the cloth. We sprawled out on the gym floor, and he told us that nobody could begin to imagine what God was getting ready for his people down here. "Just try," he challenged. "Dream your best, most fantastical dream, knowing heaven will be even better than that."

At the end he held up a key like it was a supernatural object of great power. And it was. He opened the Coke and candy machines and said that for the next ten minutes we could have all we wanted, for free. We screamed and ran in a frenzy.

Frankie's sister poked my ribs while I was chasing my second Kit Kat with an Orange Crush. "Puke in my car, kid, and I'll kill ya," she said.

Later that night I lay in bed, trying to think of the most fantastic heaven I could possibly comprehend. In the state before sleep the visions took on a life of their own. I saw God eight billion miles tall shrinking down to skyscraper size, magnifying me up to his level, going on a world tour where we rescued the helpless and stomped all the hospitals like twin Godzillas wrecking sin-sick Tokyo until nothing but rubble remained.

Then God stretched me to billion-mile size and we flew to the edges of the universe to explore the wonders there, laughing as we sped through the corkscrew of rogue stars that ran from Andromeda to the Milky Way.

Heaven was sweet old dogs that never die. Heaven was a city of crystal and gold. Heaven was an endless twilight where the beaches were vacant and the sands black. Heaven was a river of cold orange soda and deep-dish pizza stacked to the sky, each taste twice as delicious as the one before, and you never got tired or full. Heaven was your favorite moment a million times magnified and brought back to life. Heaven was far better than it was even possible to dream.

The next day Frankie told me the parents were none too pleased with the easygoing preacher that promised a heaven beyond our wildest dreams. They said that sort of foolishness had no place in church and that the youth should not be taught such frivolous things.

And if dreams and easygoing preachers didn't fit, I figured there wasn't much chance for me.

"You sure we won't get in no trouble?" Lilly Frensi asked, knotting the ski rope around my wrists.

"It's the middle of the day," I told her. "Nobody's watching." The apartment pool was in the space between two buildings, hidden from most.

"Can I wrap it around your head and tie it to your ankles?" Logan Frensi asked, a little more into it than his twin.

"Whatever," I said. "Just be sure to use it all."

Logan pushed up his glasses and went to work, trading ends with Lilly until I was totally hog-tied with bright yellow rope. They scanned the sidewalks one last time and rolled me into the shallow end of the pool.

I sank quickly and came to rest on the sky-blue concrete below. Thirty seconds passed in the cool, weightless silence. I could see the siblings fidget and bite their nails as I struggled against the restraints.

Forty-five seconds. They crouched at the edge, craning their necks to see.

At one minute I grew still, a string of bubbles rising from my lips. A garbled yelp rang out as the twins rushed the water. Just as they reached me, I shot to the deep end and popped up laughing.

It was all a trick. The ropes were loose long before I even got wet. I'd been practicing holding my breath in the bathtub for weeks. I learned all of this in a book.

While some teachers pushed junior readers, I was more interested in the mystery of time bending around black holes and the secrets of breathing fire and making elephants disappear. My plan was to grow up and be a star-gazing escape artist who searched for the secrets of how the universe worked. Miss Patti ran the library and she kept me encouraged and well stocked.

"Growing up is overrated, Jamie," she said, elementary-school perfect with her high pigtails and pastel overalls. "Stay curious. Wonder keeps you young."

After I read every book on magic and space in the Random County system, she started requesting titles for me from all over the state. Randi, Sagan, Kepler, Einstein, Hume, Kant, Kierkegaard. One dog-eared text explained that the faster one travels, the slower time moves and, at some point, should theoretically reverse.

I couldn't sleep one night, so I snuck my bike out and blasted full speed down the red dirt hill, back up and again, each trip faster, checking my watch's second hand, hoping that if I went fast enough and long enough—with a serious dose of heartfelt wishing—just maybe I could turn time back to the way things were before.

Between trips I would sit and catch my breath at the top of the hill, looking out over the town, smoke from the refinery rising through the factory lights, the clockwork of stars revolving around Polaris. I realized that turning back time on a bicycle would be more supernatural than scientific, but it felt good to try.

The experiment was over once first light started fading the moon. Nighttime was infused with possibilities. Daylight was for more practical things. I slunk back home and lay on my pallet as the sun slipped through the curtains, thinking that, in some sense, the theory proved true. Time did not reverse. But I'd found a way to make the minutes deep, to expand a moment into something rich. It was a balance between holding on and letting go, work and rest, action and being still. Time was relative, not absolute. And if time could be changed, it could be redeemed.

I trusted Miss Patti with my discoveries, and she started slipping in books on reason and faith. One spoke of the Creator's delight in hiding secrets for humans to find; therefore man's purpose was to explore and investigate. God disguised himself in dazzling darkness. His essence, the writer said, is mystery. The truly spiritual were rarely complacent. There was always another mountain to climb, another hidden facet of the face of God.

Just like the best books on space and magic, the author said true believers must never discount the impossible. There is no impossible for those who believe. I read this thinking maybe I could be a Christian after all.

LITTLE WING

[NOW]

She is clothed with strength and dignity,
and laughs without fear of the future.
—PROVERBS 31:25 (NLT)

I DRIVE OUT TO THE AIRPORT TO PICK UP MARLBORO. Rehab is over. He's coming home, and things will go back to how they used to be. And I'll zip-line over a field of sunflowers and catch up on sleep, and life will be easy-beautiful again. Or something like that.

I fish a piece of cardboard from the back of the Trooper and Sharpie Marlboro's name on it like those driver guys who pick up strangers at the airport. You know, just for laughs.

My plan is to spot him first and then hold up my sign, but the concourse is too narrow, so I stand with the sign over my chest the whole time passengers file off the plane. Dead-eyed salesmen in rumpled suits. College kids with backpacks on. A foreign mom herding a passel of kids. Some give wary looks, and I realize most people holding arrival signs in airports wear uniforms and chauffeur hats. I look like a fruit bat exterminator from Gulfport Beach.

The line trickles until the pilot passes through. "That's everyone?" I ask.

"Unless somebody's hiding," he says.

I dial Marlboro's number. No answer. No voice mail. I ask the agent at the counter. "Last one tonight, sir," she says.

The airport parking lot is nearly vacant now. I saw this movie once where the hero was frazzled, so he closed his eyes and thumped his head softly against the side of a tree. Parking lots don't have trees. But my truck cab is handy.

thumpthumpthump.

I hope I'm a hero in this movie. In the really good stories, the villian is convinced he's the hero too. So how do you know until the movie's over and you see it from a different point of view? What movie was that anyway? *Race for Your Life, Charlie Brown*, I think.

I helped send Marlboro to treatment. My replacement will probably send me. It's a dark glass, this life. We are all just sailing on life's stormy sea.

thumpthumpthumpthump.

The yards bleed together in weeds and wrecked school buses, deathtrap trailers and Cadillacs, old pink houses and potholes in the street. Rylan Heights used to be a nice neighborhood back in the day. Kind of run-down now.

I'm creeping slow, trying to find the street number. A lanky man walks the shoulder with a whole lot of swagger for somebody carrying a twelve-pack of toilet paper in a Dollar General sack. "Hey, brother," I ask, window down. "You know where 3013 is?"

He squints one way down the street and then the other,

hitching his pants up with one hand, looking like Snoop Dogg on social security. "Nice white lady and a kid?"

"Yeah, that sounds right."

"Next street over," he says, setting the sack down so he can point the way. "See, you're on Fuschia now, but next street's Fuschia too. That's Short Fuschia and this is Long."

I look in the direction where he's pointing and then back to the street sign behind us. "So I'm looking for Short Fuschia?"

"Confusing, ain't it?" Old Snoop says with a smile. "One street over, chief."

"Got it, thanks. I'll let you go," I tell him. "Looks like you're on a mission too."

As Rylan Heights goes, 3013 Short Fuschia is one of the nicer homes: blue with brown shutters, Eeyore birdbath, one of those shiny wind spinner things spiraling by the porch light. I glance over my notes before approaching. *Single mom. Depressed. $. Sick kid.* The caller got my number from a mutual friend, but everybody knows everybody in a small town. I don't remember writing any of this.

Heatwaves shimmer when she opens the door, and the whole house smells like dog. The kitchen table is piled with pill bottles and unpaid bills, and a plaque over the sink says, *All things are possible to those who believe.* "That one cost 133 bucks a month," Ellie says, pointing to the bottle of capsules in my hand. "And all it did was make things worse."

She's got an ex-husband at the prison farm and a cruel boss who cuts her no slack. But when her twelve-year-old daughter was diagnosed with a life-threatning illness, it sent her over the edge. "You have to keep believing something good can come, even from the worst," Ellie tells me. "Otherwise it's just too much to take."

It's not too hard on my part, plugging her into quality support and setting up an appointment with a doc who can help, knowing how to make that happen fast rather than the three-month lag time it usually takes. I make calls while she checks on her daughter.

"I hear you're good with kids," she says upon returning.

"Worked two seasons at the haunted house."

"So you're good at scaring kids."

"Something like that."

"Izzy loves anything Halloween. I named her Isabella, and we called her Bella at first, but then when she was six, she decided she wanted to be called Izzy. Izzy fits her. You mind saying hi before you go? She doesn't get many visitors these days."

My head feels like a cracked snow globe. The system is jacked. Everyone is suffering, and Eden is long gone. Schizophrenia and depression is one thing. Sick kids is something else. "Of course, sure," I reply. "Love to."

The hallway to her room is long and dark, family portraits from happier times and the stove light far behind me. I stand at her door knowing I'm a fraud, that my faith is weak and I fake my way through everything. Nothing feels fake now. I pray the prayer of every true crusader: *God help me not to screw this up and fall to pieces, amen.* Then I knock.

Her bubblegum-colored hair is close-cropped, and she's propped in bed with a tube trailing her arm. "Hey, uh," I interrupt, sticking my head in the door, "your mom said you might could help me with my math homework?"

"Sure," she says, closing her journal and playing along. "Whatcha having problems with?"

"Subtraction."

"Yeah, that'd be a problem if you're in college." A dust of freckles dots her nose, and the sides of her ears are pierced.

"Actually, I graduated grad school. But I'm thinking about going back for my PhD."

"In what?"

"Astrophysics. If I can get past this math thing, I know I can get us to Mars before the Mexicans."

"You're silly." Izzy laughs, waving me in.

"Not really. I'm just very immature for my age."

Her tiny room is top-to-bottom oddball trinkets, handcrafted curios, and dolls of every shape and size. Spooky cartoon supergirls guard the front of her journal, and posters of Edward Scissorhands and Einstein sticking out his tongue are tacked up over her desk. "Einstein was God's prophet, you know," I tell her, tapping Albert's head.

"How so?"

"He told us the separation between past, present, and future is only an illusion." I sit beside the bed. "Time isn't constant. It can be changed."

"I *looove* science," she says with a hand across her heart. "Hope I make it to the good stuff."

"Good stuff?"

Izzy thumps the tube in her arm and points to a bandage featuring Emily the Strange. "Like if I'm flippin' still around," she says. You forget that kids aren't so squeamish. She mimics the great physicist's stuck-out tongue. "One way or the other, guess I'll find out."

In the corner there's a guitar with silver stars down the fretboard. "You play?" I ask, changing the subject.

"Learning to, but I can't get it back in tune."

"That I can fix." I pick it up and work the tuners to pitch. It's a cut-rate model with shoddy strings, but I manage to coax it close enough to true. "Cool guitar. Where'd you get it?"

"My moms," Izzy says. "I asked last Christmas but didn't think I'd get one because things are supertight right now." She sits up straighter. "Ooh. Play me a song."

"Who you like?"

"Older stuff," she says, naming them off on her fingers. "Nirvana, Misfits, Depeche Mode, Green Day, The Cure, Hendrix—"

I interrupt her list with the E-minor lick that kicks off "Little Wing." She shuts her eyes and sits back to listen, head weaving back and forth. I noodle a bit. And then, just because my heart seems so heavy and confused, I bend the strings until they sing something closer to what I feel than I'm able to speak. I wring it out so hard I'm afraid the cheap guitar will come apart, but we work together until the final E-minor comes around again.

"Hello?" Izzy proclaims, clapping her free hand against her leg. "Like, why aren't you playing somewhere?"

"Who says I'm not?"

"So cool," she says, the words like helium until my heart blows up mountain-sized.

I hand the guitar over. "Your turn."

"Oh, no fair."

"Who ever said anything was fair?"

"O-kaay," she mutters, a not-very-convincing protest. "Like what?"

"Whatever's your favorite."

"Stupid PICC line screws up my playing," she says before cradling the guitar and sliding into a rasped-out version of "Love Song" with far more emotion than any thirteen-year-old should know, her voice cracking but full of hope, and it wrecks me in the best possible way. But there's another side, and if I could, I would run far away from this sort of beauty and pain. I look at the carpet, my shoes, Edward's scissorlike hands, and Albert's defiant gesture toward gravity and time—anywhere other than this sick kid fighting and singing about love, loneliness, and coming home. Einstein was right. Time cannot beat us forever. There must be some equation, some secret way to rise above.

"I like sad songs better," Izzy says, stopping after the second verse. "I'd rather be sad than fake."

There's a decoupage cross on her closet door made from words clipped out of a magazine:

All the world fades away, and each second is a moment to hold the rest of your life.

"Even Jesus wept," I tell her, pointing to the cross.

"That's 'cause Jesus wasn't fake," she says, leaning the guitar back in the corner. "Can I ask you a question?"

"Sure."

"What do you think happens when we die?" She says it matter-of-fact, as if we were still discussing our favorite songs. I wish I'd never put down her guitar, that I was playing "When Doves Cry" or "Wonderwall" instead of twisting a ponytail holder around my wrist and trying to figure out something to say. Finally, I answer, best that I can. "No time, no worry. No pain. Everything you ever loved and lost comes back for good." The space heater oscillates side to side while her fish tanks gurgle and hum. "At least that's what I think."

She stares past her rainbow toe socks toward the door. My eyes are fixed on a black goldfish as he weaves through a sunken castle. A smile sets in, sweet and a bit mischievous before she speaks. "That'd be a really good place."

"Really good," I reply. I reach out and Izzy presses against my hand, finger to finger, palm to palm. "Thanks for helping me with my math."

"Well, you know," she says, shifting fingers to grip my hand. "Gotta get to Mars before Mexico."

I stand, taking a last look around her room. Magic 8 Balls and cross-stitched Abe Lincoln on skates. A handsewn sock puppet of the plant from *Little Shop of Horrors* prepares to eat Yosemite Sam. "Take care," I tell her. "Okay?"

"You too," Izzy says. "And if Mama asks, just tell her we talked about Einstein and Jesus, okay?"

It's midnight, and there's a drunk on the bridge singing about the river of life. Just a shape, a silhouette against the luminous sky, his lonesome tenor ringing through the valley below.

"Water looks cold," Sergeant Riley reports.

"You'd think they'd pull this sort of stunt in the summer," says Glaser. "You can get him down, though, right, Jamie?"

"One way or another," I deadpan. "However, my attire isn't suitable for this assignment."

"What's that?" asks Glaser.

"Forgot my coat."

Riley pops his trunk and throws me a flak jacket with three stripes on the shoulders. "You don't care if I wear your jacket?" I ask, sliding my arms through the metallic green sleeves.

"Long as you don't get it wet," he says with a grin.

Their radios squawk to life: "Ten-eighty in progress, number nine." They yap back and pull at their belts. "Burglary at the Krystal. Suspect might've fired shots. We gotta run."

"Of course," I reply. "Great."

"We'll send somebody for you." Glaser thumbs the button and speaks into his collar. "Parnell, can you send Sergeant Blaine backup on the bridge?"

"Soon as we can spare one," Parnell replies.

"Best of luck," they bid me before roaring off into the night.

I make my way down the slim walkway, sirens warbling in the distance, rough water chopping at the banks below. A Sara Lee semi thunders by, shaking the steel suspension, and I am sure the drunk will topple, but he just keeps singing. I move in for a closer look. Scraggly, lean, clothes rumpled and stained with paint. He tilts his head back and echoes a hymn across the divide—that old standard about temptations and wonder, how we'll understand it better by and by.

Late-night psychiatric crisis is not the place for well-balanced practitioners. It helps to be a little screws-loose yourself. I know the song, so why not? I start singing along. When I get close enough for him to hear, he turns.

"Hey, there," he calls, eyeing the stripes up my sleeves. "You po-lice?"

"No, sir," I call back. "Just a fan of good singing. You mind if we talk?"

"You ain't here to arrest me?"

"Nope."

"Free country," he says. "Come on out, then."

It's a short jump down to some splintered old planks, holes and rot around the sides. I can see the Black River battering the span's columns, white water rushing around the edge. "How'd you get there?" I ask.

"Step down on that solid-looking piece. It'll hold. Then come this way and over them cables."

It's a long step over the cables with nothing but water below. He squats and peers through the steel. "Careful right there. You gotta know how to manuever it."

My stomach churns as the fear cuts through me. I bend low and hang tight to the girder.

"Hey, man, don't do it if you're scared," he says. "You can head on back. I'm fine."

"Give me a minute." At six-two, he can step the distance. It's a leap for me. "I'm coming."

He loops an arm around the crossbeam and holds out his hand. "Come on, then," he says. I hop over fast without thinking, grabbing his wrist for support. A three-foot-wide piece of iron runs the length of the bridge. I edge down and sit on a square of plywood, clinging to the rail. "You sing that high part real nice," he says.

"Thanks. I'm actually a baritone." Small talk happens in the strangest of places.

"Fear'll sure make you a tenor."

"Can't argue with that," I reply. "So why you out here?"

"Just thinking," he says.

"About what?"

His face is battered, but he's got the sloping, sad eyes of a bassett hound, and there's a kindness there that shines through the dark. A bottle-shaped bag rests on the beam beside him and he takes a short nip. "You a question-asking man?" he says, not unfriendly.

"Something like that. I do have to ask this one: you didn't come out here to jump, did you?"

"Into that cold water? Naw," he answers. "I come to sing."

"You came out to the bridge rail at midnight to drink wine and sing old hymns?"

"No, sir," he asserts, holding up the bag. "This here's gin."

We laugh and shake our heads. The air is charged, stars winter bright. A barge rounds the river bend, splitting the shimmer cast by the moon. He looks off into the distance, quiet now.

"Something happen here?" I ask.

"My brother jumped off this bridge in eighty-three."

"Sorry to hear that."

"Some say he wasn't ever right in the head. Never could find his place, I guess. I was two years out of high school, doing my thing." He pulls at the corner of his eye with his fist. "Folks 'round town acted like his life wasn't worth nothin' anyways. But he was a good boy. I come up here and think about him sometimes. Talk to him. Tell him I miss him."

"What's his name?"

"Daniel."

"Daniel," I repeat.

A train passes on the parallel span. We cling to the rail as it clacks by, engines and cattle cars, over the river and down the ridge, the whistle calling as the last car fades from sight.

"Sir, any minute now deputies will return to this bridge," I tell him. "I'll either have to send you to a psychiatric facility or they'll take you to jail. That's the only choices." I pause, checking to make sure he understands. "Unless, that is, you somehow slip away. I am afraid of heights, y'know."

"If you're scared of heights, why're you even out here?"

"Sometimes you gotta do it scared."

"I hear you, partner." He nods. "Can I ask you something first? You're one of them psychology people, right?"

"Not one of them regular kind." I gesture to the bridge rail and the barge. "But, yeah. I guess you could say that."

"Sometimes I hear my brother talkin' to me. I mean, I really hear his voice."

"What's he say?"

"Stuff like, *Be strong, big brother. I love you. And I'll see you real soon.*" He pauses and turns from the river back to me. "That mean I'm crazy?"

"I don't think so," I reply.

"What's it mean, then?"

"Maybe it means your brother's closer than we know," I tell him. "Maybe he finally found his place."

He looks hard into my eyes, I guess to see if I'm telling the truth or simply giving him a line. I believe what I said, so there's no need to look away.

"Gonna shoot straight with you," he says. "Sometimes I am tempted to jump off this same bridge, thinkin' maybe it'll take me to wherever he is. But I keep coming back up here and somethin' keeps telling me, 'Not tonight.'" He kicks a loose piece of slate to the water, and we watch it fall. "Not tonight," he says again.

He reaches out his hand, and for a moment I hold back, knowing he could pull us both in. "Tonight's all we got, brother," I tell him, shaking his hand. "So let's just go with that."

"You ever lost somebody close?" he asks.

"Yes, sir."

"Ever blame yourself?"

"Sometimes, yeah."

"To Daniel," he says, raising his bottle to the stars. "Wherever he is tonight."

"Wherever he is," I reply.

Daniel's brother disappears into the trees, his absence so complete I wonder if he was ever really here. The river swirls, black and cold beneath me, as a bitter wind cuts through the steel. I pull my jacket tight as the barge creeps closer, long and wide as a runway, its rim sparkled with tiny lights. The wind rages, then dies down to a breeze. On a faraway hill the radio tower glows—one glimmer, another, then three.

DAY 39

Scripture says we enter the kingdom as children, pure and unfiltered, not yet taught to conform or pretend, asking an endless array of questions and easily believing the good, seeing the future with effortless, childlike hope.

Think back to your earliest memories of God.

JESUS WALKS
DARK WATERS

And in the fourth watch of the night Jesus
went unto them, walking on the sea.
—MATTHEW 14:25 (AKJV)

I WAS LYING IN BED WAITING FOR SLEEP WHEN THE
smell of smoke hit. My toy box seethed with cinders as the first
spark caught the drapes. They went up quickly and flames licked the
ceiling, spreading along the baseboards and toward the door. G.I.
Joe action figures twisted into grotesque shapes, my Snoopy poster
peeling into char, the Lego spaceship melting, multicolored plastic
bleeding over the hardwood floor.

I shouted but no voice came. My arms and legs were paralyzed.
All I could do was watch as the fire crept closer and my parents slept.

I'm dreaming.

It felt too real to be a dream. I was in my bed, in my room at
night—only the room was engulfed in flames. Then came the horses,
sulphur and bones, slips of black shadows riding their backs and
laughing, charging closer and—

I shook loose from the dream and caught my breath.

The nightmares came most every night—house fires and phantom horses, skeletons hovering while I lay frozen, unable to separate reality from the dream. Though the visions were bizarre, in the moment they seemed more real than the real. A robot painted like a Southern Bread wrapper hurled knives at my head. Masked surgeons marked my torso for harvest. And if I managed to turn away, the pillow would trap me, stuck and unable to stir, certain I would suffocate, gasping and kicking out at the last second.

I never told anyone. Why try to describe smoky black stallions that galloped into my room at night and fire that burned while I was asleep yet awake and paralyzed? Adults already considered me a strange child with an overactive imagination.

You grow up and forget there is a secret kid world much larger and complex than you could ever explain. But in the Deep South they would tell you there is a God in heaven who sees all secret things, who walked this planet to understand.

I sat up and looked around my room. No flames. No shadows. Everything was just as it was before, the Lego spaceship ready for launch, Snoopy flying his doghouse and shaking his fist at the sky. The house creaked. My father snored. The bedside clock flicked minutes like pages in a book until they clicked to *11:59*. I tried to slow the numbers with my mind, to see how long I could make that last minute last, to witness the end of one day and beginning of another, like I was the only person awake and alive.

At midnight, I snuck into the den, turning on the television with volume low. The last moment of a movie played. An army of super-evolved apes fired machine guns while mutants sang praises to the bomb. The astronaut's bloodied hand gripped the lever that would end the world. A brilliant white light obliterated the screen before cutting abruptly to the local station's logo. There was a long and eerie pause. With a crackling hiss, the grainy old clip began to play.

A choir sang the national anthem a cappella. Jets streamed and eagles cried while statues stared into space. The secret voice of God spoke, deep and serene.

"TV 7 now concludes another broadcast day. Good night . . . and good morning."

Numbers flashed across the screen followed by a piercing tone and pattern of colored bars. "This is a test of the Emergency Broadcast System," God's voice said. "This is only a test."

After a long rush of static, I turned the TV off and crept into the kitchen. Using drawer pulls for a ladder, I climbed to the top cabinet, counted out eleven Lucky Charms, then slipped out the door to the back steps.

If I closed my eyes and listened, I heard big trucks on the highway, cicadas droning in the trees, frogs in the marsh by the pond down the hill, one dog barking far away, boxcars connecting in the train yard off Park. And if I focused hard, I could hear the nothing between the noise, the silence surrounding the arrival of God.

Just as real as the fiery horses, Jesus walked dark waters, out from the trees and up the hill. He would sit on the lowest blue step, leaning back with his elbow near my feet, and together we would listen to the still, small sounds of the night.

I'd once heard a preacher say that we show our thanks by giving a portion of all we possess, that the tithe is a tenth, but true believers go the second mile. I threw four bits of cereal into the darkness, knowing seven Lucky Charms with God was better than eleven alone. And while the whole world slept, we listened to the nothing of the night.

I had a response ready in case my parents found me. I would feign confusion, a sleepwalking spell, and they would carry me back to bed.

Night after night I returned to the steps, and they never found me. Not once. After somewhere between a minute and a million years God would stand and walk back across the water into the trees. There in the cool, dark quiet, I could breathe again. I could slip back to bed and sleep in peace.

Sometimes I wonder if I dreamed the whole thing. Sometimes I wonder if I am still even now waiting to shake out of the dream.

CITIES OF GOLD ON FIRE

[NOW]

His throne was fiery flames, and its wheels burning fire.
—DANIEL 7:9 (NHEB)

I GET A CALL TO SKYLARK AND DRIVE TOWARD WEST-
wood by mistake. I backtrack and get lost on a street I've been
down a hundred times before. I pull over and walk around the
truck until I get my bearings.

When I turn into the hospital, I am momentarily disoriented
again. I speak with some person in some room about some great
problem that eclipses everything good. Ten minutes later I cannot
remember one single detail other than his shoes. Converse High
Tops, maroon with silver stars.

My next caller waits at the corner of Twelfth and Electric,
huddled in an army jacket and looking like a lost dog. I am a beacon, a magnet, a funnel for trouble at the rock-bottom drop-off
of life.

Overdramatic, that's what I am. Better dramatic than numb.

"Curtis?" I call from the window.

"Jamie?" he calls back.

I park in the People's Bank side lot and walk over through

the rain—not driving or incessant, just a steady drizzle though skies are clear. We shake hands and his story begins: how he was managing the sporting goods store and doing all right, but then found out his wife had been unfaithful. He confronted her and she turned it against him, making him out to be the bad guy. His in-laws own the store and hold a certain influence in town. Now he's living in a boardinghouse and running from the marshal, who's trying to serve papers for back support.

"Every day I wake up and pray for the strength to get through this," he says. "Feels like I should be stronger. But I made mistakes too."

Brother Ponder once preached it's a half door to the broken. You crawl in on hands and knees.

"I'm the guy who answers the helpline every night," I tell Curtis. "And I can't hardly even help myself."

Water sweeps under the awning as a Wells Fargo truck splashes by at the curb. I shake my sleeves out and wipe my glasses dry.

"C'mon," says Curtis. "I know a place that's out of the rain."

We dart to the back door of the Asian Palace and duck under the overhang by the dumpsters, continuing our conversation there. Turns out Curtis and I went to school together. He was a junior in my freshman year.

"The world is too small, man," he says, embarrassed.

"Yeah, but I'd hate to have to paint it," I reply. It's a weak joke, but he still laughs.

A bug light burns by the back entrance, and I can see his features better now, the Cherokee hair and jutting chin. Nice fellow, best I remember. Quiet, kept to himself.

Curtis snaps his fingers and points to me. "You wasn't one of them fellas who blew up the talent show and the fire trucks had to come, were you?"

"Small world," I agree.

The rain lets up as he spins his story into its numerous dead ends. There's not much I can do but listen. Meds might help. Might not. Inpatient isn't an option, and he doesn't drink or use drugs. In the South, church is chief respite and refuge from storms, but Curtis says his in-laws run the church, too, and the one time he showed up didn't go too well. He sometimes attends the Tuesday morning men's meeting at Downtown Methodist and has been helping bring the bathrooms up to code. "Preacher tries to pay me," Curtis says. "But I won't take it unless things get bad."

I'm doing my best to stay tuned in, but suddenly I feel seasick, and the slab is like a fun-house floor.

"Hey, man," says Curtis. "You okay?"

"Just running a lot lately." I lean against the pillar. "That's all."

"Hang on. Busboy here's a friend of mine." He walks over and raps against the back door. A man steps out, wiping his hands with an apron. He exchanges words with Curtis and heads back inside, returning with two plastic containers of soup. "You like Chinese?" Curtis asks me.

"Nothing better on a cold, rainy night." I take the steaming dish and drink deep from the brim, the heat like a depth-charge in my chest.

"Pang she. Is good?" the busboy asks, leaning against the dumpster and lighting a smoke.

Of all the careers, I had to pick one filled with smoke. Wait a minute. I didn't pick anything. "Thank you," I tell him. "This soup rules."

"I know what is like to be hungry," he says. "I was on street once too."

The last drops of rain drum against the corrugated steel as the neon down Twelfth hisses. I turn up the container as a thin blue wisp slips from the side of his mouth to the sky.

There's a verse in Revelation that says the smoke of the

offering rises sweet to the nostrils of God, and I wonder if this smoke makes its way from here to heaven and somehow God, who sees all things for what they truly are, somehow receives it as honest sacrifice—of frustration and finding calm, breathing deep and letting go, of being still for one small moment and trying to tell the truth of who we are in the dark.

I don't mean to sound sacrilegious, but sometimes, when it's late and rainy, my mind thinks crazy things. I wonder if thoughts don't rise like smoke as well. "Burn up the fat on the altar," Leviticus tells us, "like the sacrifice of peace." Maybe God in all his infinite wisdom—the one who screens all thoughts from beginning to the end of man—receives these jumbled reflections and calls them sweet too.

I watch as the smoke rises and hope that somehow, someway, every wrong thing will be made right. For whatever else is on my account, in favor or debt, this one thing I know: I hope.

Curtis breaks the silence. "Some people believe crab is crab," he says, tossing his empty bowl into the dumpster. "But fresh is always the best."

The busboy nods in agreement. "Pang she," he says. "Fresh."

I offer thanks and excuse myself to a waiting call. In the truck, I lay my head against the wheel. I'm allergic to shellfish. Another mark in the long column of my careless mistakes. I heard a sermon once that said true believers can take up serpents and poison won't do them any harm. "No weapon formed against us can stand," the pastor declared. "So fear not, and keep pressing on."

I believe. Help my unbelief.

I'm dragging and my legs are heavy, so I pull into the Quik-Stop and stare through the cooler at my choices for a boost. Minutes pass. The quicksand grows deeper. No more sweetly pungent energy drinks. I grab a bottled water and head to the front. The hot dogs on the rotary are decrepit. A teenage clerk fights with her boyfriend on the phone.

There's a packet next to the register with two big red-and-black pills and a fierce-looking wasp on the label. *400% more mind-blowing energy in every pill!* it promises. I flip it and scan the warnings. Every sentence ends in an exclamation point, so it's gotta be good.

Ambulance lights flash in the distance. I toss the packet on the counter, pay, pray for strength, and press on.

A farmer suffering dementia attacks me with a rake, a schizophrenic lady has a seizure while my phone shows zero bars, the client I saw at Skylark escapes and shuts the interstate down, the town drunk is throwing rocks at cars, and the preacher's daughter hates everything.

In the movies some do-gooder saves the day with an impassioned speech that wakes a troubled person up and sets things back on the righteous path. Real life doesn't work that way. Or at least I can't get it to.

My former English professor turns paranoid and claws the side of my face. A three-hundred-pound patient falls on me when I try to pry the needle out of her fist. The clock at St. Mark's Cathedral strikes twelve.

Good night. Good morning. This is only a test.

There's a jail patient waiting, sixth floor at Westwood. The linoleum blinds me as the elevator doors open and bang shut. I cross to the stairwell and start to climb. My ears are ringing as the pulse pounds my neck. I am going through the motions, like the pilot of some distant machine.

The convict is cagey and scared, scarred up with hair buzzed close to his scalp. I offer my hand, and he flinches, yanking the tube from his IV. Blood spurts across my shirt and I stare, spaced out and frozen as the room dissolves in a flash of white light. The light fades; the bed is kicked sideways and the patient trapped underneath.

"Whoa, easy, Jamie," the doctor says, hustling me toward the sink. "I think this guy's Hep C."

I drive off down the avenue, trying to clear my mind. Library, strip mall, Slotski's Sport & Ski, flashing billboard for Powerball, just a dollar and a dream. The Powerball scene morphs into an ad for Froman's Jewelry as the light ahead turns red. The billboard changes again to a picture of a woman with hands lifted high and head back, a perfect halo around her from the brightness of the sun. The words in the sky above her: *Made for More: Step into the Life You've Been Longing For.* It's a commercial for a series at my church.

The light seems red forever as I stare at the message on the sign. The image spins into a pinhole and reemerges as a four-year-old on crutches begging me to help Children's Hospital find the cure. Finally, the words transform back to Powerball. Just a dollar and a dream.

The light turns green, and I drive, taking a right on a side street, through Lily Park to the middle school. I stagger from the truck and throw up in the sand behind the monkey bars, holding to the rail of the playground slide for support. The ground sways when I try to walk, so I lie back against the cold, molded plastic of the slide's chute. There's an empty space of sky just north of the Big Dipper, so I focus there and pray for the earth to stop churning.

The dizziness finally settles as a crimson streak stretches across the darkness through the trees. I grip the sides of the slide, push upright, and make my way back to the truck. Turning the ignition key seems like abstract algebra, but somehow I drive home on instinct and grit.

The spiral stairs rise like K2.

I collapse into bed, but my mind refuses to give in, obsessively spinning anxious thoughts. Huddling by the heater, I take two Zombien and fall into a fitful dream.

A narrow path stretches to the horizon in the hour before dawn. Everything is lifeless, the color of rust, stone towers scattered over the endless plain. The dust scratches my throat as I plod forward. There's a deep glow in the distance where the path disappears—

A jolt of pain stirs me. Every spasm sends battery acid through my veins. I'm freezing, burning with fever, and my mouth is filled with bees. I reach to shut the heater off and pass out again . . .

No matter how far I walk, the landscape remains the same: cratered, burnt and barren, red rocks rising like daggers into the sandstone sky. My arms and legs are made of lead, and my lips cracked with thirst. Keep moving. That's all I know to do—

The spasms attack in waves, each more violent than the one before. I clench my fists and try to hold on. My head is being crushed between metal plates while spikes twist into my spine. Everything goes dark and I fade out once again . . .

A steep ridge appears to the right with a switchback spiraling into the sky. If I climb the switchback, I might be able to get a fix on my position, to see if there's a town or a river in sight. Every circuit takes me higher above the land. Gravity gets thicker, and the morning light blinds my eyes, forcing me to crawl the final lap. I drag myself closer, but the weight is too much, and the source too bright. It's as if the sun crashed into Earth or Earth, like an asteroid, into the sun. If I could just steal a glimpse from the side. I cling to the rock for the longest before lifting my head. And for one brief moment, I open my eyes—

I wake up on the floor in a pool of sweat, throat scratchy and muscles tight. Small movements, slow. I remember something—the

ER one night. Benadryl. I dig it out of the cabinet and sip Gatorade with crushed-up tablets in it until I think I'm okay to drive. The streets are a blur. After five tries, I punch in my code and stumble through the back doors of Westwood ER. Dr. Black is on the phone, but when he sees me, he hangs up.

"Uh-oh," he says, suddenly at my side. "What'd you get into?"

Amy clips the back of my knees with the wheelchair, guiding me down. I try to crack some joke about how she's been waiting for this moment, but my brain can't put the pieces together, and whatever adrenaline I was running on is tapped out now. "It's okay," she says, wheeling me away. "Don't talk."

There's a swarm over me in the room. A needle slides in, and I start to protest, but the heaviness lifts and a thousand angels spread their wings and sing hallelujah.

"Can you count from ten backward?" Black says.

"Sure. Ten, nine. Eight. Sevvvvff . . ."

The lights are low when I come back around. At first I'm disoriented, unsure whether I am a child at my mother's house or a freshman in the college dorm.

"How you feeling?" Black asks, slipping through the door to look me over.

"I think I'm okay," I tell him, slowly coming around. "Am I okay?"

"Nothing a little magic IV mix couldn't fix. That and six good hours of sleep."

"Six hours?" I say, patting pockets for my phone.

Black tosses over my cell. "I took the liberty of calling in for you."

"Oh, man."

"You'd do the same for me," he says, checking my blood

pressure and pulse. "Good thing you got here when you did. You were in a pretty sketchy state."

"It was that bad?"

"It was not good," he says.

I pull myself up straighter by the elbows. The overheads hum, brighter now. "Can I tell you something weird?"

"Let's hear it."

"I had the craziest dream when I passed out this morning. I was climbing up this mountain, and off in the distance I saw a huge city, like gold on fire."

He taps the gauge and blows up the blood pressure cuff again. "Like heaven?"

"Don't know. What's that chemical that kicks in when you think you might die?"

"Dopamine, epinephrine. Oxytocin. DMT, maybe. When you go into shock, your memory bank increases, and you remember every detail clearly. How'd you feel when you woke up?"

"Peaceful, actually."

Black peels off the Velcro cuff and shines his penlight into my eyes. "What's so bad about that?" he asks.

"Nothing, I guess."

"You still taking the Zombien?"

"Yeah."

"I think I might have to lay off," he says. "The other day I painted a big smiley face on my washing machine with peanut butter. Apparently while I was asleep."

"I ate a whole box of cereal and put my clothes in the freezer."

"I tried to back my car out with the garage door closed."

"Why didn't you tell me?" I say, sitting upright. "I've been taking that stuff every day for months."

"I didn't tell you?" He scratches the back of his neck. "See, that's the other thing. It might have some weird effect on your brain."

We nod at each other in a pact that says we're both going straight from here on. I swing my legs out and stand. "What'd you give me, a blood transfusion?"

"We had a few leftover pints."

"I feel better now. Weird, but better."

"Well, you've been to heaven."

"I didn't get to go," I tell him. "I just saw it from a long ways off."

Black gives my shoulder a good-natured slap as he walks me out the door. "Closer than I've ever been."

THE SEVENTY-SEVEN
SECRETS OF LIFE

Woe to you who are complacent.

—AMOS 6:1 (NIV)

L ATE WINTER IN THE SOUTH IS SURREAL, TUESDAY
night with red skies and 65 degrees while the hospital laundry
whirs and belches white steam into the night. One smoky bulb
lights the ER's back exit. Wonder where I left my truck.

$0.00. YOU OWE US BIG-TIME NOW

I'm holding Amy's personalized discharge summary in my
right fist, and the back of my hand burns from where the needle
dripped in fluids. The hospital wristband identifies me as *9 y/o
FiFi Milinovich*, and a yellow sticker says, *Fall risk*. My face is
puffy, I'm bruised from hip to armpit, and claw marks trail down
the side of my neck. I look like an amateur storm chaser who tried
to roller blade through a tornado.

I'm not sure if I had a near-death experience or went into
shock or if I'm being melodramatic about an allergy spell fueled
by exhaustion and pills. Me. The guy who warns people about the

side effects of prescription meds every night. Humility partners with irony again. God makes sure I can never lecture or boast.

The crisis line rings. "Heard you saw Jesus," Squiggly says.

"Nah. Just where he lives."

"So's that mean you're in trouble with him or not?"

"Hope not."

"Well, look, I got this covered. Do what you need to do to get better. You're the crisis tonight."

"Not a good feeling."

"God puts us on both sides," she says. "Least that's what you told me once. Lay low. Get some rest."

With a click Squig's gone, and I'm left standing at the ER back door, still uncertain I'm not lost in some meandering dream. A thin black ladder takes me up the scaffold of Westwood's power plant. I rattle the ID bracelet and stare through the trees overlooking the old apartments. The pool is blackish green, and slim rows of silver mailboxes line the walk by the Laundromat.

I've got a dent in my head from crashing into that curved piece of handrail guarding the sidewalk and a ghost-white scar on my wrist from plowing into the sticker bushes by the creek. That third balcony from the left is where I hid during my tenth birthday party because there were too many people and it was loud. The hilltop is the first place I stayed up all night and watched the sun rise.

The past marks us in many ways. Nobody really grows up. Time passes and we just get strange. We get quiet. We get secretly hopeful for something more. I am the same kid I ever was, sleepless and dreaming, fumbling, searching, trying to find the difference between illusion and reality, fake and genuine, to separate the truth of God from all the religious nonsense and noise. The seemingly random stories of my life are just like everybody else's—not much different from the hundreds of stories I've heard in the hospitals and jails and churches of this town. We are always looking for something to complete us, to fix us, to give us a clear, simple map and make things finally make sense. In this city of pretenders, I am pretending too.

Moses zigzagged forty years. David did all sorts of crazy things. Samson crumbled, Elijah ran, John the Revelator saw the stars of heaven fall, and Jesus bewildered everyone in his time. There is no one hidden secret of how to do life. Creation made us complex. Life is more like seventy-seven secrets. Seventy times seven, even. I'd settle for figuring out just one.

A cold wind sweeps from the north and the tall pines sway in the townhouse lights. Suddenly I know it. The purpose. At least for tonight.

I rush to the one-stop superstore next to the hospital. Bicycles hang from a rack in the air, smaller ones parked in rows beneath. The smell of new tires and floor wax brings me back. I've got an emergency hundred-dollar bill tucked behind the flap in my wallet. To break it out tonight seems justified. Problem is there's only one BMX bike close to my price range, a sparkly pink-and-purple Sunshine Rambler marked from $117 to $96.75.

I roll it into the aisle and straddle the seat. It might be pink, but the suspension's rugged. That unreasonably hazardous crossbar they stick on boys' bikes always confused me anyway. I count out the few extra bucks in my wallet and try to figure the tax in my head. The store is empty, so I ride down one aisle and up the next.

A worker with a hawkish nose and brush-cut hair walks by, casting skeptical glances as I test the pedals and pull at the handlebars. Brother Benny challenged us to share the love of God more in our everyday walk. Now seems good.

"Jesus loves you," I tell him.

"Yeah, I know," he says, expression unchanged. "You buyin' that bike?"

"Maybe," I reply. "But I only got a hundred bucks."

"Hang on," he says, scanning the barcode with his price gun. "Huh, looka there." A tag spits out the bottom of his gun and he slaps it on the front fender. *$74.28.* "That better?"

"Jesus loves you because he has to," I report back. "But now he likes you too."

"Yeah," the worker says, smiling this time. "I know. This bike for your niece or sister or something?"

"No, it's mine."

"And you're okay with daisies?"

"I'm on a mission, my man. What difference do daisies make?"

"Okay, then," he says.

I pay and pedal through the superstore's magic doors and across the parking lot to the construction site near Westwood's new neonatal wing. Gathering an armful of cinder blocks, I dash down and pile them on the creek bank below. Not tall enough.

"Give no thought to tomorrow," Scripture advises. "Why just sit here 'til we die?"

I run back and forth until the blocks are stacked two feet high. Plywood sheets are scattered around the worksite, but they're all too thick or too long. I spot a black-and-orange detour sign laying behind the parking gate. It makes a wobbly metal thunder sound when I hold it by the sides and shake it. Seems perfect. I slide it under my arm and walk back fast-casually so as not to look suspicious.

It's an odd thing of beauty in the pearl moonlight, a shiny slope of sign propped against the wall of gray blocks, a gateway to the sky over the rift. A dare, that's what it is. A slap-in-the-face challenge to forget the noise.

I walk up the ramp and look out. The creek is a churn of

murky water at the bottom of a precipice, glistening bits of glass and broken toasters, tires in a heap half buried in the sand. I hear the taunts and laughter, feel the hollow in my chest. It's all still here around me. Everything is different, and it's just the same.

I shake the hospital bracelet again. I've got a perfectly good explanation for losing my mind. This is probably all a dream anyway.

I climb to the hilltop and mount the bike. There's something supercharged about setting one foot on the pedal and the other in the dirt, eye level with the rooftops and the launch ramp far below, the exact same place I sat when I was ten.

I set before you life and death, God says. Life is risk. Risk is fear. Fear is a tower in the night or a muddy canyon at the bottom of a steep dirt hill. Fear is the bully who assures you that you'll never measure up or find your way. Choose life. Live free or die. Closure is the hope that leads you home, the gift from heaven that says, *Hey, you made it. Let it go.*

I fix my eyes on the canyon. It's a dark, twisting path to the ramp. Smoke from the refinery rises through the factory lights, and the gas station flags ripple in the breeze. I hang one half second . . . and let go.

The drop-in is sheer and stony rough. Pumping the pedals, I wrestle to keep the handlebars from jerking out of my hands. I level out through the courtyard and pick up speed into the woods. The ramp is hazy, and I fight to find the lip, pulling left, then right again. And then, just before the rim, my tire catches a root, and the bike crumples. Heels over head and face in the dirt, tangled in spokes and smashing cinder blocks, skidding to a stop at the bank's edge.

I lie flat and dazed, staring at the night sky, listening to the steady rush of creek water toward the drainage ditches in town. A corner of concrete scraped my cheek, and there's blood mixed with dirt. Sitting up, I can see the avenue low through the branches, the library drop box, and a billboard for Powerball, the woman in the sun with hands lifted, insisting we were made for more.

I dust off and rebuild the ramp, turning the sign over, arrow-side up and pointing over the creek this time. "I'm with you, sister," I say, saluting the billboard and pushing back up the hill before I lose my nerve.

Sometimes you need a win. Any win. Some small way to tip the scales of justice, some old dragon to fight. Sometimes you have to do something foolish to feel alive, to kick back against this ill-fitting, frustrating, too-tiny life. Better reckless than dead inside.

The air at ground level is warm as a bitter wind rustles the treetops. All of life is a balance between push and pull, action and trust, holding and letting go. I wait. The current swirls around me as porch lights flicker and dot the night. This might be the stupidest thing I've ever done. Or the coolest. One way or another, hang on.

Deep breath. Jump.

I find the worn path between the ruts and stand in the seat to bear down, working with gravity for maximum speed. There's a flutter when I plane out to flat ground, but I grip the bars tight and make the pedals blaze.

Life is risk.

The grass blurs beneath me as I enter the trees.

Don't be afraid.

The orange slash of ramp rushes in fast.

Just believe.

I hit the steel at top speed, and it sways and pops back. The night air pierces my skin as every cold star declares the glory. And suddenly there is nothing but flight.

EVERYTHING NOW

He discovereth deep things out of darkness.

—JOB 12:22 (KJV)

THE VICTORY LAP TAKES ME TO THE FOOT OF THE hill. I look back to the creek, but it all seems different now. I feel a little stupid. But stupidly, totally alive.

"That was *awe*some," a voice interrupts. A kid stands at the handrail with a trash sack in his hand. He's eleven, maybe, toothy, rumpled a bit.

"You saw that?" I ask, riding over.

"Yeah, you're too big for that bike, though," he cracks. "You live in the apartments or the neighborhood?"

"Apartments. Used to," I tell him. "You could do it, y'know. The creek. It's no big deal. You got a bike?"

"Got stole last summer," he says, shifting the sack to his shoulder. "Why you riding a girl's bike?"

"Don't matter what you ride, if you can ride."

"Guess so," he says. "It's still a pretty cool bike."

I step off and lean it toward him. "Here." I let go of the bars. He catches the bike and sets down the trash bag.

"I can ride it?" he says.

"You can have it."

His head bobs back, eyes wide. "I can't take your bike."

"It's your bike now. I don't need it no more."

He looks it over, quiet, running his hand across the seat. "This bike's, like, brand-new."

"I took almost good care of it," I tell him. "'Cept for the jumps and stuff."

He shakes his head, talking while pulling his ear. "That don't make no sense. You're gonna just gimme this bike?"

"Somebody took yours; you get this one. Give it to somebody else when you get done," I say. "Look, take it. I'm trying to make a moment here, all right?"

"A moment?" he asks. "Why wouldya try'n do that?"

"Tell you what: I'm gonna leave it by the hill one way or another. You can make up your own mind what to do."

He swings a leg over, testing the seat. "What if they pick on me for riding a girl's bike?"

"So what if they do? Enemies make you tough. Everybody needs good enemies."

The kid shoots me a look. "They do?"

I realize that I'm muddy and scraped up and wearing Fifi's hospital bracelet. And trying to give a bike to a kid on the side-walk at night. "I gotta go find my truck," I tell him. "Have fun, okay? And watch that rail. It'll sneak up on you."

His face brightens as the reality of the exchange sinks in, foot bouncing and making the pedals spin. "Anytime you wanna ride it, come on back," he says. "Anytime."

Balancing the trash bag on the handlebars, he rides away, shaky at first, then finally straight. The full moon casts shadows in the street, the lights of town glowing over the trees.

Tires screech, and the kid calls back. "Hey, what am I gonna tell my mama?"

Twenty paces lie between us as a beacon burns from the tallest of small-town skyscrapers and the water tower rises in the east. My mind turns and tries to find the words. When the moon is full and the night is alive, you just might think irrational things. You might think that in some strange sense you have met your younger self again.

"Tell her you saw a grown man jump Chance Creek on a pink bike with daisies down the side, and then he gave it to you."

"She ain't gonna believe that."

"Then tell her whatever she'll believe."

"She usually believes me pretty good," he says. "I most always tell her the truth."

"Well, all right, then."

"Thanks, mister," the kid says. "See ya 'round." He steadies the trash with one hand and pedals away.

I turn and walk toward the hospital. Steel-gray clouds hide the moon, and in the field beyond the cul-de-sac crows signal winter's end. The streets are quiet and lights in the houses dim. One lone sprinkler swishes from grass to sidewalk and back again.

Einstein was right. Time is only an illusion. Jesus said for those who can receive it, heaven is everything now.

I reach into the stream and let the creek dirt wash away.

For just one moment, I close my eyes.

IV CODA

What is your life? For you are a mist that appears for a little time and then vanishes.
—JAMES 4:14 (ESV)

I wish I'd had the courage to live a life true to myself, not the life others expected of me.
—NUMBER ONE REGRET OF THE DYING

THERE IS NO END

That which hath been is now; and that
which is to be hath already been.
—ECCLESIASTES 3:15 (AKJV)

FUNNY SIGN," MARLBORO SAYS, AS HE STEPS OFF
the tarmac of the red-eye flight. He looks less like the
Marlboro Man now and more like Uncle Rico from *Napoleon
Dynamite*, a little banged up and weary, but hopeful overall.

"It was funnier that time you didn't show up."

"Sorry, Jamie," he says. "Couldn't do it. Not if I was gonna stay
straight. I'm done. I told corporate that you should take my place."

"What? Are you trying to kill me?" I ask. The terminal doors
swoosh open, and we step into the empty parking lot. "I'm done
too. At least for now."

"I thought crisis was in your blood," he says. "Like you were
born for it."

"Not this much of it. People are crazy, man."

Our boots echo across the concrete wasteland of white lines
and empty spaces as moths flitter under the streetlamps. Marlboro
slides in on the passenger side and eases the seat back. "It'll make
a good book someday," he says.

"Forget that." I laugh.

There's a half-minute pause as I drive down Airport Road with the windows open and wind rushing through the cab. Blue lights line the runway, flicking off like falling dominoes before lighting back again. "So what are you gonna do now?" Marlboro asks.

"Like I always wanted." I kill the headlights as the runway goes black. We ride in total darkness. "Disappear."

His smirk cuts through the gloom. "Good thing you saved your money," he says.

The alley is low and dark, scattered bits of trash kicked up by the breeze. There's a chink in the security fence wide enough to squeeze through if I turn sideways and hold my breath. The first two flights of the fire escape are missing, but it's easy enough to monkey up the frame and jump rail to the third.

I take the steps by two to the roof access. Another ladder is fastened to the far wall, leading five stories higher to the tallest building in town. A beacon on top swivels and pierces the sky while, far below, the People's Bank Time and Temperature sign flashes 64 degrees at 1:22 a.m.

There is a mystery in the darkness that connects us. Beyond matter and energy, gravity or time. Maybe there really is just one secret to life.

I am thankful for the wind and the still, small voice. For grace and mercy, each day's chance to start again. The stars are thick, and the path endless.

I grab the lowest rung and start to climb.

THANKS, DISCLAIMERS, AND STUFF YOU PUT AT THE END OF A BOOK

Too much activity gives you restless dreams;
too many words make you a fool.
—ECCLESIASTES 5:3 (NLT)

WRITING IS LIKE PUSHING A SCHOOL BUS FROM Houston to Nicaragua through a lightning storm with one dim headlight and intermittent swarms of rabid bats. It's a lonely, treacherous haul. Now and then you need a few trusted hands to help you push . . .

Adria Haley, David Gahan, D. R. Jones, Daisy Hutton, Doug Miller, Ian Kilmister, Joe Daly, Joel McIver, Joel Kneedler, John Lydon, Kathleen Dietz, Kimberly Golladay, Kristen Gathney, Kristi Smith, Laura Weldon, Leslie Peterson, Lori Cloud, Matt Baugher, Michael Holmes, Nicki Renna, Paul Frehley, Paula Major, Peter Criscuola, Rachel Smith, Robert Smith, Roger Nelson, Ronald Scott, Sean Beaudoin, Stephanie Nicks, Terence Butler, Tiffany Arbuckle, and Victoria Von Rotten. And to Bryan Norman and Deborah Wicky, who kept saying, "Jamie, baby, just be you."

God bless the ER docs, police officers, hotline operators, nurses, night stockers, EMTs, chaplains, convenience store clerks, and overnight DJs who keep the world turning while the city sleeps.

Saint Paul suggested we be all things to all people. To the addict, I tried to show up as one struggling to stay sober, and to the broken, as a drifter searching for home. But there are many facets to a fully lived life, and I am thankful for supportive friends and family and a wife who doesn't care what I write, as long as I leave out our business. She's the quiet, private kind, and I appreciate that.

Mercy Never Sleeps is based on true stories from mental health facilities, rehab centers, hospitals, and jails. Names, faces, places—everything necessary to protect the identities of those involved has been changed. In some cases, characters have been combined for anonymity and clarity's sake. We see through a dark glass in this life. So we tell our stories the best we can, knowing someday, hopefully, we will fully understand. Until then, all we have are broken bits and scattered memories, keepsakes and compasses, souvenirs of a life wandering and wondering why.

"What is truth?" Pilate asked.

Jesus did not reply.

הוהי ימחר

ABOUT THE AUTHOR

JAMIE BLAINE WRITES FROM HIS UNIQUE PERSPECtive of, among other things, having worked as a Piggly Wiggly bag boy, primate researcher, PE coach, roller rink manager, megachurch minister, midnight psychotherapist, college professor, editor, DJ, screenwriter, and rock journalist. His writing has been featured in venues such as *Salon*, *Relevant*, *Metal Hammer*, *Modern Drummer*, *OnFaith*, and the *London Scene*. He lives in Nashville, Tennessee.